T0316386

Rethinking Labour in Africa, Past and Present

This book offers a broad range of perspectives on major transformations in the research of labour in African contexts over the last twenty years. This is a groundbreaking work by social scientists and historians; adopting innovative paradigms in the study of African labourers, working classes and economies, it moves away from stringent Marxist perspectives towards more localised and fluid conceptions of materiality and productivity. Against the backdrop of increasing mobility of labour and capital, the authors demonstrate the need for a simultaneous consideration of local, national and transnational contexts.

This collection provides multiple perspectives on how African workers have negotiated changes and exploited opportunities in increasingly globalised workplaces, while at the same time confronting the impact of global capitalist expansion on local settings in Africa.

This book was previously published as a special issue of *African Identities*.

Lynn Schler is a Lecturer in African History in the Department of Politics and Government at Ben Gurion University, Israel. Her work has focused on the cultural and social history of colonialism in West Africa, with an emphasis on urbanization and community building. She is the author of *The Strangers of New Bell: Immigration, Public Space and Community in Colonial Douala, 1916-1960*.

Louise Bethlehem is Senior Lecturer in the Department of English at The Hebrew University of Jerusalem, where she currently also heads the Program in Cultural Studies. She co-edited the Routledge volume *Violence and Non-Violence in Africa*, and *Skin Tight: Apartheid Literary Culture and its Aftermath* (also published by Routledge).

Galia Sabar is a Senior Lecturer and the Chair of African Studies at Tel Aviv University. She is the author of *Church, State, and Society in Kenya; From Mediation to Opposition, 1963-1993* (also published by Routledge), and co-editor of *AIDS Education Prevention in Multi-Cultural Societies*.

Rethinking Labour in Africa, Past and Present

Edited by Lynn Schler, Louise Bethlehem and Galia Sabar

Routledge
Taylor & Francis Group
LONDON AND NEW YORK

First published 2011 by Routledge
2 Park Square, Milton Park, Abingdon, Oxon, OX14 4RN

Simultaneously published in the USA and Canada
by Routledge
270 Madison Avenue, New York, NY 10016

Routledge is an imprint of the Taylor & Francis Group, an informa business

This book is a reproduction of *African Identities*, volume 7, issue 3. The Publisher requests to those authors who may be citing this book to state, also, the bibliographical details of the special issue on which the book was based.

Typeset in Times New Roman by Value Chain, India

British Library Cataloguing in Publication Data
A catalogue record for this book is available from the British Library

ISBN13: 978-0-415-58802-7

Disclaimer
The publisher would like to make readers aware that the chapters in this book are referred to as articles as they had been in the special issue. The publisher accepts responsibility for any inconsistencies that may have arisen in the course of preparing this volume for print.

CONTENTS

Notes on Contributors

Louise Bethlehem is senior lecturer in the Department of English at The Hebrew University of Jerusalem, where she is also currently the head of the Programme in Cultural Studies. She has written widely on postcolonialism, gender and South African literary and cultural history and historiography. Together with Pal Ahluwalia and Ruth Ginio, she co-edited the Routledge volume *Violence and non-violence in Africa* (2006). Her book, *Skin tight: apartheid literary culture and its aftermath* (Unisa/Brill, 2006) is currently being translated into Hebrew. Her most recent research deals with witness and cultural memory with a particular focus on South Africa's Truth and Reconciliation Commission.

Isaie Dougnon is a Professor of Anthropology at the Faculté des Lettres, Langues, Art et Sciences Humaines (FLASH), Department of Social Sciences, University of Bamako. His research on migration and labour from Dogon Land to Office du Niger (Mali) and to Ghana has resulted in the recent book *Travail de blanc, travail de noir: la migration des paysans dogon vers l'Office du Niger et au Ghana (1910 – 1980)* (2007, Paris, Karthala) and several articles. From 2003 to 2005 Dr Dougnon carried out a research on migration and small-scale irrigation in the Northern Region of Mali. Currently, he leads the Groupe de Recherches sur les Migrations Maliennes Internes à l'Afrique (GREMI) based at the FLASH, Department of Social Sciences.

Harvey E. Goldberg is Sarah Allen Shaine Chair in Sociology and Anthropology, Emeritus at the Hebrew University of Jerusalem. His books include *Jewish life in Muslim Libya: rivals and relatives* (University of Chicago Press, 1990), *Sephardi and Middle Eastern Jewries* (edited, Indiana University Press and The Jewish Theological Seminary of America, 1996), *The life of Judaism* (edited, University of California Press, 2001), and *Jewish passages: cycles of Jewish life* (University of California Press, 2003).

Béatrice Hibou is director of research of the CNRS at CERI-SciencesPo (Paris). She holds a Ph.D. in political economy from the École des Hautes Études en Sciences Sociales (EHESS, 1995). Her comparative research in political economy focuses, from a Weberian perspective, on the political significance of economic reform, based on cases from sub-Saharan Africa, the Maghreb and Europe. Her most important publications include *La Force de l'obéissance. Economie politique de la répression en Tunisie*, Paris, La Découverte, 2006 (to be published in 2011 with Polity Press); *Privatising the State*, London, Hurst and New York, Columbia University Press, 2004; *The Criminalisation of the State in Africa* (with Jean-François Bayart and Stephen Ellis), London, James Currey and Indiana University Press, 1998.

Steven Kaplan is Professor of Comparative Religion and Middle Eastern and Islamic Studies at the Hebrew University of Jerusalem. Professor Kaplan's research concerns the religious and social history of traditional Ethiopia. He has written extensively on Orthodox Christianity, missions and the dynamics of conversion. He is also an expert on Ethiopian Jews and has written several books and numerous articles on their history in Ethiopia and adjustment in Israel. He is former Dean of the Faculty of Humanities at the Hebrew University of Jerusalem where he has recently been appointed Academic Director of the Truman Institute. During the 2007 – 08 academic year, Steven Kaplan was at the Radcliffe Institute for Advanced Studies (Harvard University) as part of a humanities cluster: 'Cultural Creativity in the Ethiopian Orthodox Diaspora in the United States'.

Terry Kurgan is an artist who lives and works in Johannesburg. Her practice is characterised by a keen interest in the confluence of public and private realm issues and spaces. Most recently, her work has engaged with the transformation of Johannesburg's inner city. She is currently working on Hotel Yeoville – a multi-media exhibition, web project and book publication (November 2009). The project aims to produce a social map of a neglected inner city neighbourhood that is 'home' to a largely invisible community of migrants from all over the African continent. Terry Kurgan has been awarded many prizes and grants, exhibited broadly and her work is represented in most major public and corporate South African collections and art publications. For more information about her work, visit her website: http://www.terrykurgan.com

Emily Lynn Osborn's research focuses on the social and political history of West Africa. She has written on the history of colonialism, state-craft and gender in Upper Guinea (Conakry). She is also interested in using alternative sources and approaches to study transformations that have taken place in the daily life and material conditions of the twentieth century. For this project on the history of aluminium casting, Osborn carried out research in six West African countries. She is currently working on a manuscript on aluminium and the artisans who work with it in West Africa.

Galia Sabar is Senior Lecturer, and Chair of African Studies, at Tel Aviv University, Israel. Her research has focused on the interplay between religion and politics in Africa. She is the author of *Church , State, and Society in Kenya; From Mediation to Opposition, 1963-1993,* London: Frank Cass, 2002. For the past 15 years she has been researching the African labor migrants in Israel and back in Africa. She is the author of *"We are not here to Stay" African labor migrants in Israel and back to Africa*, Tel Aviv: Tel Aviv University Press, 2009. Emphasizing the unique experience of women labor migrants she has recently published "Between crossing boundaries and respecting norms: Sub-Saharan African Women Labor-Migrants in Israel 1990-2005," in Wilder-Smith et al. eds. *Travel Medicine,* Oxford: Elsevier Publishers, 2008. Galia has been active in several Israeli and international NGOs including the Hotline for Migrant workers and refugees, and Israel Religious Action Center. For her work she has received, in April 2009, the Unsung Heroes Award, granted by the Dalai Lama.

Hagar Salamon is the head of the Jewish and Comparative Folklore programme and the Africa Unit at the Harry S. Truman Research Institute for the Advancement of Peace, both at the Hebrew University of Jerusalem, Israel. Focusing mainly on the Ethiopian Jews and Israeli folklore, her research concerns the transition of ritualistic and symbolic expressions, racial perceptions and life stories. She is the author of *The hyena people: Ethiopian Jews in Christian Ethiopia* (University of California Press, 1999), editor of *Ethiopia: Jewish communities in the East in the nineteenth and twentieth centuries* (Jerusalem: Ben-Zvi, 2007), and is a co-editor of the journal *Jerusalem Studies in Jewish Folklore.*

Lynn Schler is a Lecturer in the Department of Politics and Government and the Head of the African Studies Program at Ben Gurion University in Israel. Her research and publications have focused on the history of migration and urbanization in colonial Africa. She is the author of *The Strangers of New Bell: Immigration, Public Space and Community in Colonial Douala, 1914-1960* (Unisa, 2008). Her current research on the history of Nigerian seamen in the colonial and postcolonial eras examines the economic, cultural, and ideological opportunities opened up to these seamen in their Atlantic migrations, and highlights the race, class and social networks seamen constructed in the context of their work.

Pnina Werbner is Professor of Social Anthropology at Keele. She is the author of 'The Manchester migration trilogy' which includes *The migration process: capital, gifts and offerings among British Pakistanis* (Berg 1990 and 2002), *Imagined diasporas among Manchester Muslims* (James Currey, and School of American Research 2002) and *Pilgrims of love: the anthropology of a global Sufi cult* (Hurst and Indiana 2003). Recent co-edited collections include *Anthropology and the new cosmopolitanism* (ASA Monographs 45, Berg 2008), *Debating cultural hybridity* and *The politics of multiculturalism in the New Europe* (with Tariq Modood, Zed Books 1997), *Embodying charisma: modernity, locality and the performance of emotion in Sufi cults* (with Helena Basu, Routledge 1998), *Women, citizenship and difference* (with Nira Yuval-Davis, Zed Books, 1999), and a special issue of the journal *Diaspora on 'The materiality of diaspora'* (2000). Her fieldwork has included research in Britain, Pakistan, and Botswana where she is studying 'Women and the changing public sphere', and a trade union, the Manual Workers Union. Recent awards include an Economic and Social Research Council grant to study 'New African migrants in the gateway city' and a comparative study of the Filipino diaspora in Israel and Saudi Arabia, 'In the footsteps of Jesus and the Prophet', supported by a large grant from the Arts and Humanities Research Council in its Diaspora programme.

Abstracts

Dialogical subjectivities for hard times: expanding political and ethical imaginaries of subaltern and elite Batswana women
PNINA WERBNER

School of Sociology and Criminology, Keele University, Staffordshire ST5 5BG, UK
Tracing the careers of three Batswana women leaders, two of them trade unionists and one a public servant who became, first, a politician and then an international civil servant, the article explores ideas of ethical leadership in Botswana and argues that leadership is to be understood as essentially dialogical, linked to notions of dignity and responsibility, while activism has created an impetus for the women to expand their cosmopolitan political imaginaries. The article responds to feminist poststructuralist arguments regarding the possibility of gendered agency and ethical subjectivity. While rejecting Michel Foucault's 'negative paradigm' in favour of a more dialogical understanding of subjectivity, it argues that an alternative reading of Foucault's later work may provide insight into an ethics of the other, beyond the self.

Work discipline, discipline in Tunisia: complex and ambiguous relations
BÉATRICE HIBOU

By looking at tourism, textiles, and call centres in Tunisia, this article analyses the complex relationships between capitalism and political discipline. Starting from the tradition of Weber and Foucault, it shows that the multiplicity of the meanings of capitalist work and the plurality of the ways in which people live with their work stem from a deep heterogeneity in the perceptions of reality: at the same time discipline and freedom, submission and access to some sorts of freedom, rigidity and new latitude for action. In this way, capitalist labour relations can at the same time serve for domination and erode its effects. The analysis that is offered, based on extended fieldwork in Tunisia, suggests the multiplicity and the plasticity of relationships between the technologies of power, the development of the productive forces, and the methods of economic and political regulation.

Migration for 'white man's work': an empirical rebuttal to Marxist theory
ISAIE DOUGNON

Enlisted between 1920 and 1960 for mines in Ghana and and for the construction of the Markala dam in Mali, migrant Dogon workers offer a definition of colonial work that runs counter to that of Marxist intellectuals who have denounced it in all its forms. Within the colonial towns, the migrant workers established a hierarchy of tasks according to the amount of labour and the technical and social organisation required to accomplish them. This article analyses why the Dogon migrant workers glorified colonial work in these different dimensions (time, organisation, discipline). This new hierarchisation of activities places 'white man's work' at the top, and other activities at the bottom, of the scale. The following questions lie at the heart of this article: (1) In what manner does the discourse of Africanist researchers reflect the practices, the experiences, and the minds of those people who migrated and worked in colonial centres? (2) Does the 'ancestral' system of work have any influence on the differentiation and evaluation of the 'white man's work'? (3) Does the local classification of village activities have any effect upon the classification of the colonial world?

Casting aluminium cooking pots: labour, migration and artisan production in West Africa's informal sector, 1945 – 2005
EMILY LYNN OSBORN

This article investigates the history of aluminium casting, a sector of the informal economy devoted to recycling scrap aluminium. Artisans who cast aluminium make a variety of products out of scrap, including various utensils and receptacles for food preparation, such as cooking pots. While labour and its history in West Africa has garnered much historical research, as has the work of artisans who specialise in working other types of metal, especially iron, little attention has been paid to aluminium casting. The oversight is significant, because the diffusion of aluminium casting opens up a history on the transnational movement of labour and artisan production in late colonial and post-colonial Africa.

Transnationalism and nationalism in the Nigerian Seamen's Union
LYNN SCHLER

This article will examine the shifting tactics employed by Nigerian seamen in their struggles to improve their working conditions onboard Elder Dempster vessels in the late colonial period. Nigerian seamen successfully exploited opportunities arising within the context of colonialism to participate in globalised economies and cultures, exposing them to new solidarities and empowering them to seek an improvement in their lives. In crafting their onboard protests, African seamen historically forged ideological and organisational alliances with the wider world of the black diaspora. But the era of decolonisation shifted the balance of power between seamen and the union leadership as they negotiated with colonial shipping companies in the transition to independence. As ruling elites in both Europe and Nigeria took political, economic and ideological actions to secure lasting power and influence for themselves, seamen experienced a profound disempowerment. Although intent on engaging with the globalised world, African seamen were ultimately prevented from securing for themselves positions of power and autonomy as an effective labour movement in the post-colonial context.

What goes around, comes around: rotating credit associations among Ethiopian women in Israel
HAGAR SALAMON, STEVEN KAPLAN AND HARVEY GOLDBERG

This article looks at how working-class Ethiopian women, who have migrated to Israel, have sought empowerment and economic control through the establishment of rotating credit associations known as *iqqub*. In the changing world of Ethiopian Israeli women, *iqqub* associations and their specific cultural manifestations constitute a highly meaningful experience, whose building-blocks incorporate the financial, the social, the ritualistic, and the symbolic. It is a complex mechanism of tradition and renewal: its existence challenges paternalistic assumptions regarding the status of Ethiopian immigrants vis-à-vis the state and its institutions and the experience of Ethiopian Israeli women specifically. As we shall demonstrate, the *iqqub* serves as a generative focus for gender relations and the dramatic changes that have affected them. Ethnographic examination of the *iqqub* and its internal discourse expands our understanding of the dynamics of change among the group's cultural, gender, and power relations.

Park pictures: on the work of photography in Johannesburg
LOUISE BETHLEHEM AND TERRY KURGAN

This article investigates the cultural economy of an inner-city Johannesburg park through tracking the work of itinerant photographers who operate there. The authors revisit Johannesburg artist Terry Kurgan's interactions with the photographers of Joubert Park in order to raise questions relating to their material and symbolic – or 'immaterial' – labour. They point to the mnemonic or archival dimensions of this labour and investigate the visual idioms in which inner-city migrants conduct their self-fashioning, forging modes of vernacular urbanity in the photographic encounter.

INTRODUCTION

Rethinking labour in Africa, past and present

The study of labour in Africa has undergone important transformations over the last 20 years. Following a period of intense scrutiny from the 1950s to the 1980s, research on working classes, labour unions, capitalist expansion and proletarianisation in Africa experienced a decline that paralleled the political reality of the gradual marginalisation and disempowerment of the working classes and of organised labour more generally. Early approaches to the study of labour in Africa, heavily influenced by Marxist theory, underwent a process of self-examination and revision as poststructuralist and postcolonial critics exposed the Eurocentric biases underlying prevalent conceptualisations of labour-related research (see, for example, William Sewell 1993). The resulting retreat from universalist conceptualisations of class, work and productivity led researchers to eschew imposed notions of working-class consciousness and proletarianisation.

This shift paved the way to a revised approach toward the study of labour in Africa, one which bears little resemblance to the earlier phase of research born out of the first decades of African independence. The field of labour studies has not so much been abandoned as redefined. A primary focus of this reconceptualisation has consisted in the attempt to accommodate local African perspectives and experiences. This book takes stock of the important tools acquired as a result of the interventions of recent years, but at the same time reasserts the importance of a materialist orientation in the study of Africa. Such an orientation is, we feel, crucial given the exigencies of our times, an era commonly characterised in terms of globalisation and neo-liberalism. As we invoke the notion of 'African Labour' here, we question what an 'African' perspective might provide scholarship against the backdrop of the increasing fluidity of borders, transnational migrations and multicultural alliances. At the same time, we investigate what can be articulated differently from within the perspective of 'labour' while remaining open to fluidity, multiplicity and transition in its construction.

From the outset, the study of labour in Africa was intimately tied to the study of migrations. From the late colonial era and through to the period of decolonisation, colonial administrations throughout the continent commissioned studies of the working classes, hoping that the heightened scrutiny would reveal sites of potential unrest, particularly among the swelling urban working class. It was at this time, as Frederick Cooper (1996, p. 369) has written, that 'the scholarly study of wage labor and African urbanism began to be a sustained enterprise'. But while labour was on the move in Africa, the study of labour on the part of various colonial regimes sought to confine the working class in bounded entities and groupings under constant surveillance, based on categories of ethnicity, professional affiliation, the industries it served and the like. These early studies of labour were deeply enmeshed in colonial agendas which sought to maintain control over local populations, and accumulating knowledge of labour played a role in the paternalist advancement of moderated modernisation. Colonial enterprises needed a 'modernised' workforce, but simultaneously feared the consequences of local populations breaking with their so-called traditional lifestyles (see Freund 1984, p. 4). Thus, the displacement of labour from rural areas to urban centres was seen as a necessary evil that should be controlled and contained. The colonised subject, standing on the other side of the divide, experienced displacement as multiple and as acute. 'Some people were literally displaced (indigenous peoples, but also the so-called nomadic in many countries),' write Sheldon Pollock, Homi K. Bhabha, Carol A. Breckenridge and Dipesh Chakrabarty. 'Others, in particular those excited by and open to the newly introduced European knowledges, underwent a powerful cultural experience of being dislodged from "tradition"' (Pollock et al. 2000, p. 578).

The process of decolonisation opened up new directions in the study of labour in Africa. Scholars who were sympathetic to African nationalist movements now replaced those contracted by colonial regimes. Research on labour in this period shifted dramatically to a focus on labour unions (see Freund 1984, p. 7). The orientation of these post-independence endeavours was largely Marxist, but they were also heavily sympathetic to the nationalist cause in Africa. Thus, trade unions were identified as the uncontested representatives of working classes while their role in nation-building was scrutinised and debated.[1] The conceptualisation of these histories remained faithful to a universalist narrative of proletarianisation, and evidence of solidarities among labouring constituencies that were not class-based were deemed to require analysis and explanation (see, for example, Waterman 1982).

The commitment to the classic narrative of proletarianisation began to unravel in the wake of widespread disallusionment with socialist regimes both inside and outside Africa at the end of the 1970s. The corollary weakening of labour movements at the end the twentieth century led to a general crisis in labour studies, as William Sewell has noted: 'Because the organized working class seems less and less likely to perform the liberating role assigned to it … the study of working class history has lost some of its urgency' (Sewell 1993, p.15, cited in Silver 2003, p. 1). It was increasingly evident that Africans had not been transformed into a revolutionary proletariat even when engaged in wage labour within capitalist enterprises such as mining or transport industries. In addition, universalist conceptions of labour and productivity were challenged by the increasing volume of studies on women, rural populations, and the informal sector generated at this time. While debates were initially focused on why Africans did not fit the proletarianisation model, scholars eventually began to question why the model was being used at all.

Postcolonial critiques have, by now, gained prominence in the study of Africa. It is widely accepted that Africans continually reinvent their own meanings for productivity, materiality and accumulation. Theoretical formulations of identities and experiences are generated in fidelity to the local context, and emphasise openness, fluidity and transition. The study of labour has also come to incorporate a conscious rejection of essentialist categories, as Frederick Cooper's description of class powerfully demonstrates in his landmark study on African labour in the era of decolonisation. 'In this study,' he writes characteristically, 'class appears as a contigent, changing set of relationships, and also as an imaginative project' (Cooper 1996, p. 14). Whereas Cooper attempts to recuperate the notion of class to reflect the particularities of African landscapes and histories, it might equally be said that the study of Africa has largely avoided the category of class altogether over the course of the last two decades, and has focused instead on discourse, subjectivity and culture under the influence of poststructuralist thought. Labour continues to be on the move within and beyond Africa, but studies of labourers have shifted from their former rigorously materialist orientation to reflect a growing preoccupation with representation, imagery and ideology as the means through which the African working classes negotiate their place in global markets. In Mamadou Diouf's formulation:

> we must inquire into the modes on the basis of which native modernity relies on, confronts, and/or compromises with global modernity and with cosmopolitanism, the latter considered an instrument and a modality of the incorporation of the local into the global. (Diouf 2000, pp. 680–681)

Embedded in these approaches is an emphasis on agency, as we seek to understand the ways in which local vernaculars confront, resist and avoid the homogenising tendencies of modernity and globalisation. We can see how sensitivity to the particular and the local have transformed our ability to describe the experiences of Africans outside of what might be seen as premature capitulation to the homogenising tendencies of modernity. Yet, in the search for postcolonial subjects who imagine and pursue autonomous and resistant identities, we must not lose sight of the material circumstances that variously enable or block this pursuit. As Craig Calhoun (2003, p. 537) has argued: 'Crucially, differential resources give people differential capacities to reach beyond particular belongings to other social connections'. A sharpened sense of material inequality and disparity also has the salutary effect of reminding us of how we have perhaps become overly preoccupied with *detached* representations in the course of elaborating our poststructuralist and postcolonialist agendas. Cooper's observations, in an anthology that productively investigates the interface between race and class, are appropriate here:

> One reads these days too many attempts to read 'the female body' off a magazine advertisement, to locate 'the colonial subject' in a text by Kipling, to find 'governmentality' in a marriage law, or to embody 'resistance' in a passage from Fanon. (Cooper 2000, p. 213)

Cooper seeks to reorient us to the point where 'coal miners dig coal, dock workers carry loads, domestic workers clean floors'. In his view,

> To talk seriously about how whiteness or masculine respectability was constructed should not be to assume people spent all day thinking about who they were; they had other things to do. Fresh and thoughtful analysis has emerged from confronting representations with the nitty-gritty of labour. (Cooper 2000, p. 213)

For all that we are party to this return to what Cooper terms 'the nitty-gritty of labour', our new materialism does not imagine that even the most recalcitrant of working contexts is ever experienced without discursive mediation. At the same time, this optic returns us to an appraisal of materiality in everything that concerns questions of inequality, access and empowerment. The point to emphasise is that our understanding of the modes through which Africans represent and negotiate their participation in political and cultural contexts will be enriched and complicated by a sustained awareness of material opportunities as well as by the vectors resulting from articulated identities and allegiances. A broad reinvigoration of material perspectives can bring us closer to unravelling how lived agendas are set.

The invocation of 'African labour' constitutes a particularly useful exercise at this time as scholars continue to debate globalisation, and ask to what extent the increased mobility of resources and people across fluid borders of the present era constitutes 'a fundamentally new situation and a significant historical shift' as Michael Hardt and Antonio Negri (2000, p. 8) have claimed. In examining the history of labour in Africa over the long term, we can evaluate what is indeed new or different in this current era of globalisation, and what factors and circumstances might determine the role Africans will play in it (Bonner et al. 2007, pp. 137–138). In her influential study of twentieth-century workers' movements,

Beverly Silver has argued that we need histories of labour to help us understand the continuities and breaks between past and present currents of globalisation. Do labour movements have the potential to re-emerge as powerful agents of political and social change, or 'will they remain too weak and scattered' in Silver's (2003, p. 2) phrase to destabilise the forces of globalisation?

Some of the historical studies presented in this book respond to this question by reaching into the colonial past in order to understand the evolution and resolution of conflicts between African labour and European capital. The contribution of Isaie Dougnon provides a rich opportunity for uncovering the historical antecedents to the globalisation of labour markets in Africa from the colonial period, and for understanding how Africans of the past negotiated and responded to their inclusion in industries associated with capitalist expansion. According to Dougnon, from the early twentieth century onwards, Africans migrating to work in colonial enterprises embedded pre-colonial hierarchies of knowledge into their identification and exploitation of opportunities for employment in both British and French territories. Thus, Dougnon insists that we must juxtapose our reading of Africans' participation in colonial workplaces against the backdrop of both local cultural formulations of work and productivity on the one hand, and with respect to the availability of knowledge concerning alternative opportunities on the other. Dougnon's work on African labour in the colonial period productively highlights the historic ebbs and flows of globalisation, and demonstrates how collective and individual memory of colonial work in the post-colonial period must also be read through the lens of contemporary political and economic circumstances. Thus, Dougnon's work teaches us that the local has figured prominently in the construction of experience and the generation of meaning for Africans in the globalised spaces of the past.

The affirmation of the vitality and perseverance of local cultures and agents, however, must also acknowledge historic limits to African agency in determining opportunities for work or conditions of employment in capitalist markets of both the past and present. Any description of triumphant autonomy must also acknowledge the disempowerment experienced by Africans in the most pernicious colonial and postcolonial workplaces, where African working bodies and lives have been rendered superfluous in significant respects. This notion of superfluity has been used by Achille Mbembe to foreground, among other things, 'the dialectics of indispensability and expendability of both labour and life, people and things,' in the specific context of the racialised biopolitics of Johannesburg in that city's various incarnations from mining camp to post-apartheid metropolis (Mbembe 2004, p. 374).[2] For Mbembe, the inception of what apartheid-era South African labour historiography termed 'racial capitalism' (see, for example, Wolpe 1990) entailed the obfuscation of any 'exchange or use value that labour might have' (Mbembe 2004, p. 375). Racism, in Mbembe's analyis, overpowered black labour's power of self-definition. He argues:

> In the calculus of superfluity, racism was not only a way of maintaining biological differences among persons, even as mining capitalism, migrant labour, and black urbanisation established new connections between people and things. More fundamentally, racism's function was to institute a contradictory relation between the instrumentality of black life in the market sphere, on the one hand, and the constant depreciation of its value and quality ... (Mbembe 2004, p. 380)

to the very point of being worked to death.

> In a context in which native life had become the new frontier for capital accumulation, superfluity consisted in the vulnerability, debasement and waste that the black body was

subjected to and in the racist assumption that wasting black life was a necessary sacrifice – a sacrifice that could be redeemed because it served as the foundation of civilization. (Mbembe 2004, p. 381)

In considering Dougnon and Mbembe's divergent depictions of African labour as it was drawn into colonial capitalist enterprises, we confront a textured and contradictory spectrum of possibilities and outcomes for the engagement of African labour in the globalised spaces of the past, with clear implications for how we should approach the study of African labour in the globalised contexts of the present. With regard to the present, we stress that the most timely intervention which may be accomplished by a reinvigorated focus on African labour in the context of globalisation is to simply insert Africa into a field of study that has elsewhere systematically overlooked African perspectives. James Ferguson has decried the lack of attention paid to Africa in the study of globalisation, attributing this marginalisation to the fact that Africa does not fit the models or narratives constructed around the totalising impact of capitalist expansion. Ferguson invokes Susan George's caustic proclamation: 'One can almost hear the sound of sub-Saharan African sliding off the world map' (George 1993, p. 66, cited in Ferguson 2006, p. 9). Major assumptions prevalent in social theory today regarding the uniformity of globalisation can be called into question when we view these through the prism of African labour. Globalisation in Africa is distinctly uneven, and the implications of this insight for the ethical project of postcolonialism – the more equitable distribution of social, economic, political and gendered rights – are many. It is abundantly clear that the most salient inequalities remain 'intersocietally global', as we would emphasise alongside Craig Calhoun, and these are consequently not amenable to redress 'by intrasocietal measures' (Calhoun 2003, p. 534). The fact of exclusion is an integral part of this differential. As Ferguson has argued:

> That a purportedly universalizing movement of 'globalization' should have the effect of rendering Africa once again 'dark' in the eyes of the wider world suggests the intimate link ... between the question of marginalization in a global economy and that of membership in a global society. (Ferguson 2006, p. 14)

In Ferguson's succinct analysis:

> Africa's participation in 'globalization' has certainly not been a matter simply of 'joining the world economy'; perversely, it has instead been a matter of highly selective and spatially encapsulated forms of global connection combined with widespread disconnection and exclusion. (Ferguson 2006, p. 14)

It is very much to the point to observe, alongside Ferguson and others, that when the contemporary African worker experiences globalisation at all, he or she experiences it as a form of hyper-extraction of value and of vitality. African working lives, those actually engulfed by the forces of globalisation, are darkened – to revisit Ferguson's trope – by the polluting extraction of human and natural resources. Nor does extraction proceed any longer solely through the agency of its historical, that is to say, Western protagonists as the growing incursion of China into Africa suggests (see, for example, Alden 2007, Rotberg 2008). The historical figure of the black miner in a Johannesburg mine, depleted by the violent extraction of his life force, or the contemporary figure of the rural South African HIV/AIDS mother struggling with the labour of reproduction, the work of parenthood, under conditions of scarcity may be used to mark different points along this continuum. Indeed, invoking the horizon of the HIV/AIDS pandemic suggests that current studies of African labour might do well to revisit questions relating to the extraction and depredation of life under the sway of a differently inflected biopolitics (see, for instance, Sitze 2004).

It is immediately necessary to qualify this depiction, however. We do not mean to suggest that depredation or the equally unsettling alternative of quiescence in exclusion exhaust the analytic possibilities for charting labour in Africa – nor for working there. As a corrective, then, we offer a third set of figures: those of the young black South Africans whom Sarah Nuttall (2004, p. 434) has analysed as they frequent the 'privatized public space' of a shopping mall known as The Zone in Rosebank, Johannesburg whether as workers in its service sector or as consumers, or both. The overalls emblematic of their identity, produced under the idiosyncratic brand Loxion Kulcha (a rendering of the phrase 'Location Culture'), bear a design that 'improvises on the mineworkers protective garment' but '[appropriates] the utility-oriented, mass-produced overall for new cultural ends' (Nuttall 2004, p. 437). Nuttall points out that the overalls 'suture together two economic imaginaries' such that 'the history of work and of labour is less forgotten than tied to a service economy' (p. 437). The spectral figure of the mineworker might still persist residually in these representations, we suggest following Mbembe's (2004, p. 375) insights into a ghostly spectrality that is the underside of superfluity. But Nuttall's example teaches that the self-constructions and work milieus of the present enable a post-apartheid generation of black South Africans to revisit the spectrality of the mineworker in something other than a traumatic or mournful mode.

Nuttall's approach points us in the direction of complex and nuanced representations of 'economic imaginaries'. In seeking to understand African encounters with globalisation, we believe that a reinvigorated materialism can help understand why and how certain projects, identities and struggles are pursued. Through the prism of 'African labour', globalisation takes shape as both empowering and debilitating, encroaching and occluding, extracting and enriching, and we must reject any form of determinism that might hold either exclusion, depredation, or empowerment as the singular and uncontested outcome of Africa labour's engagement with capitalist expansion. By invoking the notion of 'African labour' during this time of prolonged engagement with globalisation, we are proposing a broad set of interlocking and mutually dependent questions about identity, solidarity, and opportunity, without imagining any particular end result. Thus, we seek to direct contemporary analyses of African labour to the chiastic or criss-crossing paths of materiality and immateriality, bodies and affect, the self and the social, in which work comes to be lived. A number of interventions in this volume instantiate this new materialism, whether implicitly or explicitly.

Pnina Werbner's analysis of 'dialogical subjectivity' in the careers of three Batswana women, two trade unionists and a civil servant, is exemplary here. Departing from E.P. Thompson's regarding the historicity of the emergence of class consciousness, Werbner draws Foucault's notion of *askesis* – ascetic discipline or self-mastery – into an analytical relation with the vernacular notion of *seriti* – personal and collective dignity – in Botswana. She stresses the intrinsically dialogical construction of *seriti* since vernacular conceptions of honourable ethics are realised in the public sphere in social interaction. In the Tswana saying, replicated elsewhere throughout Southern Africa, '*Motho ke motho ka batho*' or, 'a man [or woman] is a person through people'.[3] Werbner stresses that the political engagements of the women she depicts occur in a broad social setting in response to the depredation of their purchase over *seriti* when 'hard times' make 'dignity … a fragile achievement for both men and women'. As her female subjects craft ever more expansive notions of ethical leadership, imbued with the notion of *seriti*, in response to their discovery of a sense of social responsibility for vulnerable others, they emerge as actors in the public sphere, often in the face of powerful male resistance. Werbner's supple analysis of the manner in which subaltern women in Southern Africa 'create political imaginaries that make sense of their citizenship and gendered worlds in specific political or social circumstances' makes an important contribution to feminist discussions of gendered agency and ethical subjectivity. The manner in which Werbner's contribution is routed through an affective category, *seriti*, also underlines the potential value of renegotiating the terrain of the union floor – so beloved of an earlier phase of Marxist labour history – to reveal the emotional repertoires and gendered subjectivities of the men and women who cross it.

In a similar vein, Louise Bethlehem and Terry Kurgan's contribution to this volume works with the horizon of affect explicitly in mind as they offer commentary upon the production of images in contemporary Johannesburg – photographic portraits commissioned from street photographers which help to render concrete the aspirations of migrant workers for new representations of selfhood. Bethlehem and Kurgan do not overlook the conditions of material scarcity in which the 'work of photography' proceeds. They nevertheless enable us to begin to ask how scarcity is renegotiated by means of what they, following Hardt and Negri (2000, p. 28), describe as the 'immaterial labor' of commissioning the portrait of a well-formed family group, for instance. This to-and-fro movement enables Bethlehem and Kurgan to avoid an overly narrow analysis of the material and affective contexts in which Africans live and work in the inner city of Johannesburg.

The case of Johannesburg exemplifies that by mapping the flows of labour, we can gain important perspectives on the significance and potency of political borders. Particularly at a time of growing speculation regarding the diminishing significance of political borders, some advocates of a revival in labour studies have argued that field might well enable us to assess the power of borders to shape identities from a transnational perspective. The focus on labour can help us understand more clearly the role border-crossings play in promoting transnational alliances undercutting and circumventing the hegemony of nation-states. South African scholars Philip Bonner, Jonathan Hyslop and Lucien van der Walt have recently mapped out the critical potential of labour studies from a transnational perspective:

> [T]ransnational labour history does not assume that the nation-state is the necessary framework for historical analysis. It is interested in perspectives that move beyond the level of the 'nation' to look at flows of people, commodities, ideas and organizations across national boundaries. It does not seek to be comprehensive: rather it simply does not accept that its field of inquiry should stop at the 'national' border, or that a 'national' unit is a self-evident, or necessarily a particularly useful unit of analysis. It argues for approaches that examine connections across countries, continents, and cultures, for comparative studies, and for rethinking the conceptual vocabulary of labour and working class history. (Bonner et al. 2007, p. 144)

When the transnational perspective is applied to labour studies within the confines of a particular national context, it serves to problematise and destablise the nation-state as a fixed category of analysis. Béatrice Hibou's analysis of the case of Tunisia in the present volume is deeply pertinent here. Her intervention illuminates the unexpected interface between 'late capitalism' or 'globalisation' and authoritarianism in disciplining the Tunisian workforce, in defiance of accepted traditions of inherited thought on labour and the state. Her astute readings of a variety of conjunctions within the Tunisian economy enables us to understand the forces of a global capitalism as moving in conjunction with disciplinary practices within the discrete constitution of the Tunisian state. Hibou argues that the Tunisian state has de-nationalised specific zones in the economic landscape in order to create opportunities for enhanced exploitation of labour and resources.

Specifically, through the manipulation of offshore corporations or tourist sectors, the state
in Tunisia is able to apply a separate set of standards for employment and investment
ultimately increasing the state's control over economic resources and the labour force.
When considered from the perspective of labour itself, participation in these de-localised
zones provides opportunities for economic and social advancement, as well as a sense of
empowerment and transformation through their identification with a more globalised
context. Hibou's work on state and labour relations in Tunisia ultimately highlights the
process through which the borders of nation-states and nationalist identification are
constructed, exploited and policed against a backdrop of material circumstances and
opportunities.

Hibou's work reveals the plurality of logics constructing the consciousness of African
labour, and compels us to consider the local, national and transnational contexts as
simultaneously constructive in working-class experiences and agendas. Indeed, an
enormous challenge facing scholars of Africa today is the need, precisely, to reconcile the
tensions between here and there: universalism and relativism, the global and the local, and
cosmopolitan and vernacular perspectives. The study of labour can and should 'work out a
middle ground', as Dipesh Chakrabarty has attempted to do in revisiting Marx's concept of
abstract labour. Chakrabarty reminds us that labour embodies particular historical origins
that can and do remain outside of capitalism's totalising grasp to one extent or another,
such that '[Difference] lives in intimate and plural relationships to capital, relationships
that range from opposition to indifference' (Chakrabarty 2000, p. 671). Thus, rather than
seeing local actors as either engulfed by capitalism or situated outside of it, Chakrabarty
suggests that we imagine 'difference-with-capital' (p. 671). The point, for Chakrabarty
and others, is that whatever remains beyond capitalism's logic enables 'labour power to
enact other ways of being in the world, other than, that is, being the bearer of labour
power' (p. 671). In consonance with this view, we should seek to avoid the portrayal of an
either/or dynamic with regard to local and global perspectives. Mamadou Diouf has rightly
argued that 'there is neither a dissolution of the local in the global nor an annexation of the
latter by the former' (Diouf 2000, p. 702). Rather, through the experiences, struggles and
imaginaries of African labour across time and space, we can get a better grasp of how
local, national, and transnational spaces are mutually constructive of each other.

The local–national–transnational interdependence comes to life in Emily Lynn
Osborn's work on aluminum casters in West Africa, as the concomitant relationships of
labour to migration, industrialisation and urbanisation are explored. Osborn focuses on a
dynamic sector of the informal economy in West Africa that is managed by artisans who
specialise in recycling scrap aluminum into new aluminum goods, mainly cooking pots.
Through Osborn's work, we see that markets and migrations within Africa, particularly
those associated with the informal sector never wholly captured by the state, are best
understood through a simultaneous consideration of local, national, and transnational
contexts. Osborn's analysis speaks to the contingency of social and economic change
outside of state mandates, formal institutions or national boundaries, and her intervention
provides a much needed opportunity to direct studies of African labour to the informal
sector. She makes the crucial point that skilled labour is often acquired and disseminated
outside of formal institutions of learning and employment in Africa. Osborn is attuned to the
dynamic interaction between local practices of work, travel, and knowledge transmission in
the origins and growth of the artisanal diaspora she investigates. As we review how this
diaspora of sand-casters conjoins a particular material (aluminum) and a particular technology (sand-casting) we must insist, as Osborn does that transnational flows of resources
and knowledge are in constant dialogue with determinate local practices. Thus, Osborn's

portrayal of aluminum casters in West Africa provides vivid evidence that African producers dynamically integrate knowledge and practices deriving from a multiplicity of economic and cultural landscapes to identify and exploit new opportunities.

While emphasising transnational flows and crossings, we must nevertheless be careful not to overstate the diminishing significance of physical, ideological and cultural borders in transnational spaces. Despite evidence of increasing transnational migrations, gate-keeping devices are as prevalent as ever, and have even become more intractable in specific circumstances, landscapes and for particular racial or ethnic groups. The notion of the transnational relates to a specific kind of border-crossing, but the concept does not necessarily incorporate an inherent awareness of the power relations that guide or block other kinds of border crossings, such as those associated with race or gender. As Asale Angel-Ajani (2006, p. 292) has argued, 'the history of racial oppression is sorely lacking in contemporary studies on transnationalism'. Thus, African labourers might cross national boundaries, but their destination, by choice or compulsion, is often more adequately described by the notion of black diaspora. The notion of the black diaspora provides an alternative to 'the politically sanitized discourse that surrounds transnational studies' (Angel-Ajani 2006, p. 296). The study of labour must therefore always pay attention to the ways in which race and gender have interacted with class, and to focus on processes rather than reified categories. In our celebration of African labour's mobility, Angel-Ajani suggests, we must not forget to ask who is able to travel, under what circumstances, and who is left behind (Angel-Ajani 2006, p. 293).

The unionised seamen whom Lynn Schler analyses in this volume provide a case in point. Schler shows them to have successfully exploited opportunities arising within the context of colonialism to participate in transnational economies and cultures. These men were exposed to new solidarities in the process. They formulated innovative aspirations and experimented with different modes of understanding their subjectivity. African seamen, Schler demonstrates, forged significant ideological and organisational alliances with the wider world of the black diaspora. Yet their gains were bracketed and their agency limited precisely by the advent of national independence. The foreclosure of their mobility in the face of the ascendancy of new national elites in the immediate aftermath of decolonisation in Nigeria suggests how precarious the attainment of mobility might be. Forced to relinquish their power, not without struggle, to post-independent elites, the former seamen came to be bounded by more limited parameters. Although they were intent on engaging with the globalised world, the arrested mobility of the African seamen corresponded with their ultimate failure to serve as an effective labour movement in the postcolonial context.

Schler's reconstruction of the movement of seamen across space teaches us that we can maintain an awareness of both privilege and discrimination in our descriptions of labour migrations if we remember to define and map the physical and discursive spaces that labour occupies. David Harvey (2000, p. 539) has argued that the insertion of space into social theory illuminates and disrupts central propositions and derivations of the latter. The categories of inclusion, of citizenship, of belonging implicitly congeal in spatial attachments. But the grounding of subjectivity in a certain set of spatial coordinates does not mean that spatial referents are essentially fixed or immovable.

For Pnina Werbner, in a well-known article on Pakistani migrants or 'working-class cosmopolitans' that also informs her arguments in this book, notes how the ceremonial objects such as food, clothing, cosmetics and jewellery move metonymically from one space to another in order to personify 'moral "places"' through which 'new global ethnic social worlds are constituted' (Werbner 1999, p. 19, see also Werbner 1990).

The contribution of Hagar Solomon, Steven Kaplan and Harvey Goldberg, in this issue, alerts us to the fact that practices move just as readily as ceremonial objects. Their article implicitly interrogates spatial imaginings of the national, on a dual front, in the lives of diasporic working-class Ethiopian women in Israel through an examination of the rotating credit organisations in which they participate. Although some Ethiopian women have not formally entered the labour market following their absorption into the state of Israel, they have benefited from stable incomes due to the social policies of the Israeli welfare state. Through perpetuating the cultural form of the *iqqub* or credit association, these Ethiopian women elaborate new opportunities for empowerment in response to the often unwelcoming cultural and political ideologies of their host country. Analysis of the *iqqub* allows the authors to calibrate contrasting binaries linking the individual and society, certainty and uncertainty, past and present. In a slightly different framing, their study of the *iqqub* also illuminates the tensions Ethiopian women face in reconciling between an explicit desire to be seen as Israelis, on the one hand, and an implicit yearning to preserve forms of cultural and economic organisation that speak of attachment to the imagined Ethiopian 'homeland', on the other.

Looking back over the trajectories we have traced reveals the progressive fragmentation of the solid Marxist orthodoxies of a previous phase of research into African labour. But learning how to accommodate the *multiplicity* of histories, identities, and ideologies that attract Africans to defy the logic of capitalism must go hand in hand with recognising the circumstances under which Africans aspire to inclusion and empowerment in the epicentres of modernity. As James Ferguson (2006, p. 19) has argued, 'the question of cultural difference itself (everywhere, no doubt, but perhaps especially in contemporary Africa) is tightly bound up with questions of inequality, aspiration and rank in an imagined "world"'. Africans who participate in globalised spaces are keenly aware of the opportunities they do and do not have, and they perpetually manoeuvre to achieve their evolving objectives. These manoeuvres might be aimed at gaining easier access to or inclusion in the landscapes of modernity, but we can not regard this simply as either mimicry or resistance. Africans latch on to solidarities, identities, and imaginaries that offer them solutions to the problems they face. Thus, the call to rethink labour in Africa is fundamentally a reaffirmation of the materialist perspective, and a suggestion that we continually read African pursuits through the lens of material conditions, opportunities, and inequalities.

Acknowledgements

The editors would like to acknowledge the support of The Harry S. Truman Institute for the Advancement of Peace at the Hebrew University for funding a research group entitled 'African Labour in Transnational Contexts' where some of the work staged here was generated. We would like to thank our fellow participants in the group, Yael Abessira, Ruth Ginio, and Hagar Salamon for their collegiality. A particular debt of thanks is owed to Stephen Belcher for his very fine translations of Béatrice Hibou's and Isaie Dougnon's papers. His generosity and support for the project of African Studies is noteworthy.

Notes

1. The literature here is extensive. See, for example, Eliot Berg and Jeffrey Butler (1964), William Friedland (1969), David R. Smock (1969), Paul M. Lubeck (1975), Adrian Peace (1975), Richard Sandbrook (1975), Jon Kraus (1979), Bill Freund (1988 pp., 103–104).
2. The concept of biopolitics arises from the work of Michel Foucault, notably *The history of sexuality*, vol. 1 (1978, pp. 135–145) and 'The politics of health in the eighteenth century' (1980, pp. 166–182). Biopower refers to the administration of life as the object of power: the

capacity to control the production and reproduction of life itself. For Hardt and Negri, the ascendancy of biopolitics, and especially of biopolitics in concert with globalization under the constellation they term 'Empire', radically changes the manner in which power relations are conducted in that biopower 'presents power with an alternative, not only between obedience and disobedience, or between formal political participation and refusal, but also along the entire range of life and death, wealth and poverty, production and social reproduction, and so forth' (Hardt and Negri 2000, p. 26).

3. For a brilliant analysis of the Isizulu rendering of this saying that moves from its syntax to stress its ethical implications for the conduct of witness in South Africa's Truth and Reconciliation Commission, see Mark Sanders (2007, pp. 26–29).

References

Alden, C., 2007. *China in Africa: partner, competitor, or hegemon?* London: Zed Books.

Angel-Ajani, A., 2006. Displacing diaspora: trafficking, African women, and transnational practices. *In:* M. Gomez, ed. *Diasporic Africa: a reader.* New York: New York University Press, 290–308.

Berg, E. and Butler, J., 1964. Trade unions. *In:* J. Coleman and C. Rosenberg, eds. *Political parties and national integration in tropical Africa.* Berkeley, CA: University of California Press, 340–381.

Bonner, P., Hyslop, J. and van der Walt, L., 2007. Rethinking worlds of labour: Southern Africa labour history in international context. *African studies*, 66 (2–3), 137–168.

Calhoun, C., 2003. 'Belonging' in the cosmopolitan imaginary. *Ethnicities*, 3 (4), 531–568.

Chakrabarty, D., 2000. Universalism and belonging in the logic of Capital. *Public culture*, 12 (3), 653–678.

Cooper, F., 1996. *Decolonization and African society: the labor question in French and British Africa.* Cambridge: Cambridge University Press.

Cooper, F., 2000. Back to work: categories, boundaries and connections in the study of labour. *In:* P. Alexander and R. Halpern, eds. *Racializing class, classifying race.* London: Macmillan, 213–235.

Diouf, M., 2000. The Senegalese Murid trade diaspora and the making of a vernacular cosmopolitanism. *Public culture*, 12 (3), 679–702.

Ferguson, J., 2006. *Global shadows: Africa in the neoliberal world order.* Durham, NC: Duke University Press.

Foucault, M., 1978. *The history of sexuality*, vol. 1. Trans. Robert Hurley. New York: Vintage.

Foucault, M., 1980. The politics of health in the eighteenth century. *In:* C. Gordon, ed. *Power/knowledge.* New York: Pantheon, 166–182.

Freund, B., 1984. Labor and labor history in Africa: A review of the literature. *African studies review*, 27 (2), 1–58.

Freund, B., 1988. *The African worker.* Cambridge: Cambridge University Press.

Friedland, W., 1969. *Vuta Kamba: the development of trade unions in Tanganyika.* Stanford, CA: Stanford University Press.

George, S., 1993. Uses and abuses of African debt. *In:* A. Adedeji, ed. *Africa within the world: beyond dispossession and dependence.* London: Zed Books.

Hardt, M. and Negri, A., 2000. *Empire.* Cambridge, MA and London: Harvard University Press.

Harvey, D., 2000. Cosmopolitanism and the banality of geographic evils. *Public culture*, 12 (2), 529–564.

Kraus, J., 1979. Strikes and labour power in Ghana. *Development and change*, 10, 159–186.

Lubeck, P.M., 1975. Unions, workers and consciousness in Kano, Nigeria: a view from below. *In:* R. Sandbrook and R. Cohen, eds. *The development of an African working class: studies in class formation and action.* London: Longman, 139–160.

Mbembe, A., 2004. Aesthetics of superfluity. *Public culture*, 16 (3), 373–405.

Nuttall, Sarah, 2004. Stylizing the self: the Y generation in Rosebank, Johannesburg. *Public culture*, 16 (3), 430–452.

Peace, A., 1975. The Lagos proletariat: labour aristocrats or populist militants? *In:* R. Sandbrook and R. Cohen, eds. *The development of an African working class: studies in class formation and action.* London: Longman, 281–302.

Pollock, S., Bhabha, H.K., Breckenridge, C.A. and Chakrabarty, D., 2000. Cosmopolitanisms. *Public culture*, 12 (3), 577–598.

Rotberg, Robert I., ed., 2008. *China in Africa: trade, aid, and influence*. Washington, DC: Brookings Institution Press.

Sandbrook, R., 1975. *Proletarians and African capitalism: the Kenyan case, 1962–1970*. Cambridge: Cambridge University Press.

Sanders, Mark, 2007. *Ambiguities of witnessing: law and literature in the time of a truth commission*. Stanford, CA: Stanford University Press.

Sewell, W., 1993. Toward a post-materialist rhetoric for labor history. *In:* L.R. Berlanstein, ed. *Rethinking labor history: essays on discourse and class analysis*. Urbana, IL: University of Illinois Press, 15–38.

Silver, B.J., 2003. *Forces of labor: workers' movements and globalization since 1870*. Cambridge: Cambridge University Press.

Sitze, A., 2004. Denialism. *The south Atlantic quarterly*, 103 (4), 769–811.

Smock, D.R., 1969. *Conflict and control in an African trade union*. Stanford, CA: Stanford University Press.

Waterman, P., 1982. *Division and unity amongst Nigerian workers, Lagos Port unionism, 1940s–60s*. The Hague: Institute of the Social Studies.

Werbner, P., 1990. *The migration process. Capital, gifts and offerings among British Pakistanis*. Oxford: Berg.

Werbner, P., 1999. Global pathways. Working class cosmopolitans and the creation of transnational ethnic worlds. *Social anthropology*, 7 (1), 17–35.

Wolpe, H., 1990. *Race, class and the Apartheid state*. Trenton, NJ: African World Press.

Lynn Schler
Department of Politics and Government, Ben Gurion University, Beer Sheva, Israel

Louise Bethlehem
Department of English and The Program in Cultural Studies, The Harry S. Truman Research Institute for the Advancement of Peace,The Hebrew University of Jerusalem, Jerusalem, Israel

Galia Sabar
Department of Middle Eastern and African History, Tel Aviv University, Tel Aviv, Israel

Dialogical subjectivities for hard times: expanding political and ethical imaginaries of subaltern and elite Batswana women

Pnina Werbner

School of Sociology and Criminology, Keele University, Staffordshire ST5 5BG, UK

Tracing the careers of three Batswana women leaders, two of them trade unionists and one a public servant who became, first, a politician and then an international civil servant, the article explores ideas of ethical leadership in Botswana and argues that leadership is to be understood as essentially dialogical, linked to notions of dignity and responsibility, while activism has created an impetus for the women to expand their cosmopolitan political imaginaries. The article responds to feminist poststructuralist arguments regarding the possibility of gendered agency and ethical subjectivity. While rejecting Michel Foucault's 'negative paradigm' in favour of a more dialogical understanding of subjectivity, it argues that an alternative reading of Foucault's later work may provide insight into an ethics of the other, beyond the self.

Introduction: from subject to subjection

E.P. Thompson remarked famously in his opening to the *The making of the English working class*: 'The working class did not rise like the sun at an appointed time. It was present at its own making' (Thompson 1963, p. 8). The emergence of class and class consciousness, he stressed, is an *active* process, 'which owes as much to agency as to conditioning' (1963, p. 8). Class was not merely a 'structure' but a *historical* phenomenon, unifying 'disparate and unconnected events, both in the raw material of experience and in consciousness'. Echoing Thompson, Iliffe argued about dock workers in colonial Tanzania that workers developed class consciousness by the very process of working together and acting together to advance their interests (Iliffe 1975, p. 50).

A key question not pursued in this early literature on labour relations concerns the extent to which a politics of honour and distinction is at stake in trade union activism. The present article traces the historical evolution in Botswana of the notion of *seriti*, personal and collective honour and dignity, in the wider context of the emergence of what Iliffe recently has called a 'modern code of honour' (Iliffe 2005, p. 280). My approach echoes Lonsdale's (1992) analysis of the historical evolution of the Gikuyu notion of *wiathi*, self-mastery in labour, and that of the late Foucault's analysis of the changing meaning of *askesis*, self-fashioning and self-mastery, from the Greek to the Hellenistic period.

Unlike these two latter notions, however, *seriti* even in its rural setting was not only a matter of *self*-mastery, but of recognition by others. *Seriti* is, in other words, an intrinsically dialogical notion, often related to the notion of *botho*, compassion or humanity. Tswana say that '*Motho ke motho ka batho*', 'a man [or woman] is a person through people'. My article moves from a broader discussion of current debates on subjectivity and ethics in Foucault's work to a focus on the ethical subjectivities of three women, two trade unionist and one a politician.

The poststructuralist turn in the social sciences, in social history, anthropology and feminist studies, has questioned Thompson's humanist conception of the acting subject, whose consciousness is embodied culturally 'in traditions, value systems, ideas and institutional forms' (Marks and Rathbone 1982, p. 8), and defined in struggle. In a far-reaching critique of notions of experience, consciousness and agency, Joan Wallach Scott has argued that 'Thompson's brilliant history of the English working class, which set out to historicize the category of class, ends up essentialising it' (Scott 1991, p. 786). In particular, she castigates Thompson for ignoring women in his stress on an allegedly masculinist universal definition of class (Scott 1988, pp. 68–92). In this respect the project of the present article, of exploring the subjective and public ethics of subaltern and elite women public actors in post-independent Botswana, must necessarily contend with feminist responses to the early Foucault's deconstructive unmasking of the modern individual as the product of socialisation, subjection and insertion into highly coercive, inescapable discursive formations. These construct embodied subjects and subjectivities,[1] allowing at most for a 'plurality of resistances' (Foucault 1980, pp. 95–96).

Recent feminist scholarship has, however, questioned the constraints of this 'negative paradigm' of the subject, limited to describing subversive strategies or partial resistances to hegemonic normative regimes. Acts which 'transcend their immediate sphere in order to transform collective behaviour and norms', Lois McNay suggests, require a '*more dialogical understanding of the temporal* aspects of subject formation' (2000, p. 4; emphasis in the original). She thus proposes theorising a creative, active subject transformed not merely discursively (i.e. in language) but through embodied action, self-narrativising and a capacity to imagine the social creatively (McNay 2000, p. 4 and passim).[2] A limitation in McNay's own work, however, is that she bases her critique on Foucault's first volume of *The history of sexuality*, and thus does not attend to his later theorising of an ethics of the self (Foucault 1987 and 1990).

In her recent monograph on the Islamic pietist movement in Egypt, Sabah Mahmood draws on Volume 2, *The use of pleasure* (Foucault 1987), to theorise the possibility of embodied agency shaping an ethics of the self, fashioned through self-mastery and voluntary self-subjection to a transcendentally authorised, normative aesthetics of female conduct (Mahmood 2001, 2005). Moving beyond Judith Butler's notion of agency as resistive performativity (Butler 1993),[3] Mahmood draws on Bourdieu's and in particular Aristotle's notion of 'habitus' as a learned, embodied ethical disposition. She ignores, however, what may be considered Foucault's *ethical theory of leadership*, first hinted at in Volume 2 and developed more fully in Volume 3 of the *Sexuality* series. This would have allowed her to illuminate further dimensions of the women's pietist movement she studied, and, in particular, their mastery of knowledge and desire as authorising their assertion of public leadership positions.[4] Foucault's approach, particularly in the final volume, is critical to an understanding of his theory of ethics, not simply as aesthetic self-fashioning through personal asceticism, but as a theory of alterity and power. A hint of this appears at the end of Volume 2: in the Greek city of the fourth century BC, abstention and renunciation by older men of physical relations with boys, Foucault argued, stemmed from:

> [t]he respect that is owing to the virility of the adolescent and to his *future status as a free man*. It is no longer simply the problem of a man's becoming the master of his pleasure; it is a problem of *knowing how to make allowance for the other's freedom in the mastery that one exercises over oneself and in the true love that one bears for him.* (Foucault 1987, p. 252, emphasis added)

Individual freedom, albeit restricted to 'free men', is defined here in negative terms for the first time in Foucault's *oeuvre*, as being a conscious abstention from coercive power over an Other. Beyond that, in the Greek city a man's claim to authority was based both on his status and on his capacity for self-mastery and self-governance, so that 'ethics implied a close connection between power over oneself and power over others' (Foucault 1990, p. 84). In this model, which posited 'a close connection between the superiority one exercised over oneself, the authority one exercised in the context of the household, and the power one exercised in the field of agonistic society' (Foucault 1990, p. 94, see also 1991, pp. 357–358) the self-mastery of desire legitimises authority in a hierarchical series of nesting social formations – over the self, the household, the city.[5]

The dissolution of the boundaries of the Greek city during the Hellenic period gave rise, however, to a new kind of ethics – more cosmopolitan and egalitarian. This created, Foucault argues, a 'crisis of subjectification' in which 'heautocratism' – 'the principle of superiority over the self as the ethical core' – needed to be 'restructured' and 'reelaborated' although it 'did not disappear' (Foucault 1990, p. 95). Political space had become much vaster, more discontinuous and less closed, with multiple centres of power (p. 82). The correlation between identity, status, functions, powers and duties was sundered (pp. 85, 93), and the Cynic and Stoic philosophical response was to fashion oneself as a rational, virtuous subject, *irrespective of status or external power*. For the Stoics, political activism was seen as a free life choice, based on judgement and virtuous reason (p. 87), a matter of rational negotiation within a complex field of relations (pp. 88–89 and passim). An early Cynic, Epictetus, renounced marriage and all private ties because *qua* philosopher, 'his family is mankind', so that 'responsibility for the universal family is what prevents the Cynic from devoting himself to a particular household' (p. 158). For the Stoics, by contrast, heterosexual marriage was natural, universal and hence obligatory. Marriage was defined as egalitarian, reciprocal and ethical (p. 163). A wife was the 'valorised' other, identical to the self (p. 164).

Several conclusions may be drawn from this genealogical movement in Foucault's thought: first, he shows that a concept such as *askesis* (ascetic discipline) may change its significance historically while retaining some of its earlier connotations; second, the subject as rational agent and political actor is rescued from the straightjacket of an all-determining discourse; and finally, the notion of ethics moves from being almost entirely monological, focused on the autonomous self, to being dialogical, egalitarian and cosmopolitan.[6]

Citizenship, honour and dignity in modern Botswana

Post-Foucault, we may conceive of subjectivity as the product of subjection and creativity co-existing historically in dialectical tension. In the present article I consider the careers of three women, one a senior civil servant-turned-politician and the other two trade unionists in the Manual Workers Union, a public service union of government employees. I locate their rise to positions of leadership in two epistemic shifts in the history of citizenship in Botswana. The first relates to the grounding of citizenship in the right to a living wage and, with it, the right to dissent, to legally challenge the developmental state; the second identifies a transformation in the meaning of citizenship arising from the immediate need to save the lives of ordinary citizens, which draws further legitimacy from a global movement re-envisioning health rights as human rights.[7] Both, and especially the latter, have entailed new subjection regimes as well as new entitlements, modes of governance and individual responsibility.

Chronologically, the first shift was associated with the nascence of a collective working-class ethos and identity in Botswana, rooted in a series of historical events which shaped both individual and collective discourse and consciousness of being a worker in what Thompson, as we saw, has called a 'historical relationship' – in this case, with the black, African-governed, postcolonial state. The second arose in response to the HIV/AIDs pandemic in Botswana. Both shifts were associated with emergent cosmopolitan as well as local reflexive discourses. Inserted differentially in Botswana's changing historical and political landscape, the three women portrayed here sought, in different ways, to act and think in terms of wider social universes of discourse, expanding their current understandings of citizenship in the face of state failure to deliver what they came to regard as basic rights.

This process highlights the fact that subjectivities need to be grasped in temporal and creative terms – they are made and remade dialogically through tests and ordeals overcome. I mean 'dialogical' here in two senses: first, to refer to women's political engagement and struggle within the wider social field; and second, as reflecting vernacular notions of honourable ethics as they have come to be incorporated historically into Botswana's political discourse and 'modern code of honour' (Iliffe 2005, p. 280). My notion of dialogical may be referred to Charles Taylor's argument (1994, p. 27 and passim) that in the shift from feudal notions of honour to notions of citizen dignity, secure hierarchies of ranking and respect have been replaced by the need for recognition, and that winning that recognition might fail (1994, pp. 34–35). So too in modern Botswana. As Botswana has become more egalitarian and democratic, dignity (*seriti* in Setswana), from being embedded in rural notions of ancestral protection, prestige, gender and seniority, has come to be a fragile achievement for both men and women. If, as McCaskie proposes, the 'Asante historical subject existed in dialogical consciousness', embedded in implicit collective 'background understanding[s]' (McCaskie 2000, pp. 43–44), it is likely that modern Ghanaians, like modern Batswana, must win recognition in the public arena, and that this attempt may, and often does, fail.[8]

Seen in dialogical terms, then, I aim to show that the activism of the three women described here emerged in response to hard times they encountered, in contention with authoritarian or conservative voices and the perceived predicaments of vulnerable others. In ethical terms their dignity (*seriti*) is linked by them to a sense of their rights and responsibilities as compassionate citizens (an ethos captured by the Tswana term *botho*). Notions of dignity, distinction and compassion define the qualities of the rightful leader in Botswana's modern-day political discourse, as they did for chiefship in the past (Schapera 1956, pp. 137–138). Modern citizenship itself is a discourse that emerges dialogically; it is not frozen in a timeless set of principles, but encapsulates 'specific, historically inflected, cultural and social assumptions' as these emerge over time (Werbner and Yuval Davis 1999, p. 2 passim, P. Werbner 1998).

I use embedded personal narratives to illustrate my argument. In doing so, I draw on a long tradition of African scholarship which stresses the centrality of narrative for recording the history of ordinary subjects alongside the 'morally determined, intellectually convinced, pioneers of a new Africa' (Lonsdale 2000, pp. 6–7).[9] 'No action', Lonsdale argues, is 'conceivable outside of narrative (2000, p. 8). African narratives of selfhood embody different genres of telling the past, Richard Werbner argues. These emerge inter-subjectively, embedded in wider social relations (R. Werbner 1991).

A common historiographical strategy in Southern African scholarship is that of telling women's life stories or microhistories, whether in order to recover their voices (Kompe 1985), to exemplify social change, highlight (racial) difference, or connect the global with the local (cf. Marks 2000). Thus, for example, Deborah Gaitskell portrays the individual lives of mission women, white and black, and relations across the racial divide (Gaitskell 2000a, 2000b).[10] The shift in such narrativising by African historians has been, Hay argues, 'from queens to prostitutes' – from heroic narratives of prominent individuals to narratives of silent victims (Hays 1988). One problem in such micro-histories, as Shula Marks points out, is to underline both the commonalities and contrastive positioning of the women portrayed (Marks 1988).[11] As C. Wright Mills has argued, the sociological imagination arises from the capacity to recognise that one's personal troubles are shared by others and determined by wider structural forces, that the personal is also the political. Hence the biographies of particular individuals,

> cannot be understood without reference to the historical structures in which the milieux of their everyday life are organized ... that is why culture and politics are now so intimately related; and that is why there is such need and such demand for the historical imagination. (Wright Mills 1959, p. 87)

The cases portrayed here are exemplary in the sense that they link the emergent recognition of shared predicaments to a widening sense of social responsibility, a move from the private domain to public activism, and the expansion of political imaginaries encompassing increasingly widening discursive horizons. My argument is thus that for the women portrayed here, a sense of social responsibility for a vulnerable other is not simply pre-given. It is discovered through ordeals, which test human capacity to act. This is an argument I have put elsewhere (see P. Werbner 1999a), in my development of the notion of 'political motherhood', first outlined by Jennifer Schirmer (1993) in her foundational analysis of women's resistance movements in San Salvador and Guatemala. Political motherhood, as I have interpreted it, refers to the active move of women from their traditionally defined domains of *seriti* in familial care and social responsibility – from being a mother and wife – to being actors in the public sphere, often in the face of authoritative male resistance. Such processes lead them to 'discover' their role as public actors when they face hard times (Schirmer 1989, 1993, pp. 58–59).[12] Writing about the rise of large-scale women's protest movements in South Africa, Gisela Geisler writes that in their heyday during the 1950s, they were predominantly 'motherist'. Hence Lilian Ngoyi, the first president of the Federation of South African Women, a multi-racial organisation, 'called on women to be at the forefront of the struggle in order to secure a better future for their children' (Geisler 2004, p. 67). As Tom Lodge too argues: 'The most powerful sentiment was matriarchal, captured most vividly in the magnificent phrase of Lilian Ngoyi's: "My womb is shaken when they speak of Bantu Education"' (Lodge 1983, p. 151). It was only later that more explicit feminist agendas were developed by women.[13]

In theoretical terms this means that the subject, from being the object of subjection, becomes an acting agent over a lifetime. This transformation, it is argued here, occurs in active participation, in the challenge posed by hard times, by the encounter with oppression and discrimination, or the misfortunes of vulnerable others. Particularly in the case of women, activists often begin as wives and mothers in the domestic sphere, only 'discovering' their role as public actors when they face hard times. Ultimately, this activism leads them to engage with more universalist knowledge regimes and gendered or human rights discourses. In this article I extend the comparison of the argument on political motherhood further by examining the unfolding ethics of contemporary African women activists. My acquaintance with all three women portrayed here has been long-term, based on many conversations and shared participation. Each of the women was interviewed formally once (in 2001, 2005 and 2006) at some length. The trade unionists are both elected officers, *primus inter pares,* firsts among equals in the union's collective action; the politician by contrast is highly placed enough to initiate major policies in her own right.

Generational consciousness: three women

While it may be true that postcolonial African women have moved into the public sphere in confronting hard times, these hard times have differed considerably for elite and subaltern women. Two of the cases discussed here trace the evolving subjectivities of subaltern women workers in Botswana in their involvement in the collective struggle for a decent wage. For an elite woman in Botswana, her subjectivity has evolved as she has felt compelled to respond to the HIV/AIDS pandemic ravaging her country, and the world. In each of these three cases, the women's life histories reveal a dialogical movement in which they reach consciousness and self-consciousness of wider global or cosmopolitan discourses, whether of labour or human rights.

One could equally well, of course, talk about Batswana men who faced the same sorts of ordeals, but I believe that a dialogical understanding of women's subjectivities as leaders is important precisely because the distances they have had to travel from being private mothers to public actors are often much greater, and because their interpretations of global discourses are inflected by their femininity. We see this in the remarkable autobiography of Emma Mashinini, a pioneering black woman trade unionist and activist in apartheid South Africa (Mashinini 1989). If, as Nancy Fraser argues, 'many of us who had been "women" in some taken-for-granted way have now become "women" in the very different sense of a discursively self-constituted political collectivity' (Fraser 1992, p. 179), this discursively constructed counter-hegemonic identity has nevertheless come alongside an identification with, and command of, broader discourses of social justice *which encompass men as well as women.* In this sense, the 'her-stories' presented here are not intended to relegate women to a 'separate sphere', isolated and apart from men (Scott 1988, pp. 20–21).

The Batswana women who figure in this article were born just before the moment of Botswana's independence, in 1966. All three thus grew up in a time of scarcity and relative poverty, before Botswana's diamond wealth created a boom in personal consumption with its associated politics of desire. Although two of the women have relatives in South Africa, all three were, and still are, committed Batswana citizens, dedicated to the country's project of nation-building, and sharing its ideology of development, as promoted by successive Botswana governments. If they oppose government policies, it is for the sake of just citizenship as they envision it. To the extent that they are also cosmopolitan subjects, they see the wider world as embodying values of justice and human rights which they believe should apply at home. All three have become leaders in their own spheres of action. Their careers, while not perhaps typical, portray the encounter of positioned individuals with their own, black, elected government in changing historical circumstances.

Seen sociologically, the women are thus part of a single 'generation' in the sense defined by Mannheim (1997). Mannheim argued that generational consciousness is always positioned temporally and socially. This means that those exposed to the same historical and cultural circumstances have, he proposes, a generational 'location'. In this sense members of a generation are 'sited'; they are 'held together by the fact that they experience historical events from the same, or a similar, vantage point' (Edmunds and Turner 2000). At the same time, however, people may respond quite differently to the same historical events in terms of their class, status and political attitudes. In other words, their interpretation of these events may differ quite markedly. They may be liberal or conservative, religious or secular. This creates, according to Mannheim, generational 'units' or identity cohorts within the broader generational cohort (Mannheim 1997, p. 306–307).

In addition to generation, then, actors may also be positioned by class and status, as the cases below illustrate. I begin my account with the personal life story of a union activist, who rose to be vice chairperson of the Manual Workers Union of Botswana, based on research conducted between 2005 and 2007.

Subaltern subjectivities

The Manual Workers Union of Botswana is the union of so-called 'industrial class' workers, employees of government, local government and parastatals in Botswana.[14] They occupy the lowest ranks in government service, working as cleaners, porters, drivers, hospital orderlies, messengers, storekeepers, cooks, agricultural extension workers, pump attendants, night watchmen, gardeners and such like. They are uneducated, relatively speaking, and they work in unskilled or menial jobs for very low pay. Not surprisingly, many of the Union's members, at least 50% and probably more, are women. If anything, women trade unionists occupy even lower employment positions than their male comrades. They are certainly below other public service women employees such as teachers or nurses. Unlike nurses in South Africa who constituted the nascent black middle class (Marks 1994), they identify with the international workers movement.

Despite the low wages of its members, the Union was remarkable during the time of my study, in 2005, for being the largest in Botswana – at its peak, in 2003, it had some 70,000 paid-up members, and even in 2005, in the face of an extremely painful factional split, it still had some 45,000 paid-up members. For a small country of 1.5 million people, these figures are impressive, especially in a period when union membership in the West is in decline. In Britain, for example, only a quarter of all workers belong to trade unions. This comparison underlines the immense achievement of the Manual Workers Union in recruiting virtually all government industrial class worker employees into the Union. Its success was partly due to the fact that Union dues were low, five pula, about 50 pence ($1) a month (they have since risen), yet the income from this paltry sum had made the Manual Workers Union rich – its officers had invested Union income wisely, in property and shares. Hence, paradoxically, the Union of some of the lowest-paid workers in Botswana was also the wealthiest in the country, and the best organised.

Trade unions in Africa were historically leading civil society actors in the colonial era, mobilising different ethnic and even national groups in demand of basic rights, united in opposition to colonial regimes. This was made evident in early anthropological studies of miners on the Zambian Copperbelt (Epstein 1958), and on the railways in East Africa (Grillo 1973, 1974). Trade unions were at the forefront of the liberation struggle against apartheid in South Africa,[15] Namibia (Moorsom 1977), and, since the 1980s, in Zambia

(Bratton 1994, pp. 66–67, 71–72), and Zimbabwe (Raftopoulos and Phimister 1997). In Ghana, railway and other public workers developed an independent, radical consciousness, across ethnic divisions, during the colonial era which persisted after independence (Jeffries 1978).

African nationalism arose on the back of such inter-ethnic alliances, only to be subsumed and suppressed after independence. In his magisterial survey of the 'labour question' in French and British Africa outside South Africa, Frederick Cooper (1996) documents the emergence of an emancipatory discourse of self-governance, citizenship and labour rights, and the growing international links of African unions to international labour organisations, during the period following World War II.

In Botswana in the early years after independence, unions, never strong, were actively discouraged and the demand for workers rights construed as unpatriotic, striking at the country's development effort.[16] It thus took an act of moral courage to challenge the status quo from the lowly position of a manual unskilled worker. Such workers were not the subject of common esteem. Seretse Khama, the first president of Botswana, extolled rural work while suppressing the demands of miners and government public manual workers. Thus, in a speech made in 1976 to celebrate 10 years of independence, Khama said that:

> the future of Botswana lies in the rural areas, in the land, where our forefathers eked out a living, where the majority of our people still eke out a living, and where we must make life more attractive not only for ourselves but for many future generations. To do this – to develop our rural sector – we must, first and foremost, appreciate the *dignity of labour,* and be instilled with a clear social conscience. We must come to grips with our true identity as a traditionally rural people who are being lured to the towns by the largely false promise of a better style of life and a more secure standard of living … Botswana is a democratic country founded on the ideal of *kagisana* (harmony) … rooted in our past – in our culture and traditions. (quoted in Vaughan 2003, p. 134, emphasis added)

Dignity, in Setswana *seriti* or *tlotlo*, is here represented as a feature of rural 'traditional' labour. Against that, the struggle of manual workers in modern non-agricultural work is for dignity and a fair wage in manual work outside the rural sector. There was a redemptive quality to the self-conception of struggle in the Union, the sense that their ultimate aim was to liberate the poor and oppressed – this, despite the fact that daily activities were marked by nitty-gritty, pragmatic negotiations over wages and rights. Members of the Union never tired of telling me that despite their poverty and lack of education, they could 'teach' the other unions and occupational associations in Botswana how to be unionists, how to protest, how to mobilise effectively.[17] This was a source of pride and distinction for them. The redemptive quality of their vision may be linked to their almost universal affiliation to churches, whether established churches like the Congregationalists (UCCSA) or Catholics, local 'Spiritual' churches, 'Zionists' or Pentecostals. Many of the leaders stressed that they had cut their teeth in church preaching and organisation. Indeed, the 'dignity of labour' bears Christian connotations, rooted in Puritan ideas of vocation and calling (Constantin 1979). The ILO headquarters in Geneva has a large mural painting by Maurice Denis entitled 'The Dignity of Labour', commissioned in 1931 by the International Federation of Christian Trade Unions, showing Christ in his Nazareth workshop talking to a group of workers, dressed in twentieth-century work clothes, who are easily identifiable as key leaders in the Christian Trade Union movement (WTO Building 2007, p. 12).

Their moral courage in claiming their rights as workers was displayed by the Manual Workers Union in what has come to be mythologised as a glorious history of struggle. The struggle proved that although Union workers may be uneducated, they cannot be intimidated, above all because they are rights experts. Knowing their rights has made them unflinching, tenacious negotiators who have gained the respect of university-educated, top Batswana civil servants. The achievement is all the more notable in a developing country in which open public protest is rare (Maundeni 2004). Botswana, a multi-party democracy since independence, started off as one of the poorest countries in the world, and for this reason, anti-state protests were defined as a betrayal of the solidarity needed to build a new nation. Against the grain, the Union demanded a fair wage from government. At the time, in 1990, its members were earning as little as 80 pula a month, which amounted in those days to not much more than 30 pounds sterling.[18]

The 1991 strike, which lasted for four or five days, was a remembered heroic fable of worker solidarity.[19] It took a further 10 years, until 2000, to achieve the minimum wage settlement demanded in that strike (by then in many ways the victory was a pyrrhic one), and it involved the Union taking the government to the High Court of Botswana and then to the Court of Appeal. It was during these heady days that Lilian Mamoshe[20] chaired and led the Union in her region before becoming, in 2004, a nationally elected vice-chair of the Union.

Lilian was a messenger in one of the government offices. She was excluded from school at 16 when she became pregnant and was a union leader by the age of 22. By the age of 30 she had been widowed, left to bring up four children.

I first noticed Lilian as an outstanding singer of Union songs, sung in Setswana, the language in which all union affairs and public meetings are conducted.[21] Many of the songs were written in Setswana by a former labour unionist and activist, Klass Motsedisa, later Labour Commissioner,[22] and their words speak of oppression and of the fight for workers' rights and liberty. There was (for me) an element of *déjà vu* in the songs,[23] of bygone eras and dead ideologies, but sung with passion, they re-emerged like a phoenix from the ashes, to bear real meanings in the real world. 'We work in suffering/Creating Botswana's wealth/We work, not eating/We die in poverty.' Or in another stanza: 'We die of hunger/Without healthcare/Without a home/Or education for our children.' And finally, 'We live in grief/We live wretchedly/We live like strangers/We live like beggars.' There is a certain twist in the songs: we, the workers, create the wealth of the new nation yet we live like beggars and strangers in the land of our forefathers. As one song goes: 'We (only) want our rights/In a land that is ours.'

The only solution to this injustice is to join the Union and fight for liberty. So the singers sing in Setswana, in a translated version of the English song: 'The Union is our shield – we shall not be moved/We are protected by it – we shall not be moved/Just like a tree that's planted on the waters, we shall not be moved.' There is sometimes a local colouring to the songs as when the workers sing: 'If you see workers (or women) sleeping in the bush/[know that] All they want is their rights.' Every Union meeting begins with a song and a Christian prayer, followed by more songs. And it ends with a song and a prayer. Prayers are sometimes passionate and highly politicised. The workers stand up, often dressed in red Union T-shirts, and sing, harmonising their voices naturally, as in a church choir. It is indeed a moving moment, a moment of uplifting, of hope, of unity and solidarity. Members are used to this kind of natural harmonising of different voices since almost all, as mentioned, are active members of Christian churches. Union and church are in Botswana deeply symbiotic.[24]

The singing conjures up a consciousness of faraway worlds – of workers' struggles in Europe at the birth of the industrial revolution, but also elsewhere in Africa, particularly Southern Africa. Here in Botswana, however, there is no doubt that the struggle is very concretely against one's own government, and not against white privileged capitalists. It is the workers' own black government which is oppressive. Workers work for the government and experience on a daily basis this oppression and the hardship caused by their meagre salaries. Lilian told me about their protests: 'We were called the ones who sweat, "*magaposetito*", that was the slogan, we would wipe our brows.'

For Lilian, who was not a great reader, the songs were a bridge to those other worlds of struggle, to a wider consciousness. She told me: 'When you sing these songs, you feel very happy, that you are very strong and it gives you the bones (i.e. the strength), like medicine. You feel at one with other workers.' As a woman, she had suffered. She was the victim of arbitrary rules which first removed her from education, then left her without compensation when her partner, who never married her, was killed in a road accident. Even when he was alive, although he professed to loving her deeply, he was, nevertheless, something of a philanderer. She managed her household and brought up her children alone. But she did not see her agency in her womanhood. She told me:

> I'm a man. I've never gone to those things of the women's wing. I just act like a man. I chaired the region for many years. Men like performing, standing in front of people. Women, I've noticed, like being the secretary, supporters behind the scenes. ... To me, I've never been in these women's councils pushing men away from us. I don't like working on one side – from experience, when we women get together we fight. There is a lot of jealousy, yes, even witchcraft – too much. Men like a big base, they want to be respected, honoured (*ba batla seriti, ba batla go tlotlwa*). Women are not so worried about that. They show off, they just show off. ... That's not *seriti* [lit. powerful dignity], just to shine. Myself, I want to act like a man.

She prided herself on her oratorical skills. When she stood up in front of an audience, she said, she was listened to intently, she held her audience.

At my request, she described the time of the great strike, the moment of remembered heroism.[25]

> I started on 122 pula a month. When we went on strike, in 1990 [the strike began in November 1991] I was on 322 [or 276, unclear] pula. Myself as a politician I had once been in a seminar with Mr Marambo who taught me about inflation and the poverty datum line, which was 276 (pula) a month, which means I was being paid at the poverty datum line. That is why I had the strength to teach my colleagues why the salary was so low. I was the vice chair of the region, but in fact acting as chair because the chair was never there. ... Sometimes I attended the Union General Council. When we came close to striking I started to attend. The decision came after the government went back on their agreement (with the Union)[26]. Some members didn't really understand, many had never been to school ... we just made a simple example, so they could understand. We took three plates, and we put *bogobe* [traditional porridge], in the first plate just one teaspoon, in the second four teaspoons and in the third a huge quantity. The huge one represented the Ministers and Perm Secs, the medium [plate], the supervisors. (We the workers had just one teaspoon).

Her account highlights the common stress by union leaders that although they are uneducated, they understand their rights. Lilian goes on to stress her own personal struggle against injustice in the workplace.

> We had a lot of general meetings. Here, they knew me, first when there was a lady who was our administrator, at the District Office, who was very corrupt and I exposed her. When you are a chair you have to arrange for the meetings, cases and so on.

She described the solidarity and commensality as memorable aspects of the strike:

> We went on strike for four days. It was long [for us] because it was our first time to strike. ... we were at the DC's office every morning, just to stay down, with our breakfast and scoff tins of lunch and we sat on the ground, on the grass, sleeping, but with exact times: we ate breakfast at 8, lunch at lunch time, all (of us) together. The DC was instructed to fire us from the place, to expel us, (so) then we went outside to the trees, there are some big trees outside

the magistrate's court ... (that is) also where political rallies are held, we went under the trees. We agreed that all of us every morning should come and report there. We took the register. First we prayed, then we sang union songs, me and my secretary, we are both Roman (i.e. Catholics).

Communication and coordination across the whole country was a key challenge, and strikers required ingenuity and cunning to overcome the obstacles put in their way. They were helped by the (Catholic) church:

> The DC had left an instruction that we could not use the phone, so there was no communication. In those days there were no cellphones in Botswana. So we went to see the father at the mission to tell him our problem – can we use your fax and your phone? He even came and prayed for us the second day. That was after we'd been expelled. There were so many journalists, and Radio Botswana.
>
> Then we phoned (the organising secretary) to know the news. What the government was deciding. So we could stop the strike. That time Mabustane [a place in the Kalagadi] was under me and then all the way to the Barolong farms and Moshupa. The regions were very big. 'Where are you?? Roger Roger, under the tree! Go on, Roger'. It was very tough, we tried our level best, we stole the roger roger [i.e. the walkie-talkies] from the government – radio communication [i.e. the people working in that department], they stole it. And when we talked to Mabutsane all the other places could hear us.
>
> All of us were fired, on the third day, the government announced they were firing us. On the fifth day when we went to work we found the letters dated two days previously.

Her vivid memories underline the enormity of the achievement the strike represented for union members. Although the strike itself was brief, it was followed by nine years of litigation and political struggle in Parliament, represented by the opposition parties, and through the press and media: 'The cases (against government, in the high court) went on and on ....'

Although she does not see herself as acting like a woman, and indeed has easy relations with male Union comrades, Lilian's victimisation on this occasion is very much that suffered by assertive women in lowly positions. She told me:

> The Union destroyed my future because of the strike. I am unlucky with bosses, every time I meet a tough a boss who refuses to promote me. I'm at the top notch of A2, right on the bottom scale. My bosses refuse to promote me. I would prefer to be a field assistant. They think I'm a bully, that I'm tough.

Lilian does not allow men to dominate her. She demands respect. She expects that her dignity and self-dignity, her *seriti*, be recognised. She is no longer the young girl expelled from school. But in her position as a manual worker, even as an elected national officer of the Union, she seems repeatedly to be forced into a clash of wills with dominating men. While she was the elected regional chair, she led the Union, she had the power of office. She represented members and settled their disputes with management, with great skill. As she told me, 'to be the chair of a region is tough'. But it is also rewarding. In her new, somewhat ambiguous status as elected vice-chairperson, she often felt marginalised and continuously struggled to find a role and a voice. Eventually, in November 2006, she was compelled to leave the Union after a confrontation with two of the union leaders, one a former colleague and friend, who had 'insulted' her. She began supporting the breakaway rival union. But through it all, through all her struggles, she saw herself as first and foremost a unionist, being a unionist was 'in her blood' (*Union e mo madi a me*) as another woman told me (Y.N. 16/7/05, Gaborone), part of a heroic self-narrativising that gave meaning to the daily slog and vision to her life.

Lilian's greatest ordeal as a worker came about as a result of a familiar conflict the world over: the clash between boss and underling. As a messenger for many years at the local offices of the Ministry of Commerce,[27] she had seen bosses come and go. As a Union leader, she had dealt with many of them in her feisty way. Her latest boss was particularly difficult, and she had a series of encounters with him culminating in a public stand-off which led to an extended series of disciplinary hearings. These exemplified the tenacity a unionist must have in their dealings with government. It also exemplified the vulnerability of manual workers who lose their jobs in a time of high unemployment and government lay-offs.

The case of the offending beret

The incident that sparked the case against Lilian happened during a public meeting of the local branch of the Ministry of Commerce with the Permanent Secretary. Lilian attended the meeting wearing a beret and refused to remove it when asked to do so by the head of the local branch of the Ministry of Commerce (she explained later that she had not groomed her hair). In retaliation, he had her physically removed to the back row. Then followed a series of confrontations and internal disciplinary hearings which ended with the decision to fire her. When I first discussed the case with her, she was cavalier about it, invoking the length of time she had worked at the Ministry of Commerce, which she felt gave her a measure of job security. Gradually, however, it became evident that her boss was determined to get rid of her. She had heard that he was accusing her of bewitching him and had even treated the walls of the office against sorcery. He would not allow her to enter his office.

Despite her reluctance to mobilise the Union officers, and especially the charismatic Organising General Secretary whom she regarded as an all-too-dominant male (though she had great admiration for his negotiating skills), she asked fellow unionists to represent her. In a series of meetings involving the Permanent Secretary and his deputy over a prolonged period, her case was repeatedly heard, and the decision that her firing had been illegal repeatedly reiterated by the Permanent Secretary and his deputy. But her boss dug his heels in and, having been suspended initially with pay, her salary was stopped and she was compelled to manage for several months without any income at all. In effect, she was destitute. She had no savings, no unemployment benefit (which does not exist at present in Botswana), no income from the Union, which does not support unemployed members, and no job. The house she was living in was rented and belonged to her employers, and three of her four children were still attending school and could not be easily shifted.

Just before the last scheduled hearing, her boss had a road accident while driving with two colleagues in a Ministry of Commerce vehicle. He was laid up in hospital seriously injured. Lilian told me over the telephone that the final hearing had been delayed. She also told me that colleagues in the local branch of the Ministry of Commerce had been coming to her with information about the boss – in particular, that he had bought a vehicle without tendering, breaking regulations and hence subject to charges of corruption. She felt sure his days in the Ministry were numbered. His accident, she speculated, had convinced him that her witchcraft powers were huge, but although she heard rumours about this, he had not come out with a public accusation, since witchcraft accusations are against the law in Botswana.

After so many dashed hopes that the case would be settled, Lilian finally rang me up one day to tell me that she was going back to work on Monday[28]. Her boss had been ordered by the Permanent Secretary to pay her lost wages over several months from his own salary and she had been reinstated. When he asked why she had refused the 'reasonable request' (as set out in her job contract) to attend prayer meetings, she showed him the Constitution of Botswana, she told me, which guarantees freedom of creed and assembly. During this time she continued to be an elected officer of the Union, critical of some decisions made by the executive and yet dependent on its representatives to help her fight her own case.[29]

I asked Lilian how she was welcomed by the other workers when she finally returned to work? 'So well,' she said, 'They say I am a hero' (*mogaka*, i.e. the bravest, a champion). Her boss was still in hospital, being treated for severe injuries. One of the other passengers had injured his back and was also still hospitalised several months after the accident.

It is, perhaps, ironic that a year later, Lilian had made friends with her boss, supported by the local chief, also a friend or even distant relative. On a recent trip to Botswana, in 2007, I found her position amazingly transformed: her boss had even selected her to represent the local manual workers in her department at a national meeting to discuss changes in the structure of public salaries. Yet a year later she had once again clashed with him, over his treatment of a fellow woman worker, and once again been suspended without pay. When I last talked to her, in July 2008, she reported that she had joined another union which was handling her case while her boss had finally been transferred.

Lilian's case is exemplary rather than unique. Winning such cases for relatively uneducated manual workers in confrontation with their educated, Westernised bosses, has been the reason for Union support among its rank and file members, the basis for its formidable reputation. Suspected attempts by the current government (or the ruling party, the BDP) to infiltrate and undermine the Union's strength through factional challenges, accusations of corruption and splits, have had to contend with the belief of ordinary rank and file members, based on past experience, that only the Union could protect their interests and their vulnerable, low-paid jobs.

Subjection and agency

Lilian's case illuminates the complexity of self-knowledge and personal agency that manual workers in post-independence Botswana may develop. On the one hand, Lilian sees herself as an actor and leader, hence a man; on the other hand, she is a vulnerable victim, suspected and discriminated against, hence a woman. In Botswana subjectivities are perceived to be affected interactively, with people's hostilities and animosities impacting physically on a subject's sense of self (see Klaits in press). They are also formed through interaction with a close circle of kin and ancestors (R. Werbner 1989, Chapters 1 and 3).

Clearly for Lilian the strike was an empowering moment of heightened consciousness, solidarity and camaraderie, an ordeal successfully overcome. The Union is the primary source of her identity as an acting subject. Nevertheless, she is also active in other village committees. Indeed, as a civic-minded villager, she has fostered good relations with the local chief. In 2007 she was engaged in setting up a local Community Based Organisation to help HIV/AIDs orphans. She is a long-term supporter and member of the BNF, the main opposition party. She also dreams of leaving her job and going to work in England, so she can afford to build a house in her natal village. Although herself a manual worker, some of her closest relatives are middle-class nurses, teachers and civil servants.

The active participation of women in the strike and in the union more generally supports Iris Berger's observation, against the argument that women workers tend to be 'incompletely' proletarianised, that in Southern Africa the predicament of very low wages for men, and women's responsibility for basic household livelihood, have created 'a basis for solidarity between men and women' and women's trade union militancy (Berger 1986, pp. 220–221).

The complexity inherent in African workers' identities and subjectivities is highlighted in studies that challenge simplistic assumptions about popular worker mobilisation and strikes, or the emergence of a long-term proletarian consciousness.[30] Repeatedly, unions are revealed to be fractionised by internal racial, class and educational divisions, with clerical and skilled workers often suspected of being stooges or sell-outs. In the early colonial period, sustained consciousness was said to be weakened by workers' double rootedness as circulatory labour migrants.[31] Local and national union interests often diverge (see Cheater 1986, Kapferer 1972), leading to suspicion of official political rhetoric. Workers are also subjected to appeals in the name of broader, national interests, as in Botswana. Recently, anthropologists have challenged the supposed homogeneity of Botswana as a 'Tswana' nation, and have highlighted the need to study marginalised social groups and intersections of ethnicity, class and gender.[32]

Despite their multiple affiliations, however, these ambiguities seemed to be absent from the Union officials' worldview. In their confrontations with government the Union, like Lilian, drew on a rights ethic that presumes that justice should and must prevail, that their rights are fundamentally and intrinsically sacrosanct. These rights are defined internationally, by the ILO convention and by long traditions of labour struggle.[33]

It is worth asking, nevertheless, whether union leaders' pride in their capacity to win against the full might of the state despite, as they repeatedly stressed to me, their lack of education, echoes postcolonial narratives of subalternity, or whether it merely mirrors more familiar class narratives of conflict? Throughout the Union meetings I attended, including those convened to protest the firing of 461 diamond miners, which included teachers' and many other unions, the stress was on the fact that the Botswana government did not respect international human rights and labour laws; it had not yet, as it were, come of age, and it thus thought it could oppress workers with impunity. This narrative is one which is no longer bothered about a colonial past, in the sense that it demands full accountability and responsibility from the people's own African government. Although mention was made by one miners' union leader of the 'white' ownership of De Beers, most speakers universally pointed out that Debswana, De Beers' daughter company, was in reality owned by the Botswana government and it was thus government that was ultimately responsible for the injustice suffered by the miners.[34] In all these conversations and meetings the pre-independence past seemed totally irrelevant and long forgotten. Colonialism was never mentioned and was never invoked as an excuse for current failings. What was mentioned repeatedly *was a new cosmopolitan world of rights*, including workers' rights, which the state should acknowledge and respect (on this, see P. Werbner 2008).

In demanding procedural accountability from government and the right to strike, organise, unionise and negotiate for fair wages, workers are also inserting themselves into a complex bureaucratic and legal regime, which defines the limits of their rights as citizen workers. In this discourse on the dignity of labour prior notions of *seriti* as self-respect and embodied selfhood, dignity and well-being in the rural context have been incorporated into demand for worker respect and well-being.[35]

Elite postcolonial subjectivities

I turn now to my second case, of an elite postcolonial leader in Botswana. Joy Phumaphi is currently vice-president of the World Bank, and had also served a stint as Assistant General Director of the World Health Organisation in Geneva, having been the Minister of Health who introduced universal, free anti-retroviral (ARV) treatment in Botswana.[36] Ms. Phumaphi comes from a very different background from Lilian Mamoshi and her struggles have consequently occurred on a much larger stage.[37] She was born into one of the elite families in Botswana, which rose to prominence after independence. Her parents were founder members of the Botswana Democratic Party, which has won all the elections and ruled Botswana since independence. Her mother, a national charity worker, was mayor of the capital city, and her father rose rapidly in the civil service to become the permanent secretary of several ministries before leaving the civil service to be appointed the first ever African member of the International Board of BP and an ambassador. At 18, Joy was already head of the student union. She married a young lawyer, now a high court judge, trained as an accountant and worked as a civil servant.

Nevertheless, as a young child, Joy told me, she experienced both the hardship of poverty and the exclusions of race and minority status, growing up in Francistown, a white settler-dominated provincial town in Botswana. These experiences left an indelible trace and shaped her political outlook, she reflected. Lilian had told me: 'If you are suffering a lot you have to struggle. I don't like to see people suffering, being abused because they don't know their rights.' This sense of responsibility for the suffering of others, of *botho*, compassion, is one that motivated Joy's public activism and which she linked to their rights as citizens and to human rights.

When she became Minister of Health in Botswana the young nation was in the middle of the worst crisis of its short history. The HIV/AIDs pandemic, entrenched after growing almost imperceptibly for 10 years, was claiming more and more lives, with no cure in sight. There was medication on the market, anti-retroviral therapy (ARV), which could keep the disease at bay. A two-tiered health system was in effect in place, which protected the wealthy salariat. Those on private medicare, mainly civil servants and businessmen, were able to access ARV medication, while for the rest of Botswana's citizens, the disease spelled certain death. Yet most civil society activists, including middle-class academics with whom I spoke to in 1999 and 2000, just shrugged their shoulders in despair. Botswana was too poor to afford the drugs, one feminist activist told me, and anyway, people would not adhere to the complex drug regime involved.

Although in retrospect the move to introduce universal free anti-retrovirals in Botswana may now seem obvious, it can be seen as a turning point in the history of citizenship in the country. At the time, in 1999, it required a combination of strategic planning, courage, conviction and vision to go against the prevailing wisdom in order to overcome the hesitations and paralysis affecting the government, the Ministry of Health and the country as a whole. In the many conversations with Joy it became evident that it was not her training, education, work or even family background as such that made her a quiet revolutionary. It was a long-term conviction, which she expressed several years later in an interview with *The Times of India* in relation to her work at WHO on maternal and child mortality:

> It is a moral, political and social imperative to ensure that people don't die when you have a fairly easy solution to prevent this. Women give life to save the future and they are entitled to the gift of life. It is a basic human right.

So too in Botswana, once it was clear that medication was available that could prolong adult lives and save the lives of young babies, it was, she believed, a basic human right of all citizens to access the drugs freely. Her conviction can be seen in the context of a growing global movement to recognise access to health and free medication as a basic human right in the late 1990s.[38] In South Africa the international drug companies had in 1999 withdrawn their case against the use of generics, but no African country at the time provided free, universal anti-retrovirals and access to regular testing, counselling and medical care.[39]

In her struggle to introduce free ARV treatment in Botswana, Joy had to overcome gridlock and scepticism in the Ministry of Health, to persuade the president of Botswana of the reality of the looming economic disaster, to enlist the international drug agencies to become partners in the fight against AIDs in Botswana, to set up new systems of health care where none existed before. In short, it required all her skills of tact, diplomacy, administration, organisation and business management to overcome a myriad of hurdles, to bring NGOs, donor agencies, civil servants and government on board, and beyond that, to appeal to all Batswana citizens to heed the dangers of the disease, even to believe in its existence.

Joy is an extremely modest, soft-spoken woman, but as a politician she was not afraid to heap scorn on the antediluvian views of fellow MPs. This was exemplified in a speech on mental health she made in Parliament on 19 July 2001, following comments by two male MPs that 'there was nothing wrong in saying that a person is sane or insane', what 'benefit' is there in euphemisms? MP Phumaphi's response was scathing:

> The same benefit that you derive from not being called a bastard or from not being called a *kaffir* or any other derogatory term is the same benefit that is going to protect your dignity and protect you from discrimination and from being looked upon as a lesser human being than others is the benefit that this particular group is going to derive from the removal of the [']euphemisms['] that the Honourable Member is referring to. (Leslie 2006, p. 119)

The essential lead taken by the then President Mogae in mobilising the nation for the struggle against the disease has meant that the narrative of her own pioneering contribution is often left untold.[40] She is a loyal wife and mother who has brought up four of her own children and has fostered or adopted some sixteen others. But she is clearly a formidable negotiator and administrator, moved by her sense of conviction and responsibility for vulnerable others. Her sense of dignity means being open and accessible to others,[41] never allowing her status to blind her to the misfortunes, to the 'face' of the other, of those less fortunate than her. Hers is a liberal, cosmopolitan normative discourse, apparently quite different from that of activists in the Manual Workers Union, one she has evidently recovered for herself, deeply integrated into a coherent worldview. Although she does not use words like exploitation and oppression, she is on the side of the oppressed, the impoverished and the marginalised. They too, she argues, have a right to live as free agents, to make their own decisions about their future, to have a future.

Unlike Lilian who sees herself ambiguously as both man and woman, Joy embraces wholly her identity as a woman, humanist and feminist. She accepts the fact that she operates in a world in which men often dominate, and that this entails being a certain type of leader in this highly politicised environment: one who acts strategically, with tact, a clear vision, and meticulous attention to detail.

Botswana's achievement in creating a much improved universal health system to deliver medication, and to test and monitor the treatment of HIV and AIDS patients, has undoubtedly liberated citizens from a life of suffering and early death. It has come along with a major educational thrust demanding that citizens change their sexual habits. Yet it needs also to be recognised that this epistemic shift, which has created the grounds for an expanded notion of citizenship, has also created, in Foucauldian terms, a new subjection regime of monitoring and surveillance, backed by scientific knowledge and complex structures of governance.

Cosmopolitan working classes

The question is: do all cosmopolitans have to be members of such an elite? Recent research in Africa has begun to look at the role of contemporary African elites, intellectuals, civil society pioneers and activists (e.g. Yarrow 2008, R. Werbner 2004, 2008, Hodgson 2008).[42] To conclude this article, I want to defend my argument, put elsewhere, that in a cosmopolitanising world of increased mobility and so-called space-time compression, there can be working-class cosmopolitans too who share a global subjectivity. To consider this possibility, I turn now to a portrait not of a migrant worker, as in my previous article on this subject (P. Werbner 1999b), but of a trade union employee who became a worker representative in modern Botswana. During my study in 2000 and 2005, Elsinah Botsalano was Coordinator of the Women's Wing of the Manual Workers' Union. In this role she had risen to become the elected representative of the Southern Africa region and elected 'Titular' for the English-speaking African Region in an international labour union, Public Service International (PSI).

Elsinah, like Lilian, was of Barolong origin, a tribal group spanning Botswana's international boundary with South Africa, and half her immediate family lived across the border. She came from a settlement in the Kalahari, and she began her career in the trade union as a typist, in 1982. Later, she organised workshops on women's issues, and trained as an accounts officer. She was one of a team of four Union employees, who ran the Union on a day-to-day basis.

As the Union's strength grew, it reaffiliated to the Botswana Federation of Trade Unions,[43] and to Public Service International, an international trade union of public workers with its headquarters in Geneva, despite the heavy costs of membership. PSI represents millions of workers worldwide. It comprises five major regions, Africa and the Middle East being one such region. As Titular, Elsinah travelled regularly to Geneva and Johannesburg for PSI executive meetings, workshops and seminars. She also travelled to Italy for an ILO course, and to Beijing for the UN International Conference on Women, as part of the Botswana delegation. She was part of Union struggles against redundancies and looming privatisation of the public sector.

Elsinah is, I suggest, a working-class cosmopolitan, relatively uneducated and thus deeply conscious of the inequalities in Botswana; part, perhaps, of a tiny labour elite; well-travelled and knowledgeable about the kinds of rights to which low-paid workers, and women in particular, are entitled. She and her fellow trade unionists have made a genuine difference to the alleviation of poverty in the lives of ordinary Batswana women, indeed arguably far more so in *economic* terms than other initiatives of the women's movement.[44] In the capital city, Gaborone, her position in the established church, the UCCSA (the United Congregationalist Church of South Africa, formerly the LMS), its committees and women-run burial society, which included many wives of the great and the good in Botswana, seemed to prove her membership in the bourgeois middle class of the capital. Yet she is not really a sophisticated cultural cosmopolite, and although she was part of the Botswana delegation to Beijing, she is often marginalised by the group of highly educated elite women activists, feminists and global travellers who shared that experience with her. Although she is, quite explicitly, a feminist who promotes gender equality within the Union, and despite her international status and role as coordinator of the Union's women's wing, as an employee, Elsinah accepts that her role as a labour activist in Botswana is to lend unquestioning and loyal support to the charismatic organising secretary of the Union, a man who during my research in 2005 was regarded by ordinary rank-and-file members – and even by many government negotiators – as having almost mystical powers to settle disputes, as he travelled up and down the country.[45]

Elsinah is an example of a new type of cosmopolitan – the *procedural* cosmopolitan or cosmocrat: a person of competence who knows all the regulations (*tsamaiso* in Setswana), is familiar with constitutional structures; a skilled negotiator who is meticulous in her observance of rules and procedures. She enunciates the Public Service International ideology which promotes women and youth participation and is imbued with political correctness; for example, when I asked her if she was a Kgalagadi, a lower-status group living in the Kalahari where some members of her family lives, she explained that no, she comes from the relatively high-status Barolong tribe, but added that she would not mind being a Kgalagadi.

How does Elsinah exemplify the cosmopolitan? When she travels, she rarely ventures out beyond the Geneva airport hotel or the PSI offices located near the hotel, mainly for lack of time. Despite the arduous air journey from Botswana of some 20 hours to Geneva, she stays only as long as meetings last, usually a couple of days, moving between her hotel and PSI headquarters (in France, on the border with Switzerland) by public transport. Like most other workers in Botswana, virtually the whole of her *per diem* allowance is saved up to support her immediate and extended family back home, and she is almost always called back urgently to attend to the day-to-day mundane business of the Union, or to care for the illness of her own children, her ailing mother[46] or one of her numerous siblings. Her brief forays abroad, however frequent, mean she never feels at home there; she is not a connoisseur of art, music or foreign cuisines. Nor is she a pioneer, a mover-and-shaker in global affairs, although her election as Titular is a first for Botswana. Instead, she is an actor in an emergent bureaucracy of global governance, and, given her class background, a person who has advanced quite remarkably into global affairs through the esteem of colleagues for her dedication, religious piety and procedural knowledge. She is a person of evident moral integrity and meticulous commitment to fair procedures. She achieved her position as elected Titular for the English-speaking African Region of PSI in the face of competition from far more educated trade unionists, men and women, civil servants in local and central government, and despite Botswana's insignificance by comparison to larger African countries like neighbouring South Africa, where PSI's headquarters are housed in Johannesburg. Her achievement is all the more remarkable because in public meetings she is often soft-spoken and diffident, frequently the tireless behind-the-scenes worker lending support to an event rather than being its charismatic leader. As chair, she is practical, down-to-earth and matter-of-fact. If she expresses emotions, this is only when she joins in the singing of trade union songs or leads public prayers.

Like the other women portrayed here, Elsinah is weighed down by family commitments. In addition to her children, husband and living parents, she has at least a dozen living siblings and half-siblings, resident on both sides of the border, who regard her as an elder sister, and expect her to take command at family funerals or in illnesses. She juggles her commitments to them, the Church, and the Union as best she can, always on the run. Her consciousness as a worker (and feminist) has emerged, over time, in work, particularly in the endless round of meetings negotiating workers' rights, and in repeated legal adversarial action: with the government, in the High Court and the Court of Appeal, and with internal union dissenters and trouble-stirrers who on occasion have questioned her own integrity. As in her family commitments, she is dedicated and loyal – above all to the Union and its leader. Her consciousness has evolved through constant learning, but her instinct is always to play safe, not to rock the boat; instead, to follow the rules and procedures.

Conclusion

Writing about South African labour leaders such as E.S. Sachs of the Transvaal Garment Workers' Union and Ray Alexander of the Cape Food and Canning Workers' Union, Iris Berger suggests that 'any sense of identification with others is not simply a given fact, inherent in people's material lives, but rather needs to be constructed conceptually, emotionally and historically' (Berger 1992, p. 11). In South Africa's long history of repeated mass strikes, protests and marches, the theme of trade union activism as historically leading to a sense of expansive agency and personal empowerment is one repeatedly stressed in the scholarly literature. As Jennifer Fish comments in relation to post-independence South Africa: 'Domestic workers' unionisation – while replete with struggles for both recognition and financial viability – continually reflected women's agency' (2006, p. 120). Yet as Emma Mashinini notes almost as an aside in her story of her struggle to build a trade union and gain recognition for it in the face of apartheid, despite her national achievements and international recognition; despite the fact that the majority of black workers were women, when it came to electing the National Executive of the newly formed COSATU or its logo, women were absent, so that, as Mashinini concludes, 'it means that our presence – our efforts, our work, our support – was not even recognised' (1989, p. 118).

Botswana's short history is far less conflictual and thus lacks, on the whole, the mass populist element so prominent in the historical activism of its big neighbour. Nor have worker politics been imbricated in race politics as they almost invariably were in apartheid South Africa and other colonial societies. Nevertheless, my article has argued, in Botswana too there are many public actors, among them women, whose subjectivities have been formed in interaction and confrontation with the government and state, in response to local conflicts, injustices and crises.

Schirmer has warned against a Eurocentric tendency to elevate Western feminism as 'a superior understanding of the 'truth' (1993, p. 63) vis-à-vis other forms of women's activism. Instead, as this article too argues, the need is to reveal the alternative scripts and conjunctions that emerge, in action, in particular contexts, as subaltern women in the global south create political imaginaries that make sense of their citizenship and gendered worlds in specific political or social circumstances. In the face of poststructuralist, post-Butler feminist suspicions of essentialised unities of self, class or gender, the article thus follows Schirmer and McNay in arguing for the need to reclaim concepts such as agency, consciousness and experience, but as sited, embodied, participatory, dialogical and conjunctural.

In his book on postcolonial subjectivities in Africa, Richard Werbner reminds us of the slipperiness of the cluster of terms around the idea of the subject. Nor, he says, 'can we claim to have resolved the ambiguities by imposing a standard vocabulary,' given the richness of the literature around these terms' (R. Werbner 2002, p. 3). Nevertheless, he argues, we can say, broadly, that subjectivities are political, moral and realised existentially, in consciousness (ibid.).

The emergent postcolonial subjectivities I have portrayed here draw on modern discourses: of class oppression, normative cosmopolitanism, labour rights or human rights and contemporary Christian humanist religiosity. But as I proposed at the outset, the easy opposition between overdetermined subjects and free autonomous individuals, cannot be sustained. Instead, the article has highlighted a dialectic between autonomy and heteronomy, emancipation and subjection, by tracing the evolving ethics and postcolonial subjectivities of both subaltern and elite women in Botswana. I have argued that these subjectivities need to be understood dialogically, as historically inflected in struggle, in the face of hard times, and that therefore it can be said that there is no subject in and for itself, 'no subjectivity prior to intersubjectivity' (ibid., p. 1). Above all, the women I described here sought dignity and self-worth through a sense of responsibility for more vulnerable others.

Acknowledgements

This article is a revised version of a keynote address presented at the conference on 'Self and Subject: African and Asian Perspectives', 20–23 September, 2005, Ferguson Centre, Edinburgh, and to a workshop convened by the ESRC Programme on Non-Governmental Public Action (NGPA) on 14–16 March, 2006. I am grateful to participants in both events for the comments and encouragement, and to the ESRC for its financial support. The article also responds to comments from reviewers in JSAS and CHHS.

Notes

1. See, in particular, Foucault (1972, 1977, 1980).
2. McNay argues that Bourdieu's notion of embodied habitus allows for the capacity to change in the encounter with the 'field', a complex and changing social formation. She also appeals to Ricoeur's notion of narrativity and Castoriadis's notion of the radical social imaginary to spell out the possibility of agency outside discourse.
3. Butler argues that there is no subject prior to discourse so that: 'The paradox of subjectivation is precisely that the subject who would resist such norms is itself enabled, if not produced, by such norms. Although this constitutive constraint does not foreclose the possibility of agency, it does locate agency as a reiterative or rearticulatory practice, immanent to power, and not a relation of external opposition to power' (Butler 1993, p. 15). Foucault in fact sees resistance as *invoking* power: 'if there was no resistance, there would be no power relations' (1997, p. 167).
4. Attention to this dimension of Foucault's work would have enabled Mahmood to incorporate aspects of her ethnography left untheorised, in which she describes the emergence among pietist women of leaders (*diyani*), experts in the interpretation of Koran and Hadith, who claim the (hitherto masculine) right to lead the prayers, in some cases even when male imams are present. These women also lead active lives in proselytising and fund-raising for philanthropic purposes. One of them even filled the place of a male leader while he was jailed, and later she herself was jailed. Pious women also claimed far more authority within the family and one told Mahmood she would divorce her husband if he prevented her from engaging in pious activism.
5. Women and slaves were of course excluded.
6. Foucault appears to fudge the relation of the ethical Self to the Other in an interview in 1984 as well as the transition he identifies from the Greek to Hellenistic period, arguing merely that mastery of one's desires guarantees that a person will rule with moderation and not become a tyrant. Nor does he ever fully theorise the cosmopolitanism of the Stoics and Cynics (see Foucault 1994). Elsewhere (1983) he argues for individual autonomy through 'self-fashioning' in isolation.
7. On the global negotiations surrounding the right to free medication and health see Petchesky (2003).
8. On the dialogical see also Bakhtin (1984). Bakhtin means by dialogical the fact that personal worldviews always contain implicitly a consciousness of others' views in a never fully resolved argument, which arises in response to moral ordeals and crucibles (see Holquist and Clark 1984). Jeffery Nealton (1998, Chapter 2) compares this to Emmanuel Levinas's dialogics which – like the present article – posits the necessity of subjection to alterity along with responsibility for the other.
9. Lonsdale (2000) thus rejects Fanon's sceptical view of agency in *Wretched of the Earth* (1970) based on his belief that only violent revolution would free the self from mimetically reflecting the colonial master.
10. Anthropological examples include Shostak (1981)
11. Often interviews are combined thematically, as in B. Bozzoli (1991).

12.   In San Salvador and throughout much of Latin America, women moved into the public domain to protest against the disappearance of sons, daughters and husbands, kidnapped by the military dictatorships. In Israel, Northern Ireland, Cyprus or the former Yugoslavia, women entered the public sphere to protest against their exclusion from decisions about war and peace, and the terror and injustices that occupation and ethnic violence were causing. In England in the nineteenth century, Christian women initially entered the public sphere as philanthropists, concerned with the plight of the poor and destitute. Without ever being feminists, they became experts on matters of social welfare and fought for major legal reforms. Through their activism they created a much expanded public sphere in which matters of personal welfare were included, and were increasingly debated by political parties and financed by the state. In my own work on political motherhood among diasporic Pakistani women in Manchester (P. Werbner 1999a, 2002, Chapter 10), I traced the way male resistance to their philanthropic fundraising drove charitable women into the public sphere. From defining themselves as privileged do-gooders, the women became self-conscious anti-war activists who demanded the right to have an independent voice in the diasporic public sphere.

13.   See Wells (1999) on early women's campaigns. For a recent review of feminist movements in post-independent Southern African countries see the special issue of the *Journal of Southern African Studies*, 'Women and the Politics of Gender in Southern Africa' (Walsh et al. 2006).

14.   Recently, the union has amalgamated into a single federation with the Civil Service Union BOPEU. In 2005 the Union's name, the National Amalgamated Local and Central Government and Parastatal Manual Workers Union, was changed, dropping the 'Manual', to allow it to recruit workers from a wider range of occupations, but the name did not stick and during most of my visit in 2007, the Union was exclusively for industrial class workers and was still called the Manual Workers Union for short.

15.   For a comprehensive review see Berger 1992, J. and R. Simons 1983, also Good 2002, pp. 175–176, 182–186.

16.   On the strike in Pikwe see N. Parsons et al. (1995, pp. 320–322); on civil servants organising see R. Werbner (2004, p. 168–174); on unions generally see Selolwane (2000) and Molokomme (1989).

17.   See, for example, Peace (1975) on the mutual stereotypes of different classes of African workers and then sense of factory shop-floor unionists that they were the true opposition to oppressive management. Peace (1979) argues that low-paid workers in Nigeria were far more closely embedded in and hence aligned with the peasantry and urban masses than they were with the more highly-paid salariat in Nigeria.

18.   Perhaps not coincidentally, Unity Dow challenged the state on the new citizenship law in the High Court on 4 May 1990, in a landmark case for women's rights in Botswana.

19.   The strike is discussed by both Mogalakwe (1997) and Maundeni (2004) who both recognise its significance in the development of civil society. Their instructive account has laid the foundation for future studies. It should be noted in relation to their accounts that although the Union did not win its appeal in the Court of Appeal, the court reprimanded the government for not honouring agreements negotiated between the Union and State representatives, and reinstated all the workers with full rights. Second, that government attempts to lure workers away from the Manual Workers Union into the civil service (which at that time was prohibited from unionising) with the offer of pension rights, failed, with most Union members preferring the five-year gratuity system.

20.   A pseudonym.

21.   Minutes of meetings were written in English after the event.

22.   I interviewed Motsediso in his home in Palapye in 2005. He is a prominent member of the Botswana National Front, an opposition party with, in the past, Marxist tendencies.

23.   I speak of my own youthful experience as a member of the youth labour movement in Israel, who had witnessed the passion with which such ideologies were celebrated in the past.

24.   On this symbiotic relationship between the Methodist church and the labour movement in another context see Thompson (1963).

25.   Virtually all studies of trade unions mark the passage of time via a union's historically significant strikes. This seems unavoidable, if repetitive, since these remembered mobilisation events shape members' consciousness.

26.   This was negotiated by the National Joint Industrial Coordinating Committee (NJICC), a negotiating mechanism set up in agreement with the government. The final decision lay with

the Ministry of Finance, who had rejected the agreement that had been reached by the Committee.

27. In fact, she worked in the offices of one of the other ministries.
28. I was in England at the time.
29. In November 2006, however, as mentioned, she was excluded from the Executive Committee, and, after she went to the Press, from the Union. In her view this was because she had been questioning and challenging the lack of transparency in the financial decision-making process and strategies adopted by Union officers (see the *Monitor*, 20 November 2006, pp. 1–2). She intended to join the rival, breakaway union and to carry her 'region' with her into the newly-established union.
30. See, for example, Simons and Simons (1982), McCracken (1988), Cheater (1986, 1988) and, for an overview, R. Werbner (1988).
31. On this in Southern Rhodesia, see, for example, C. van Onselen (1976), who argues that, cumulatively, over time, ideologies of worker resistance came to be established, rooted in the industrial landscape despite a labour repressive system and the failure of individual strikes.
32. On ethnic minorities see, for example, Solway (2002), Durham and Klaits (2002) and Motsafi-Haller (2002); on the marginalisation of the disabled, Livingstone's exemplary study (2005); on the intersection of gender and class see Griffiths (1997).
33. ILO Conventions 48, 87, 98 and 151 on freedom of association and the right to unionise give unions the right to strike and the civil service to unionise. Although ratified by Botswana in 1997 and 1998, conventions 98 and 151 were only passed in Parliament in an amended labour law in 2004. They were published in mid-2005 after some delay, and were being implemented in 2006, with several major 'associations' (such as the Teachers and Civil Servants) unionising. Unions in Botswana may employ full-time administrative staff but, until the change in the law, elected union officials were required to work full-time in the industry that the union represented. This rule severely limited union leaders' professionalism and effectiveness, and was criticised by the International Confederation of Free Trade Unions (ICFTU). The law also severely restricted the right to strike. Legal strikes are theoretically possible in Botswana after an exhaustive arbitration process, but in practice none of the country's strikes has been legal. Sympathy strikes are prohibited. After much delay, the Trade Unions and Employers' Organisations Act was changed to limit the Minister of Labour and Home Affairs' powers in labour issues.
34. The government owns 51% of the shares in Debswana.
35. It is beyond this article to discuss *seriti* here in all its complexity. It differs, however, from the Gikuyu notion of *wiathi* described by Lonsdale, which refers to moral value attributed by Kikuyu to control over their labour in self-mastery, a precondition for gerontocratic rural sub-clan authority, and secondarily to freedom (Lonsdale 1992, p. 356), a notion which later, in the context of labour migration and struggle for independence, was expanded to include worker strikers' 'struggle for self-mastery' (p. 416) Mau Mau fight for self-mastery and freedom (p. 446) and even the *wiathi* right to vote (p. 461). *Seriti*, by contrast, is, like charisma, an embodied notion of the self as inherited 'shade', protected by the ancestors, which stresses dialogical features of respect and self-respect, compassion, and generosity, as well as vulnerability to attack by others (see R. Werbner and P. Werbner, forthcoming).
36. In 2007, she was appointed Assistant Director to the World Bank in Washington.
37. For a further portrayal of Joy Phumaphi see R. Werbner (2008).
38. See Petchesky (2003). Athough she was involved in the Doha negotiations in 2001, her conviction of the need for universal free ARV preceded these.
39. Botswana was the first country in Africa to implement a nationwide anti-retroviral programme. Four years later, 95% of patients, including those using the private sector, are reported to be receiving treatment, and the programme is often held up as a test case for the rest of the continent. Teenage pregnancies are down by 70% and life expectancy rates are rising. In a study on treatment adherence and drug resistance, researchers at the Botswana-Harvard AIDS Institute found little evidence of treatment fatigue – becoming less vigilant about taking the pills over time – and patients are said to have so far demonstrated better or at least the equivalent adherence of their western counterparts. Universal testing has also been introduced. See a recent presidential press release and http://www.plusnews.org/Report.aspx?ReportId=39685

40. My husband and I happened to be in Botswana during the early part of this struggle for hearts and minds in 1999 and 2001, and I have subsequently interviewed her about it, though there is much still left to be told.
41. Schapera (1956, p. 139) notes that great chiefs were supposed to be 'easy of access'.
42. On African intellectuals, nationalism and pan-Africanism see Mkandawire (2005).
43. It subsequently left the BFTU and helped establish a rival federation in 2007.
44. In Botswana, the women's movement is mainly concerned with rights issues. See Selolwane (1998, 2000), Geisler (2006). Legal rights do, of course, have economic implications. However, as most of the contributors to the special *JSAS* issue argue, despite highly progressive constitutions and legal reform, implementation is still a challenge across the whole spectrum of family law reforms. Moreover, few of these movements outside trade unions significantly impact on the economic circumstances of poor women. In South Africa, for example, the demand for inclusion of domestic workers in the Law on Unemployment Insurance, likely to have huge benefits for women, was spearheaded by the South African Domestic Service and Allied Workers' Union, who joined a coalition organised by the Commission for Gender Equality as Jennifer Fish (2006, p. 107–128) shows.
45. Lilian, who had once been one of his most loyal supporters and admirers, had lost faith in him.
46. Her mother subsequently died, in 2007.

References

Bakhtin, M., 1984. *Problems of Dostoevsky's poetics.* Ed. and trans. C. Emerson. Minneapolis: University of Minnesota Press.

Berger, I., 1986. Sources of class consciousness: South African women in recent labor struggles. *In:* C. Robertson and I. Berger, eds. *Women and class in Africa.* London: Africana Publishing, 216–236.

Berger, I., 1992. *Threads of solidarity: women in South African industry 1900–1980.* London: James Currey.

Bozzoli, B., 1991. *Women of Phokeng: consciousness, life strategy, and migrancy in South Africa, 1900–1983.* London: James Currey.

Bratton, M., 1994. Civil society and political transition in Africa. *In:* J.W. Haberson, D. Rothchild and N. Chazan, eds. *Civil society and the state in Africa.* Boulder, CO: Lynne Reinner, 51–82.

Butler, J., 1993. *Bodies that matter; on the discursive limits of 'sex'.* London: Routledge.

Cheater, A.P., 1986. *The politics of factory organisation.* Gweru.

Cheater, A.P., 1988. Contradictions in modelling 'consciousness': Zimbabwean proletarians in the making. *Journal of Southern African studies* (special issue on 'Culture and consciousness'), 14 (2), 291–303.

Constantin, C., 1979. The Puritan ethic and the dignity of labor: hierarchy vs. equality. *Journal of the history of ideas,* 40 (4), 543–561.

Cooper, F., 1996. *Decolonization and African society: the labour question in French and British Africa*. Cambridge: Cambridge University Press.

Durham, D. and Klaits, F., 2002. Funerals and the public space of sentiment in Botswana. *Journal of Southern African studies*, 28 (4), 777–796.

Edmunds, J. and Turner, B., 2002. *Generations, culture and society*. Milton Keynes: Open University Press.

Epstein, A.L., 1958. *Politics in an urban African community*. Manchester: Manchester University Press.

Fanon, F., 1970. *Wretched of the earth*. Harmondsworth: Penguin.

Fish, J.N., 2006. Engendering democracy: domestic labour and coalition-building in South Africa. *Journal of Southern African studies* (special issue on 'Women and the politics of gender in Southern Africa', eds. D. Walsh, P. Scully and D. Gaitskell), 32 (1), 107–128.

Foucault, M., 1972. *The archaelogy of knowledge*. London: Routledge.

Foucault, M., 1977 [1975]. *Discipline and punish: the birth of the prison*. Trans. A. Sheridan. London: Penguin.

Foucault, M., 1980. *The history of sexuality, vol. 1: An introduction*. New York: Vintage Books.

Foucault, M., 1983. The subject of power. *In:* H. Dreyfus and Paul Rabinow, eds. *Beyond structuralism and hermeneutics*. Chicago, IL: University of Chicago Press, 208–226.

Foucault, M., 1987 [1984]. *The uses of pleasure: the history of sexuality, vol. 2*. London: Penguin.

Foucault, M., 1990 [1984]. *The care of the self: the history of sexuality, vol. 3*. London: Penguin.

Foucault, M., 1991 [1984]. *The Foucault reader*. Ed. P. Rabinow. London: Penguin.

Foucault, M., 1994. The ethics of the concern of the self as the practice of freedom. *In:* P. Rabinow, ed., R. Hurley and others trans. *Ethics: subjectivity and truth. Vol. 1 of The essential works of Michel Foucault, 1954–1984*. New York: The New Press, 281–301.

Foucault, M., 1997. *Ethics, subjectivity and truth*. Ed. P. Rabinow, trans. R. Hurley and others. London: Penguin.

Fraser, N., 1992. The uses and abuses of French discourse theories for a feminist politics. *In:* N. Fraser and S. L. Bartky, eds. *Revaluing French feminism: critical essays on difference, agency, and culture*. Bloomington, IN: Indiana University Press, 177–194.

Gaitskell, D., 2000a. Hot meetings and hard kraals: African Biblewomen in Transvaal Methodism, 1924–60. *Journal of religion in Africa*, 30, 277–309.

Gaitskell, D., 2000b. Female faith and the politics of the personal: five mission encounters in twentieth-century South Africa. *Feminist review*, 65, 68–91.

Geisler, Gisela, 2004. *Women and the remaking of politics in Southern Africa: negotiating autonomy, incorporation and representation*. Nordiska Afrikainstitute.

Geisler, G., 2006. 'A second liberation': lobbying for women's political representation in Zambia, Botswana and Namibia. *Journal of Southern African studies* (special issue on 'Women and the politics of gender in Southern Africa', eds. D. Walsh, P. Scully and D. Gaitskell), 32 (1), 69–84.

Good, K., 2002. *The liberal model and Africa: elites against democracy*. London: Palgrave Macmillan.

Griffiths, A.M.O., 1997. *In the shadow of marriage: gender and justice in an African community*. Chicago, IL: University of Chicago Press.

Grillo, R., 1973. *African railwaymen: solidarity and in an East African labour force*. Cambridge: Cambridge University Press.

Grillo, R., 1974. *Race, class, and militancy: an African trade union, 1939–1965*. London: Chandler.

Hays, M.J., 1988. Queens, prostitutes and peasants: historical perspectives on African women, 1971–1986. *Canadian journal of African studies*, 22 (3), 431–447.

Hodgson, D., 2008. Cosmopolitics, neoliberalism and the state: the indigenous rights movement in Africa. *In:* P. Werbner, ed. *Anthropology and the new cosmopolitanism*. Oxford: Berg.

Holquist, M. and Clark, K., 1984. *Mikhail Bakhtin*. Cambridge, MA: Harvard University Press.

Iliffe, J., 1975. The creation of group consciousness among the dockworkers of Dar es Salaam 1929–50. *In:* R. Sandbrook and R. Cohen, eds. *The development of an African working class*. Toronto: University of Toronto Press, 21–48.

Iliffe, J., 2005. *Honour in African history*. Cambridge: Cambridge University Press.

Jeffries, R., 1978. *Class, power and ideology in Ghana: the railwaymen of Sekondi*. Cambridge: Cambridge University Press.

Kapferer, B., 1972. *Strategy and transaction in an African factory*. Manchester: Manchester University Press.

Klaits, F., in press. *Death in a church of life: moral passion during Botswana's time of AIDS*. Berkeley, CA: University of California Press.

Kompe, L., 1985. Union women. *In:* J. Barrett *et al.*, eds. *South African women on the move*. London: Zed Books, 97–118.

Leslie, A.N., 2006. *Social movements and democracy in Africa: the impact of women's struggle for equal rights in Botswana*. New York: Routledge, Taylor and Francis.

Livingstone, J., 2005. *Debility and moral imagination in Botswana: disability, chronic illness and aging*. Bloomington, IN: Indiana University Press.

Lodge, T., 1983. *Black politics in South Africa since 1945*. Harlow: Longman.

Lonsdale, J, 1992. The moral economy of Mau Mau: wealth, poverty and civic virtue in Kikuyu political thought. *In:* B. Berman and J. Lonsdale, eds. *Unhappy valley, book two: violence and ethnicity*. Oxford: James Currey.

Lonsdale, J., 2000. Agency in tight corners: narrative and initiative in African history. *Journal of African cultural studies* (special issue in honour of Professor Terence Ranger), 13 (1), 5–16.

Mahmood, S., 2001. Feminist theory, embodiment, and the docile agent: some reflections on the Egyptian Islamic revival. *Cultural anthropology*, 16 (2), 202–236.

Mahmood, S., 2005. *Politics of piety: the Islamic revival and the feminist subject*. Princeton, NJ: Princeton University Press.

Mannheim, K., 1997 [1952]. The problem of generation. *In: Collected works of Karl Mannheim*, Vol. 5. London: Routledge, 276–320.

Marks, S., 1994. *Divided sisterhood: race, class and gender in the South African nursing profession*. London: St. Martin's Press.

Marks, S., 2000. Changing history, changing histories: separations and connections in the lives of South African women. *Journal of African cultural studies*, 13 (1), 94–106.

Marks, S. and Rathbone, R., 1982. Introduction. *In:* S. Marks and R. Rathbone, eds. *Industrialisation and social change in South Africa*. New York: Longman, 1–44.

Mashinini, E., 1989. *Strikes have followed me all my life: a South African biography*. London: The Women's Press.

Maundeni, Z., 2004. *Civil society, politics and the state in Botswana*. Gaberone: Medi.

McCaskie, T.C., 2000. The consuming passions of Kwame Boakye: an essay on agency and identity in Asante history. *Journal of African cultural studies* (special issue in honour of Professor Terence Ranger), 13 (1), 43–62.

McCracken, J., 1988. Labour in Nyasaland: an assessment of the 1960 railway workers' strike. *Journal of Southern African studies* (special issue on 'Culture and consciousness'), 14 (2), 257–278.

McNay, L., 2000. *Gender and agency: reconfiguring the subject in feminist and social theory*. Cambridge: Polity Press.

Mkandawire, T., 2005. *African intellectuals*. Dakar: CODESRIA in association with Zed Books.

Mogalakwe, M., 1997. *The state and organised labour in Botswana: liberal democracy and emergent capitalism*. Aldershot: Ashgate.

Molokomme, A., 1989. Political rights in Botswana: regression or development? *In:* J. Holm and P. Molutsi, eds. *Democracy in Botswana*. Athens, OH: Ohio University Press, 163–173.

Moorsom, R., 1977. Underdevelopment, contract labour and worker consciousness in Namibia, 1915–72. *Journal of Southern African studies* (special issue on 'Protest and resistance'), 4 (1), 52–87.

Motsafi-Haller, P., 2002. *Fragmented worlds, coherent lives: the politics of difference in Botswana*. London: Bergen & Garvey.

Nealton, J.F., 1998. *Alterity politcs: ethics and performative subjectivity*. Durham, NC: Duke University Press.

Parsons, N., Henderson, W. and Tlou, T., 1995. *Seretse Khama 1921–1980*. Braemfontein: Macmillan.

Peace, A.J., 1975. The Lagos proletariat: labour aristocrats or populist militants. *In:* R. Sandbrook and R. Cohen, eds. *The development of an African working class: studies in class formation and action*. Toronto: University of Toronto Press, 281–302.

Peace, A.J., 1979. *Choice, class and conflict: a study of southern Nigerian factory workers*. London: Harvester Press.

Petchesky, R.P., 2003. *Global prescriptions: gendering health and human rights*. London: Zed Books.

Raftopoulos, B. and Phimister, I., 1997. *Keep on knocking: a history of the labour movement in Zimbabwe, 1900–97*. Harare: Baobab Books.

Schapera, I., 1956. *Government and politics in tribal societies*. London: C.A.Watts & Co.

Schirmer, J., 1989. Those who die for life cannot be called dead: women and human rights protest in Latin America. *Feminist review*, 32, 3–29.

Schirmer, J., 1993. The seeking of truth and the gendering of consciousness: the COMADRES of El Salvador and the Conavigua widows of Guatemala. *In:* S.A. Radcliffe and S. Westwood, eds. *Viva: women and popular protest in Latin America*. London: Routledge.

Scott, J.W., 1988. *Gender and the politics of history*. New York: Columbia University Press.

Scott, J.W., 1991. The evidence of experience. *Critical inquiry*, 17 (4), 773–797.

Selolwane, O.D., 1998. Equality of citizenship and the gendering of democracy in Botswana. *In:* W.A. Edge and M.H. Lekorwe, eds. *Botswana: politics and society*. Pretoria: J.L. van Schaik, 397–411.

Selolwane, O.D., 2000. Civil society, citizenship and civil rights in Botswana. *In:* S.M. Rai, ed. *International perspectives on gender and democratisation*. London: Macmillan, 89–99.

Shostak, M., 1981. *Nisa: the life and words of a !Kung woman*. Cambridge, MA: Harvard University Press.

Simons, J. and Simons, R., 1983. *Class and colour in South Africa 1850–1950*. International Defence and Aid Fund for Southern Africa.

Solway, J.S., 2002. Navigating the 'neutral' state: 'minority' rights in Botswana. *Journal of Southern Africa studies*, 28 (4), 711–730.

Taylor, C., 1994. The politics of recognition. *In:* A. Gutmann, ed. *Multiculturalism*. Princeton, NJ: Princeton University Press, 25–74.

Thompson, E.P., 1963. *The making of the English working class*. Harmondsworth: Penguin.

van Onselen, C., 1976. *Chibaro: African mine labour in colonial Zimbabwe, 1900–1933*. London.

Vaughan, O., 2003. *Chiefs, power, and social change: chiefship and modern politics in Botswana, 1880s–1990s*. Trenton, NJ: African World Press.

Walsh, D., Scully, P. and Gaitskell, D., eds., 2006. *Journal of Southern African studies* (special issue on 'Women and the politics of gender in Southern Africa'), 32 (1).

Wells, J., 1991. *We have done with pleading: the women's 1913 anti-pass campaign*. Johannesburg: Ravan Press, History Workshop 3.

Werbner, P., 1998. Exoticising citizenship: anthropology and the new citizenship debate. *Canberra anthropology*, 21 (2), 1–27.

Werbner, P., 1999a. Political motherhood and the feminisation of citizenship: women's activism and the transformation of the public sphere. *In:* N. Yuval-Davis and P. Werbner, eds. *Women, citizenship and difference*. London: Zed Books, 221–245.

Werbner, P., 1999b. Global pathways: working class cosmopolitans and the creation of transnational ethnic worlds. *Social anthropology*, 7 (1), 17–37.

Werbner, P., 2002. *Imagined diasporas among Manchester Muslims*. Oxford: James Currey and Santa Fe: SAR.

Werbner, P., 2008. Introduction. *In:* P. Werbner, ed. *Anthropology and the new cosmopolitanism: rooted, feminist and vernacular perspectives*. ASA Monographs 45. Oxford: Berg.

Werbner, P., 2009. The hidden lion: Tswapong girls' puberty rituals and the problem of history. *American ethnologist*, 36 (3), 441–458.

Werbner, P. and N. Yuval-Davis, 1999. Women and the new discourse of citizenship. *In:* N. Yuval-Davis and P. Werbner, eds. *Women, citizenship and difference*. London: Zed Books, 138.

Werbner, R., 1988. Epilogue: knowing the power of agency. *Journal of Southern African studies* (special issue on 'Culture and consciousness'), 14 (2), 323–329.

Werbner, R., 1989. *Ritual passage, sacred journey: the process and organization of religious movement*. Washington DC: Smithsonian Institution Press.

Werbner, R., 1991. *Tears of the dead: the social biography of an African family*. Washington, DC: Smithsonian Press.

Werbner, R., 2002. Introduction: postcolonial subjectivities. *In:* R. Werbner, ed. *Postcolonial subjectivities in Africa*. London: Zed Books, 1–21.

Werbner, R., 2004. *Reasonable radicals and citizenship in Botswana*. Bloomington, IN: Indiana University Press.

Werbner, R., 2008. Responding to cosmopolitanism: patriots, ethnics and the public good in Botswana. *In:* P. Werbner, ed. *Anthropology and the new cosmopolitanism: rooted, feminist and vernacular perspectives.* ASA Monograph 45. Oxford: Berg.

Werbner, R. and Werbner, P., forthcoming. Into dignity, out of the shadows: a comparative analysis of seriti in Southern Africa.

Wright Mills, C., 1959. *The sociological imagination.* Oxford: Oxford University Press.

WTO Building, 2007. *The WTO building: The symbolic artwork of the Centre William Rappard headquarters of the World Trade Organization.* Geneva: World Trade Organisation.

Yarrow, T., in press, 2008. Life/history: personal narratives of development amongst NGO workers and activists in Ghana. *Africa,* 78 (3), 334–358.

Work discipline, discipline in Tunisia: complex and ambiguous relations†

Béatrice Hibou

CNRS - CERI/SciencesPo, Paris, France

By looking at tourism, textiles, and call centres in Tunisia, this article analyses the complex relationships between capitalism and political discipline. Starting from the tradition of Weber and Foucault, it shows that the multiplicity of the meanings of capitalist work and the plurality of the ways in which people live with their work stem from a deep heterogeneity in the perceptions of reality: at the same time discipline and freedom, submission and access to some sorts of freedom, rigidity and new latitude for action. In this way, capitalist labour relations can at the same time serve for domination and erode its effects. The analysis that is offered, based on extended fieldwork in Tunisia, suggests the multiplicity and the plasticity of relationships between the technologies of power, the development of the productive forces, and the methods of economic and political regulation.

In the spate of liberal discourse, the question of labour in developing countries that experience massive interventionism, as is the case for Tunisia, is confined to criticism of regulation that is too tentative and too protective of employees and the need for improved flexibility in remuneration and especially in jobs. Within Tunisia, another thesis is widespread, due to the hold exercised by Marxist or dependentist thought dating to the years of the struggle for independence and the years of nation-building. This thesis emphasises the elective affinities that might exist between economic liberalism and authoritarianism. Individuals come under the control of Authority through, on the one hand, the alliance of the regime with the 'parasitic bourgeoisie', thanks to the system of incomes and the submission of labour by the 'marginalisation of social factors', and on the other with 'international capitalism' (Bédoui 2003, Fehri 1998).[1] This interpretation highlights the point that the profusion of local processes, not directly tied to security, help to shape the contours of the domination and discipline of the population through the way in which it is put to work. Starting from their Marxist orientation, these authors show that

---

†Translated by Stephen Belcher. Stephen Belcher is an independent scholar who works on African oral traditions. He has published *Epic traditions of Africa* (Indiana UP,1999) and *African myths of origin* (Penguin, 2006).

political authority is not alien to economic relations: the rationalisation of the techniques of power and economic rationalisation are concomitant phenomena.

They share in part, then, in the analysis proposed in this article, starting from the tradition of Weber and Foucault.[2] By looking at tourism, textiles, and call-centres, I would hope – and in a manner that is opposite to the Marxist tradition but not necessarily to the work of Marx himself[3] – to display the multiplicity of relationships between the technologies of power, the development of the productive forces, and the methods of economic and political regulation. I would also like to suggest, on the one hand, that the 'material conditions' and the 'constellations of interests' are far from being the ineluctable determinants of political evolution, and on the other, that it is impossible to separate spheres – capital, the regime; capitalism, political domination – that are fixed and precisely defined (Weber 2004).[4] My thesis, based on nine years of field research, on interviews, and on participatory observation,[5] shows that capitalism and discipline cannot be dissociated, while at the same time neither can be reduced to the other.

Offshore and tight-supply-lines

The Tunisian economy remains organised around a dual model of production, with a dynamic, although unstable, offshore sector,[6] and an onshore sector largely dominated by agriculture and less sophisticated services. Foreign investment accounts for only 10% of productive investment, but represents more than 34% of the total exports, and around 65% of manufactured exports; it creates 17% of the jobs and covers 80% of the current accounts deficit.[7] One can thus understand the critical nature of these foreign investments.

The advantages of dualism

For the authorities, the advantages of this model are clear in terms of foreign exchange earnings and jobs, and also in political terms: this dual organisation avoids putting Tunisian producers at risk, exercises no pressure to accelerate structural reforms, does not exacerbate the protectionist demands of entrepreneurs, and allows the central authority to preserve its leverage for action on the national scale.[8] This positioning can be understood as being entirely a technique of power. Subsidies, favourable interest rates, disregard of defaulted debt, and successive programmes to support investment can be interpreted as instruments that allow the survival of non-competitive Tunisian companies and the maintenance of dualism (Dimassi and Zaïem 1987, Signoles 1985b).[9] These practices continue today, despite free-exchange agreements and international pressure to liberalise the economy. The incentives offered to investors in the offshore zones, first set up in the 1970s, are renewed almost automatically, and the Tunisian authorities negotiate very aggressively to maintain a system which should have been abolished in 2002. Officials will declare quite openly that 'Tunisia seeks foreign direct investment (FDI) for exports, not for the domestic market.' Off the record, they will round out the speech by pointing to the vitality of investment returns, the need to protect non-competitive national industries and the gains that have been made.[10]

In fact, everything is brought to bear to attract offshore investments: real salaries are subject to pressure to keep them low, although they remain relatively high; the unions are largely controlled by public authorities; the amount of time needed to establish a new company is relatively short, and official organisations such as the Agence de Promotions des Investissements (API: Agency to Promote Investment), and the Foreign Investment Promotion Agency (FIPA), offer services – providing documents, the procedures to follow, information on legislation in progress – that investors find desirable.[11] The effects of this policy are undeniable: aside from privatisations, all the FDI occurred in the offshore zone (Economic and Financial Mission of the Embassy of France in Tunis 2004a). Inquiries show that for the investors, the choice of Tunisia is the result of a long series of factors, among which order, political stability, and personal safety always appear near the top.[12] While foreign investors in the offshore zones are able to avoid the essential elements of administrative regulation in Tunisia, and are free, in part, from social requirements, they do share with the majority of their Tunisian counterparts an ethos which considers stability, security, order, and discipline to be the safest values, and makes consensus the social quality *par excellence*. In light of the criticism that complains of the lack of any multiplier effect of the offshore investment on the domestic industrial fabric, dualism – and thus also the strategy of isolating the foreign investments – seem effective (Michalet 1992, Barbier and Véron 1991, Ferguene and Ben Hamida 1998, Signoles 1985a): the exports are produced in autarchy, and Tunisian authorities do not consider this at all problematic.

Jean-Pierre Cassarino (2000) has shown how this dualism is organised: application of the rule of 20%, according to which offshore companies may, with authorisation, distribute up to 20% of their output in the domestic market, would have been made difficult by the various administrative and customs formalities and the regulations established by the 1993 law, and also by the decree of 1997 that was intended to improve the situation. The authorities were fully aware of what they were doing when they adopted this strategy. The partitioning has been pushed fairly far in Tunisia; unlike the operations in other countries, customs clearances take place within the company. This procedure betrays a security-oriented conception of offshore activities, and a fairly basic vision of the control which is meant to be direct and administrative. This vision is corroborated by the existence of other extremely strict rules applied to offshore companies: entry is forbidden to non-employees, the company's name is not written on the buildings, the walls are built high enough so one cannot see into the factory from outside, and the companies are compelled to work with their doors locked and the windows barred . . . which also raises security problems.[13] While some companies do apply these rules with particular zeal, the rules themselves were defined by the legislator and are applied by a bureaucracy that has an absolute vision of surveillance and impermeability.

However surprising it may seem, this partitioning can also be found in tourism. The ghettoisation of this activity is the fruit of the state's strategy, for reasons very similar to those in the offshore sector.[14] At a period when there was no thought of tourism within the country, the geographic concentration of establishments on the coast, in specifically defined areas and generally far from urban areas, is the consequence of strict planning and a rational vision on the part of the state acting as an engineer. Tourist zones were defined and the land was developed and improved by the administration according to plans they had drawn up; to benefit from the many incentives offered to this sector, it was absolutely necessary to invest in one of those zones (Miossec 1997, Sahli 1990, 1990, Meddeb 2003).[15] Today, partitioning is also to be observed in a preference for clubs and self-contained entities: medical tourism, golden-age tourism. This trend was set in motion by the large tour operators (Azarya 2000), but is perfectly agreeable to the Tunisian authorities. Within the hotel complexes, contacts between foreign tourists and Tunisians are discouraged, and the latter are in fact not allowed onto the hotel grounds or into the bars and nightclubs that lie within them. While in the period of the 1960s and 1970s, young Tunisians who went to nightclubs sometimes had their heads shaved by the police, during morality campaigns, later a law penalised any Tunisian who might bother a tourist.[16] All these measures, some taken by the professionals, others by the public authorities, reveal the same intent. An image of Tunisia that is safe, sleek, without theft or confidence games or sexual pick-up serves simultaneously to guarantee the success of family-oriented, popular tourism and the assurance of foreign exchange income and international recognition. Despite the intrinsically international nature of the sector, Tunisian tourism remains principally in the hands of national agents (World Bank 2002): foreign operators are only rarely directly involved and, as also happens in the textile–clothing sector, their influence, which is quite large, is exercised mainly through the orders they place.

To a certain extent, call-centres can be considered the reproduction of the offshore system within the service sector, most particularly in telecommunications.[17] A sector that did not exist a decade ago now counts 130 companies, at the end of 2007, and employs nearly 10,000 people. These companies are mainly due to foreign entrepreneurs (28 billion dinars invested in the total of 32, or 87.5%) who outsource their services. But the small centres set up by Tunisians also do business through contracts made with foreign companies. Neither category works for the domestic market.

This dualism reinforces and legitimises the disciplinary mechanisms through 'capitalist putting-to-work'[18] of workers and employees, the strict localisation of activities, and a rigorous control of the movements of goods and especially of people. The offshore sector is entirely a part of the national economy that, despite all adjustments and successive programmes of liberalisation, remains heavily protectionist, and thereby also easier to supervise and to standardise. Paraphrasing Janet Roitman and Gerard Roso (2001), one might say that the Tunisian authorities favour the offshore sector so as to remain national.

The tight-supply-line and the disciplinary government

This is not the final limit of the disciplinary dimension of international capitalism. The short-supply-line, just-in-time delivery, and labour flexibility that characterise current global capitalism are primary concerns for a country such as Tunisia that aims to attract to its offshore zones rootless companies whose production involves a worldwide line supply and also relies on foreign orders. This applies quite obviously in the textile sector, and also in the call-centres which are dependent upon foreign customers and short-term contracts obtained in the international markets, and for the tour operators who view tourism as an industrial mass product, standardised and subject to the same price-lowering pressures (charter, low-cost, last-minute etc.). The companies require most of all extreme flexibility in labour and the possibility of easy reorganisation of work assignments. Quite clearly, Tunisia offers them these conditions, in industry as well as in services. There is the use of repetitively renewed fixed-term contracts by ever-changing personnel, and the use of structures such as subcontracts, subdivision of the labour force into multiple companies that allows avoidance of laws governing hiring and firing, the extended employment of trainees, flexibility in very cheap 'first jobs', a lack of tenure, a tolerance by the authorities of labour arrangements that are in part informal, or even entirely black market, in foreign companies as well, and all sorts of other arrangements. All this renders labour rights extremely flexible, despite the laws that protect the rights of employees.[19] This flexibility is never called into question, even when negotiations drag on, when strikes occur, when leaders are locked up or when factories are occupied.

This situation is acknowledged by those who uphold the principles: the World Bank emphasises that Tunisian regulations are well suited to the needs of companies, that the regulatory and administrative environment is rather favourable, and that labour flexibility has been achieved (Casero and Varoudakis 2004, World Bank 2003). European companies looking for outsourcing opportunities agree among each other on the reduction of salary scales and the incentives for offshore investments (DREE 2002). Labour flexibility is not a new phenomenon in Tunisia; it goes back to the liberalisation of the 1970s. At that period, it was accomplished through intensive use of apprentices, part-time workers, and overtime work. Nowadays, the methods for flexibility have diversified and involve the systematic use of subcontractors and work agencies, and very short-lived companies. Within the factories the strategies involve the reorganisation of the labour force and the use of piece-work systems; in the service sector, we find the creation of multi-function jobs.[20]

Flexibility is one aspect of the more general tight-supply-line organisation that symbolises the new disciplinary formula of capitalism (Coutrot 1998, 2002, Boltanski and Chiapello 1999). The tight-supply-line looks not only at the delivery of goods; it is, above all, a reorganisation of labour and the individualisation of wage-relations. Jean-Pierre Durand (2004, 77–78) explains that:

> dans l'acceptation du principe du flux tendu, il n'y a plus besoin de chef disciplinaire: la discipline est dans le flux tendu ... Accepter le flux tendu, c'est accepter la discipline qu'il impose; alors il n'y a plus besoin de maîtrise disciplinaire. Voici la signification profonde du concept paradoxal d'*implication contrainte*: le salarié pris dans le tourbillon du flux tendu se mobilise et s'implique parce qu'il n'a pas le choix, le flux requérant toutes ses facultés pour être maintenu tendu. D'une certaine façon, on pourrait dire en plagiant les slogans de Mai 1968 que le 'flic est dans le flux'. C'est-à-dire que le contrôle social d'hier effectué par un chef ou une maîtrise n'a plus lieu d'être puisque le salarié se conforme aux exigences du flux tendu en ayant accepté son principe de fonctionnement.

> Within the understanding of the principle of the tight-supply-line, there is no longer a need for a disciplinary centre; the discipline is implicit in the tight-supply-line ... To accept the tight-supply-line is to accept the discipline it requires, and hence there no longer exists any need for disciplinary control. Here lies the deep meaning of the paradoxical concept of *constrained involvement*: the employee caught in the whirlpool of the tight-supply-line gets to work and is involved because he has no choice; the supply flow requires all his abilities to be maintained as taut. To some extent one might say, plagiarising the slogans of May 1968 [the year of extreme student unrest and protests in France: trans.] that 'le flic est dans le flux' ['cops come with the flow']. This means that the social control exercised in the past by a boss or a management system no longer needs to exist since the employee adapts to the requirements of the supply-line, having accepted the way it works.

On the workers' side, this principle is further recognised by the acquiescence, however involuntary, to temporary work (Elbaz 2007, esp. 91–96): small jobs, or jobs well below the skills of the worker, starting with jobs in call-centres for university graduates, that are seen as the entry point for 'a real job', and this enables the workers to accept the very difficult and uncertain working conditions, not to mention the very low pay scale. The hope of getting a real job, the desire to prove that one can move up the ladder within the company, makes these workers particularly docile, eager, and highly 'motivated'.

Social control and putting Tunisians to work

This way of putting Tunisians to work is obviously not limited to a tight-supply-line system of organisation; it also affects the much more ordinary organisation of labour in small and mid-sized companies and in workshops.

The 'capitalist putting-to-work' of the Tunisians

In the Tunisian case, the disciplinary function of the work-system is made more effective by the fact that companies' organisation is modelled on the workshop.[21] This model works just as well for small companies with a few employees and for those that work in part or in whole in the informal sector. Paradoxically, foreign offshore elements are equally involved insofar as the Tunisian side of the business is only concerned with the matter of paying the workers and keeping a hardware accounting (meaning an accounting of the goods that come in and go out of the company), without being really involved in its own management or even proper accounting.[22]

The 'capitalist putting-to-work' involves ordinary techniques:[23] continual monitoring of work-stations, enhanced in major companies by the use of the Internet; a relatively long work-day – eight to nine hours a day, six days out of seven in the textile sector, and up to 10 hours in call-centres; the establishment of procedures and standards; a centralised and hierarchical work organisation that allows very little space for delegation or for individual initiative; overlapping checks and external audits in the largest companies. In the case of call-centres, for example, the phone-workers have an 11-hour shift, with only one hour off for a meal and six ten-minute breaks, but the breaks are neither scheduled nor mandatory and depend on the assessment of the call volume by the station manager.[24] The work is highly supervised; calls should not last more than five minutes, and the time between two calls should not be more than 15 seconds. In cases where the call-placer is supposed to record his comments, this theoretical time for rest and computer adjustment is most often used for work. Other classic techniques, still in the call-centres, involve subjecting the staff to continuous assessment in the form of statistical indicators of quality or of speed in operations, as well as periodic assessments of skills and knowledge.

There is also a practice specific to Tunisia that reveals, perhaps more than others, the disciplinary nature of Tunisian capitalism. The questionnaire, legally required, obliges employers to question their employees on absences, sicknesses, work incidents, and shortcomings and to keep a written record.[25] Even though this was not sought by companies, it has become customary because of the central importance which the labour inspectors accord it: should there be any conflict between the employer and one of the employees, the inspector will ask to consult the questionnaire which is considered reliable. Should some mistake or absence not be mentioned, the inspector will find in favour of the employee, to the detriment of the employer. The role of the questionnaire can be understood: while for the employer, it represents an internal monitoring imposed from outside and a tool for imposing discipline on the labour force, for the authorities it represents a way to play the role of intercessor while still watching over the company and its agents.

The recurring complaints of company heads about the lack of punctuality of the Tunisian employees, absenteeism, irregularity in work, the lack of discipline of the employees, and their 'cultural' need for a boss, about their irrationality must be understood in this context, which can explain their untimely resignations or their 'over-extended' leaves taken during Ramadan or during the summer months.[26] During interviews, the heads of foreign companies often assured me that 'you don't find the discipline of the Tunisian political order at the level of the workplace'. Tunisian employees are not to be considered 'completely committed, mentally, emotionally, and physically' to the company; they do not demonstrate 'a belief in the culture and the mission of the company'. In other words, they are not 'engaged'.[27]

One can interpret these remarks in the Marxist tradition, following E.P. Thompson: such behaviour does not stem from indolence, laziness, childishness, or some indiscipline peculiar to Tunisians, but should be interpreted as an act of rebellion, of resistance, the refusal of the discipline that is being imposed, and a partial rejection of constraints. It might also be understood as the expression of a 'labour force that is only *provisionally* and *partially* invested in the industrial way of life' (Thompson 2004, p. 82, emphasis added). One should see in these defects neither a critique of capitalism, nor protests against the loss of autonomy and humanity at work, but rather the attempt to resolve the conflicts between the world of work and the world outside the workplace.[28]

But one could also read these remarks as a political construction produced by a mythical projection – that of an undisciplined people that needs, in politics as in business, a leader – that justifies the domination and company paternalism in the same way.[29] This perception is widely fuelled by the Tunisian authories through moralising discourse. As early as 1988, Ben Ali was saying: 'It is high time for laxity to make way for discipline, and for every Tunisian man and woman to get to work.' The internalisation of discipline is also accomplished by a discourse centred upon work as a basic value and the immorality of leisure and unruliness: 'Work is not only earning a living, but also constitutes an attribute of citizenship just as much as the bond with the land'; 'It is imperative for us to restore respect for work as a value of our civilisation, our society, our economy. We must once again give to work its value and its sacred character as the best means to fulfil oneself and to contribute to the glory of the nation. There can be no progress without serious unremitting labour.'[30] These quotes ring a pale chime on other authoritarian situations: Mussolini's Italy, the Portugal of Salazar, and present-day Malaysia (Gentile 2004, Valente 1999 and Ong 1987). The organisation of labour and the surveillance of the population are all the more inextricably entwined because the interiorisation of the discipline derives not only from economic process, but also, as Max Weber demonstrated in his writings on capitalism, because it stems from an ethos projected by institutions, by discourse, by a style of government.[31]

A confirmed and diffuse paternalism

Social control of the labour force is achieved by a diffuse paternalism. This is sometimes openly assumed, as was admitted by the owner of a company I was interviewing, who said quite simply: 'We are in a paternalistic society, and I have to admit that it benefits me.' More often, however, the paternalism is denied, although it remains no less real. As illustration, consider how these managers of modern companies reject the suggestion: 'It's not paternalism, it's a permanent dialogue' – as was stated by a high-placed manager of Poulina, quoted by Yousfi *et al.* (2005, p. 65). But we are entitled to doubts when we consider the daily discourse within the company:

> Poulina is the fertile hen, then, and she's laid her eggs and each time an egg becomes a chick she assigns it an activity to meet the needs of the family. And then time passes, and the family continues to change. Poulina then becomes a grandmother, and she is satisfied with watching over the family, giving advice, and keeping in touch with her chicks by drawing up the strategies and general policies of the Corporation.

The conglomerate makes this statement right away on its internet site –www.poulina. gnet.tn – cited by Yousfi *et al.* (2005, p. 31). 'Poulina is our mother,' says a worker, while the manager of an affiliate agrees through a 'Poulina is an organic group, very similar to a large family with written rules' and an official specifies, 'the fact that he is the only one responsible, that he alone can allow deviations, is very important … As for the way the system works, certain aspects are highly formalised with procedures, and then a flexibility that is guaranteed by Mr Ben Ayed' (Yousfi *et al.* 2005, pp. 55 and 65). The aid system relies heavily on social surveillance:[32] paternalist employers sign off on their employees' bank credit, serve as their guarantor, or may themselves offer consumer credit; they are willing to make salary advances; they contribute to health-care costs; they use their network of acquaintances to help make an appointment with a doctor or an official.

But the function of this paternalism is above all discipline at work. Company managers choose certain employees to subcontract production while being completely controlled; they use and abuse the metaphor of the family within the company; they 'control them to help them' and behave like a father educating his children; they keep track of the employee's lifestyle, with, for instance, a ban on smoking 'for their own good'. The owner is the only one allowed to waive the rules and to allow employees to do the same.[33] Given these conditions, owners say that they prefer to recruit employees from the neighbourhood or through connections with the women who are already working in the factory, precisely for these reasons of control and knowledge of the environment.[34] That is also one of the reasons that explains why the fathers of the young women acquiesce in the work; the daughters remain under the control of the local company and there is no significant upheaval in the sexual segregation that structures traditional space and activities. Besides, the gendered division of tasks and fields of activity is only moderately changed. Through research into the way families share decisions, an anthropologist showed that women still maintain their traditional prerogatives, and despite all the actions taken on their behalf since independence, women still have not mastered the skill of strategic decisions, that are the critical points in family life and in the public space (Melliti 1996).

Foreign companies also join in this paternalism. No doubt, this is how we must interpret the comments reflecting overt culturalism: 'they are children,' 'they like to be ordered around,' 'the one giving orders must do it severely, he must be authoritative'; 'they like to have a father with a stick'; 'the company is seen as something outside themselves; they want immediate gratification, that's all; and if there is any sense of ownership, it isn't strong enough to bring a feeling of responsibility as well'.[35] People agree upon the role of the ideal head of the company: paternalism helps to legitimise the disciplinary organisation of the labour force and a security-oriented vision of factory work. However, this paternalism is not only part of the way the companies work, and it does not come only from capitalist economic logic. It is all the more vital because it is based, as Max Weber reminds us, upon an ethos, on a kind of human, on a specific construction of the State. In Tunisia, this paternalism results in part from a collective imagining, political in origin but widely held, of the strong man and the 'need for a leader' that the 'reformist tradition' keeps building up, and in part also from the myth of the State outside of society and of its corollary, the 'culture of riot and sedition'.[36] Capitalism and disciplinary authority form a whole, particularly because the individuals share an ethos that sees in discipline the path to the stability and security that are necessary to avoid the ever-possible disorders (Khiari 2003, Le Saout and Rollinde 1999). But this whole is hardly the synonym of homothetic relations and of convergent evolution between capitalism and the disciplinary exercise of power.

Social control taken over

Another element needs to be raised in this analysis of the disciplinary character of capitalism: the subordination and bureaucratisation of the Tunisian labour movement. Workers have been represented since independence through a single institution, the Union Générale des Travailleurs de Tunisie (UGTT). But in the 1960s and 1970s, and even at the start of the 1980s, the union was a living force, an independent political agent, the only institution in competition with the single party. However, since the end of the 1980s, the headquarters has become nothing more than a transmission belt, a belt that is essential for the political authorities, although the function is not always carried out with the docility and efficiency that they might desire. The union is now only one component among others of the central authority – no doubt a basic element, and occasionally expressing the desire for autonomy, but constrained by the limits that have been set upon it and that it knows with some precision. The permanent conflict and the real competition between the union and the single party have disappeared. What remains is a role as intermediary and often nothing more than as an appendix to power (Zghal 1998, CERES 1989, Zeghidi 1997, Hamzaoui 1999, Khiari 2000, 2003, Camau and Geisser 2003). These changes are very clearly noted in the world of work. 'Before there were two powers to manage, the union and the political authority; now there is only one. If you have a problem with the UGTT, you call the governor, and everything gets settled,' as one employer explained to me. 'The UGTT exists for its symbolic value, but it poses no threat either to the political authority or to the company,' added another. 'One good thing that Ben Ali did was defeating the union', said another interlocutor even more clearly.[37] These remarks are not at all ambiguous, and neither is the way in which President Ben Ali himself sees strikes: 'Recourse to a strike, although guaranteed by law, is the indicator of a lack of efficiency in dialogue, and of a need in that area, because in a democratic society, *social peace is a critical imperative that must be the aim of all the stakeholders in society, and whose creation depends upon the degree of efficiency of the dialogue and the mastery of its channels.*'[38] Paternalism and neutralising the union go in lock-step.

Social control is not expressed only by the submission of the UGTT and by paternalism within the companies. Other practices allow, at one and the same time, the integration of discipline at work and reinforcement of the structures of political control. For example, young women in the textile industry are recruited from the area around the factory by the women who are already working there: 'That way, you can go see the family and the neighbourhood and keep better track of them.' The control works both ways: for the company, it is clearly more useful to have direct contact with the family and the neighbourhood and to know why there may be absences or lateness; it also makes it easier to bring the workers in on Sunday or in the evenings during emergencies.[39] For the families, it becomes easier to keep an eye on the young women, via the neighbourhood, the relatives living there, authorised intermediaries, or directly when the company is sited in the parents' location.[40]

One might make the same analysis of the supervalorisation of the family's importance, and more generally, of the fact that position in the social hierarchy vastly outweighs personal abilities. Surveillance also operates in apprenticeships or in the practice of spreading the work, meaning tightly controlled subcontracting (J. Maalej quoted by Denieul 1992, p. 69, Zghal 1992, Yousfi *et al.* 2005). This is quite simply the consequence of the codes of social living, as I was reminded by an owner of a small business, who was challenging me:

> Your questions focus too much on the relationship with the administration, but that is not the only problem area, and you might even say that for an offshore company the administration isn't really a big issue. What I find really problematic is my relationship with all the private partners, the suppliers, the customers, the workers who come for repairs, the drivers.[41]

None of these practices are political. Recruitment is primarily a question of relationships, playing on the networks of family, locality, friends, neighbours. The favouritism of job agencies, when it is involved, seems to be less partisan than regional. The choice of markets, obtaining contracts, and the selection of subcontractors, are also part of these relationships. In Tunisia, the company is not the site for political control. In some cases, 'there are lots of informers', as a number of businessmen told me. Nevertheless, there is no desire on the state's part to have them hired. They are not 'placed there by the power' to watch over things, but once hired by the company employees may be approached by the police or by other authorities, so they can supply information in exchange for cancelling a warrant or for administrative assistance or for financial benefits. In other cases, 'it really has nothing of a police state'.[42] In fact, UGTT units are rare in private companies, and RCD (Rassemblement Constitutionel Démocratique: the single party) units even rarer. As for the customs official, the only representative of the administration who is permanently present in the company, he does not play that role, and when he does step outside his professional responsability, it is for strictly personal – and lucrative – reasons.[43] The only slight exception to this apolitical aspect of the world of labour is in the use of SIVP [*stages d'insertion à la vie professionnelle*: professional entry-level training programmes]. This is in fact a public subsidy granted to private companies that may hire unemployed graduates, a subsidy which involves paying a substantial part of the salary. Call-centres make intensive use of these SIVP jobs, and are often successful in renewing them. Now, to take advantage of this sort of job, which some have defined as 'semi-public', it is essential for the call-employee, and more generally for any young person who might be hired, to be in good standing with the Party, the *omda* [mayor: trans.] or the neighbourhood council, and most particularly not to have been identified with the opposition or more clearly a trouble-maker (Hibou 2006a). That said, this surveillance involves the hiring, and not the world of work as such.

One can understand that a company, in contrast, for example, with associations, does not need to be observed. There is at least a double reason for this 'omission' of the obsession with security. In part, Tunisian society is already under such tight control that it would be hard to find a single place in which there is not some part of society already under surveillance (Hibou 2006a, esp. pp. 95–130, 163–193): the male and female workers are already known to neighbourhood councils; the heads of companies are known to the employers' federations, the tax agents, or social security. Moreover, everyone has a perfect knowledge of the disciplinary rules, which they have long since internalised. People know what they may and may not say, and they rarely dare to argue in the workplace. And, in part, the company is not a subversive site, it is not considered a dangerous place because it is controlled and 'secured' in a different way, by the discipline of a sort of capitalism.

The permanence of power relationships

The occasional, but recurring, application of repressive measures, or of openly security-oriented measures against the 'capitalists' suggests that, contrary to the tenets of the Marxist creed, capitalism cannot be summed up in its disciplinary aspect, and that other dynamics are in play. When the administration imposes rules that cripple the tourism sector – for instance, by banning Tunisians from certain places or by setting the tax-rate on drinks at an exorbitant level – a power struggle between the professionals and the ministry is inevitable, even though it may remain hidden. A similar situation arises when an owner is summoned by the governor and ordered to make one or another of his female employees remove her veil, while the governor shows, by means of a list that just happens to be lying on the table, that he knows exactly how many women go veiled in every company in his district. This is the case when a governor calls the manager of a factory to demand that he skim a few dinars off every salary paid to his employees, or when, on his first day of work in Tunisia, a foreign company representative is visited by persons who come to recommend associations or companies that are close to the central authority.[44] Undeniably, such practices run counter to the other basics of capitalism (autonomy of decisions, economic or financial or sectoral considerations; observance of the hierarchy within a company etc.), and because foreign investors are well aware of this sort of interference and consider it a negative factor, there are not all that many prepared to settle down in Tunisia.[45] Those who do so are rarely the affiliates of major corporations. Rather, they are small and medium-sized enterprises from Europe or executives from large corporations setting up their own businesses, hoping to recoup something after hard times in their countries of origin.[46]

The historical sociology of the economy, whether inspired by Karl Marx or by Max Weber, reminds us that capitalism is conflict, less because of the fact of resistance on the part of certain agents than because of the multiplicity of logics operating throughout the system and the fluidity of relationships that it induces.[47] Jean-Louis Rocca's research on Chinese capitalism, and the use he makes of the concept of 'putting-to-work' of Henri Lefebvre are interesting because they recall, very specifically, how nowadays the capitalist logic by its nature implies conflicts, contraditions, violence, inequalities, injustice, and crises. In Tunisia, where the watchwords are 'safety', 'stability' and 'social peace', the conflicts inherent in the capitalist logic are still not unknown. They have simply been obscured by the many practices of disciplinary normalisation, and particularly by the constructive of a largely fictive consensus. Here, I would like to show how those conflicts are more frequent than the monotony of Tunisian social and political life might wish it to seem, and thus to suggest that the disciplinary dimension of capitalism is not enough, by itself, to account for its nature and the logic of its system.

Tensions and quelling work-related conflict

The intensive resort to courts is a first symptom of these tensions. No figures exist, to my knowledge, but during my interviews, 'field' representatives of the UGTT stressed this practice, and not one businessman I interviewed said that he had been able to avoid lawsuits, particularly in the area of labour relations management. The employees enjoy a court system that finds most often in their favour, and for the same reason the employers generally revile it. But this situation does not mean necessarily that court orders are carried out, perhaps rather the opposite: the economic authorities, and especially the police (loosely defined) are very sensitive to the purely financial and economic aspects of capitalism.

The foreign manager of an offshore company summed up the situation thus: 'nowadays, the authorities act with more finesse; they are more realistic and less nationalist, because they assess the power relationships quite clearly'.[48] Indeed, it is principally a question of power relationships, as is suggested also by the problems faced by businessmen who want to fire people. To observe that, in the end, they did get what they wanted and that the 'regime' did act in favour of the 'capitalist interests' does not mean that there are neither negotiations and agreements nor tensions and opposition. Job flexibility, for instance, entailed lengthy struggles, and the courts and various administrative procedures were involved in the attempt to stem the scourge of unemployment, with a goal of 'defending society' that, as Michel Foucault has said, ran counter to liberal logic. It is in this spirit that we must see the obstacles preventing the firing of employees, particularly in the case of foreign companies, or the obstacles set up by the administration to prevent owners from starting lawsuits against their employees, the pressures of police or the governor's office to avoid sanctions against an employee and to help the employee return to work in the plant, the multiple financial and regulatory arrangements set up to encourage employment.[49] All these negotiations show that social stability is largely a façade of harmony, and that the role of latent conflict should not be dismissed.

Public authorities intervene directly only when discontent reaches a certain level, to avoid any social upheavals. It is not unreasonable to interpret this non-involvement of the authorities in conflicts as a disguised form of support to the employers. However, it is difficult to make such a clear distinction between the administrative and the political realms, even when there is a tendency towards administrative autonomy. The tensions arise rather from a complex play of divergent interests, for example (and simplifying greatly), between, on the one hand, defence of the middle class, the central support of the 'disciplinary regime' and, on the other, defence of the capitalists who are the central pillar of the 'developmental regime', meaning that facet of the Tunisian state that aims, through its choice of economic policies and its direct interventions, to assist the development of the productive sectors. Each also grows out of a different rationale for action, for example (and simplifying just as much), between protection and maintaining a living standard, on one side, and on the other, competitiveness, or again between employment and the pursuit of foreign exchange, between security and attractiveness. The government is riddled by all these logics at the same time: everything may be done to meet the requirements of companies, while at the same time everything will be tried to prevent lay-offs. The public authorities are quite aware of tensions in the labour market and of the fears that unemployment arouses among the people.

In recent years, the increasing number of interventions have been linked to the increase in hunger strikes, the occupation of factories, or wildcat strikes.[50] The authorities take all the more trouble to prevent these conflicts coming to light, because they strike a responsive chord in people. But the management is quite real: all measures are taken to settle the problem as close to the source and as soon as possible, through intervention by the UGTT, of representatives and governors of provinces, of the RCD networks, the labour inspectors and the general secretaries of townships, as well as with the financial support of the Caisse Nationale de Sécurité Sociale (CNSS – the National Social Security Fund). Discipline is restored gently, and quite often very insidiously. Protests only appear in public if the employers' behaviour is clumsy, if not fraudulent, or if the authorities have misunderstood the situation, or if the local social context allows political protest movements to slip through the cracks.[51] Still, the discontent is not political, not organised, not a form of opposition. People fight to keep their job and to preserve a certain social safety. Even when the conflict is made political, through the intervention of organisations such as the Conseil National pour les Libertés en Tunisie (CNLT) and especially the Ligue Tunisienne des Droits de l'Homme (LTDH) or Raid-Attac Tunisie, negotiation is the strategy that wins out: repression is applied only to the members of those organisations, and works mainly through intimidation. Negotiation and damage-control are the keywords.

The serious events which have occurred since January 2008 in the region of Gafsa confirm the vitality of the social malaise, and at the same time show how this vague discontent has not been politicised. The region is known for being especially poor, but also rebellious, and it was there that in 1984 the bread riots started. This time, it was employment policy that sparked the explosion. Phosphates, the only resource in that region, went up in price, and the Phosphate Company of Gafsa organised a competition for jobs. On 7 January 2008, release of the competition results meant the end of quiet in the area. The many young men, unemployed and looking for work, organised themselves to denounce a recruitment that was smaller than expected (64 instead of 81 people) and especially the corruption, favouritism, and cronyism that had marked the process. At Redeyef, Oum Laraïs and Mdhilla, they organised sit-ins, hunger strikes, and demonstrations, they blocked the rail-line and the miners started a strike in solidarity with them. For three months, Carthage took no action. Then at the beginning of April, the situation got worse because, faced with the inaction of the central authorities and their inability to find any strategies of negotiation and appeasement, the movement wanted to communicate its demands to Tunis. After violent confrontations, that led to one death and dozens of injuries, the security forces arrested several leaders from the young men and the union representatives. Faced with very strong local reaction, these people were quickly released, but the demonstrations rapidly resumed and led to several severe sentences in a 'strategy of the periphery',[52] a classic and effective technique that led to trials for the leaders of the movement. These events are extremely important. They reveal a social malaise among the people, and at the same time a strong desire to be involved through jobs, the wish for state interventionism to be continued, a social criticism of the connection-dependent paths to employment; also, the lack of politicisation of the events, despite the involvement of dissident union representatives, stands out. The crisis in the south also shows how the authorities wanted at all costs to limit the demonstrations to the area of Gafsa, to avoid a linkage between this spontaneous social unrest and the political opposition, and to deny that the conflicts and social and economic discontent were in any way widespread. Repression was not, and is still not, the main goal of the Tunisian authorities. They are rather overwhelmed by conditions they cannot control, by the inefficiency of their redistributive system in that area, and their goal is mainly to contain the discontent. The novelty of the events lies in the failure to find grounds, and especially agents, that could allow negotiation and mediation: the traditional lines, beginning with the single party and the UGTT, were not able to attach themselves to the movement and to organise at least an appeasement, if not an end, for the movement; as the young people involved had never been at work, the CNSS couldn't get involved; since the area was devastated, there were no alternative economic options to present, beginning with the public sector; tax incentives for investment in the region, established after the springtime movement and the summer of 2008, have so far been ineffective in attracting growing companies or doing much beyond symbolic gestures. We now face a situation – a new one, however limited – in which the conflicts and tensions can no longer be hidden or smothered, but can only be reduced by attempts at emigration that is now illegal because of the restrictive European policies and by involvement in smuggling and black-market trade (Elbaz 2008).

The multiplicity of interior logics

That economic or security-oriented policies are meant to reinforce the disciplinary nature of capitalism does not negate the 'regime's' effectiveness in managing the behaviour of 'its' businessmen. Incompleteness or the plurality of logics may be an explanation; so too are the fluidity of social formations and the relationships among variables. The contingency of situations derives directly from the multiplicity of the goals, the way they are described, and the understanding of various notions such as security and development. Max Weber's analysis of modernity protects us from single-cause and functionalist analyses and from teleological interpretations:[53] the disciplinary exercise of power is the contingent consequence of multiple processes deriving at the same time from the disintegration of prior forms of socialisation and from innovations that affect economic or judicial strategies just as much as the methods of domination or the practical orientations of various social strata.

On behalf of businessmen, for example, many strategies are deployed, not always voluntarily, to reduce the impact of unions: the development of fixed-term contracts, temporary work, piece-work, and so on allow them to give 'tenure' only to people whose minds are 'on the job'. It is also possible to buy off the employees with money or the hope of promotions, to prevent them forming a union chapter; more or less frequent contacts with the local elected representative or the governor allows them to 'get the message through'. More generally, the decrease in the union's influence in Tunisia can be explained by the improvement in working conditions, by the application of ostentatiously paternalist and anti-union policies, by the development of subcontracting and outsourcing through the proliferation of small units that have not been organised into unions, and, in the most modern companies, particularly the foreign ones, by a modification of the managerial structures that softens the forms of command.[54] In this context, both employers and foreign observers might feel that the subjection of the union by the central authority is a major contribution to their business strategy.

A historical analysis of the labour movement showed us that the UGTT was something quite different, and principally a political actor. It was specifically for political, not economic reasons, that it was brought under control: a potential competitor for power had to be disciplined and mastered. An institution such as the UGTT has a memory, and the memory leads to micro-decisions and especially interpretations that no longer square with the power relations and the actual situations of the present day (Lallement 2003). This memory grants less space to class struggles than to national unity, to the construction of the nation-state, and to contributions to social harmony (Khiari 2003). Misunderstandings are at present the rule, and the political acquiescence of the union leadership helps the current capitalist dynamics; but dissension within the UGTT and the growing gap between a leadership that has been co-opted by the central authority and a base that is growing increasingly activist on behalf of employees could jeopardise this convergence.

The same applies to the dualism described above. The intentional policies of the Tunisian state are not the only explanation of the 'success' of this strategy of confinement of the offshore companies. The strategy results from many factors. An industrialist who sets up in the offshore sector will have no interest in penetrating an unattractive domestic market that is segmented and not well integrated, and he will do his best to keep to a minimum his involvement with an administration that is considered too hesitant, to avoid the 'non-market' factors that a foreigner has great difficulty in grasping, to avoid bad debts and the 'culture of unpaid bills'.[55] Similarly, in the area of tourism, the nature of the clientele, the strategy of the tour-operators, and the development of 'Club' or 'all-expenses-included' packages, the weakness of demand outside the hotel complexes, the administrative burdens, the Tunisian lifestyles and so on. All these factors combine to create the ghettoisation of the tourism described above.[56] The thesis that dualism was consciously conceived and intentionally established thus seems too unequivocal. It does not take into account the multiple rationales, some of them peculiar to Tunisian society, others deriving from global economic and financial strategies, and sometimes again from distorted perceptions or from very specific interests.

In short, the disciplinary nature of capitalism cannot be read as the expression of a particularly receptive 'attentiveness' of the 'regime' to the expectations of Tunisian businessmen. The power relations are undeniably advantageous to capitalism, but they serve it not in the sense of 'being in service to' but rather insofar as they can be used in business planning (Foucault 1994d). The difference is substantial, and it throws into relief one of the contributions of a Weberian analysis, that Michel Foucault has taken for his own without necessarily specifying the point.[57] Running against the Marxist thesis that power is principally subordinate to relationships of economic interests, and thus that domination is only a function or a tool of exploitation, it suggests some distrust of any established certainties on the meaning or function of any given institution, and emphasises rather the attention paid to the diversity of uses that can be made of the same institution depending on circumstances, historical changes, and the players.

The multiple channels of negotiated accommodation

Within the area of labour as also in that of economic success, repression as such is thus exceptional. The system instead involves very fine mechanisms for control and ordering that may, at very specific and necessarily rare occasions, turn into outright harassment, punishment, and exclusion, but that most often are expressed through pressure and sometimes trouble-making, by the operation of favouritism and arbitrary actions, by advancement of individual interests, by petty and continual administrative obstacles and interferences, and more often by a strict delimitation of the economic and social possibilities. Under these circumstances, the question that arises most acutely is that of 'voluntary servitude' (in Etienne de La Boétie's expression): what is the hold on the people and the system? If the principles of absolute obedience and naked force are not central, then what is involved? A sense of belonging? Negotiations and agreements? Probably a mix of those factors, which have been materially enabled by a multitude of imperceptible and insidious mechanisms that lead finally to an environment that creates at the same time constraints and benefits, economic opportunities and occasions for dressage, conditions for domination and for emancipation.

One might here recall the particularly meaningful remark by a businessmen: 'what weighs us down is what protects us'. The mechanisms that are perceived as constrictive are desirable, because they are at the same time protective and lead to wealth and security. What can be seen as 'attentiveness' can also prove to be a tool for control; conversely, that which may seem a form of submission may also be the consequence of the convergence of different motivations and interests. A transit through labour relations and company management gives us a step forward in understanding 'what Tunisians care about' by suggesting the ambivalences of domination, the multiple channels through which the political element slips into actual power relations, and the specific modes of accommodation to constraint and oversight.

Consent and habit

A first mode of accommodation consists of simple consent. What may be seen by outside observers as a constraint, if not coercion, a force for regularisation and discipline, is most often experienced as something ordinary, meaning that it is like rules that have been internalised.[58] Only the widespread nature of incidents, the ban on unavoidable discussions, or the appearance of contradictions between active principles make these practices unpleasant, if not intolerable. In Tunisia, as elsewhere, this internalisation can be explained first by the absence of any questioning of the environment in which individuals work and live. There is neither consent nor refusal: most of the time, people are in no way bothered by job requirements, by the political business deals, by the company's exercise of discipline, or that of the administration or any economic organisation, or by the exercise of supervision by the police. People may even enjoy this, as Marx reminds us in one of those excursus that are closer to Weber's writings than to the doctrine of the Marxist vulgate, less careful than was the founding father to recognise the ambivalence of situations. In his 'First critique of political economy', he shows that 'capitalism rests upon the involvement of desire, of exploitation, and of violence' (Bayart 2004, p. 322), and he sums up his analysis with a particularly felicitous expression: 'I pluck you while providing you pleasure' (Marx 1972, p. 170).

Later, when people do feel intermittently or temporarily bothered by the situation, the internalisation works through the widespread apoliticisation of the participants, and thus their dim perception of the mechanisms of dressage.[59] These methods, which cannot be dissociated from the specifics of economic policies, of social programmes, of assistance and subsidies, are not necessarily seen as what they are. So long as they do not lead to massive rejection, to confrontations, so long as individuals accept them because in one way or another they benefit from them, there is no critical distancing. Most Tunisian businessmen do not think in political terms when they complain about the incessant interference by the administration, by the fund-raising appeals from the party and its many satellite organisations, or when they deplore the workers' absenteeism. Most employees do not think in terms of politics when they deplore the growing uncertainty of the job market and the spread of liberal standards. Either of these parties needs some traumatic event or some exasperating incident (often with personal application) to make these minor grievances and irritants turn into resistance, and thus into political action. Finally, and most importantly, this consent can be explained by the way – even when unconscious and involuntary – in which the economic agents participate in the disciplinary power. As can be seen from the examples given above, it is not so much a question of 'creating dependencies' as of playing upon them.

A second mode of accommodation is to be found in the painless, and thus almost invisible, nature of the constraints and even of the coercion, that is made possible by the way in which the interventions and the exercise of power have become so routine. Or, to speak like Max Weber, by their *Veralltäglichung* (dailiness), and in Etienne de La Boétie's terms, by 'habituation'.[60] 'The nail is hammered in bit by bit'; 'It's a kind of non-violent interventionism, and we don't even feel it'; 'It's natural, it's always been this way': these comments all show how invisible the dressage and normalisation have become.[61] In the world of work, as throughout social relations, the tactics of power are not necessarily visible because they are mediated through beliefs and representation. The internalisation of the constraint is so strong that it also leads to the elaboration of a certain ethic, or moral rhetoric, based on the values of labour, of the nation, or of the country, of prosperity and growth, of the citizen's moral duty.[62] 'In Tunisia, we believe in family and in community', 'it is for the good of the nation'; 'we're doing this for the country'; 'this is what Muslim solidarity means', and so on. The exercise of power is also interpreted in terms of religion, or of national unity, or of Tunisianness, which all serve to link everyone in the fabric of social relations, in the chain of microscopic dependencies. Morality campaigns, the Islamisation of social life, or the discourse on the Tunisian tradition of moderation all share in this process of mediated discipline.[63] In this context, the process of normative conditioning is imperceptible; having been transformed, it becomes acceptable.

Between belonging and keeping a distance

The dynamic of the relations of strength and the interplay of power relations constitute a third mode of accommodation. The absence of any 'revolt' against a relationship of domination or of systematic surveillance in no way signifies acquiescence. There may be forms of resistance that shape the relationships within a company, within society, between the company and the central authorities, without challenging the general economy of system of control and domination. These forms of resistance or of 'counter-behaviours', using Michel Foucault's expression, will define, at a given time and on a given topic, behaviours that do not necessarily tend to normative behaviour. They express the state of relations of strength at a specific time, but they are neither powerful enough, nor established and fixed enough to allow labelling the behaviour or assigning an identity to it. Within the company world, as within society, one rarely sees any opposition or dissidence or revolt. As one of my Tunisian interlocutors put it, 'the capitalists don't like waves and risk, they'll never become dissidents',[64] while another added, 'the businessmen will never go underground'.[65] The fact that some employees are constantly absent on the occasion of holidays or family events, or that some white-collar workers 'don't belong' to the company does not mean that they are part of the opposition.[66] There may be strikes, even hunger strikes, movements across sectors or at specific places, social conflicts, but they need not lead to criticism of social and economic practices, and even less to those of the mechanisms for discipline and surveillance. These strategies of accommodation allow the actors to convince themselves that they are 'only slightly affected by the negative aspects of the regime' and that 'things aren't really so bad'. There is a sort of 'ideology of silence' (Halperin 1985, p. 5, cited by Brown 1998, ch. 4) which is an ethos that protects the individuals who do not want to go into opposition to the dominant order, while still not giving up their own beliefs. This analysis parallels that of Alf Lüdtke in terms of *Eigensinn*, the capacity to distance oneself and to feel indifferent, the capacity to create an autonomous space for oneself, and a 'self-isolating' zone. He describes workers in Nazi Germany who did not participate in large numbers or very actively either in resistance or in supporting the system, but who developed a subtle behaviour of distancing themselves and of indifference, an art of evasion that allowed them to 'breathe', that made it possible to survive or to maintain their habitual way of life (Lüdtke 2000, esp. chs 2, 3 and 4).

As the saying goes, 'one obeys but one doesn't apply the rule', the behaviour of individuals oscillates continually between participation and withdrawal, between the attempt to exercise some level of power and subordination, between the 'loan of oneself' and 'reclaiming oneself', between 'involvement' and 'my space'. One's work or social identity is more often experienced as a sort of doubling, a controlled duplication of the relationships to oneself and to others, or in other terms, 'a constant effort to reappropriate one's own being' at work as in society.[67] This form of behaviour will only turn into rejection when a drop in living conditions, or in the services provided, or in working conditions becomes too great, and if, in other areas, the fears encounter demands that are more political. To avoid being torn apart and to come to terms with these situations, every individual engages in a perpetual negotiation with him/herself and with others, on the meaning of his/her involvement so that what objectively is constraint becomes transformed into a voluntary involvement.

What Jean-Pierre Durand calls a 'paradoxical contentment' can cover all the relationships in the polis: as 'the implication is constraint, escape from the paradox is to be found through the voluntary construction of the acceptability' (Durand 2004, p. 373) of work and of life in society. Otherwise said, surveillance and domination do not prevent individuals from inventing for themselves space in which to manoeuvre, their own spaces for action. The relationships deployed in these worlds allow both discipline and the softening of discipline, as well as the existence of free spaces: 'To work is to operate continuously in the tension between the established norms and personal autonomy, to develop the conditions that allow one to bear the constraints of work' (Flamand and Jeudy-Ballini 2002, p. 9). There is no brutal domination, either from 'capitalism' or from the 'regime', except for the test cases that constitute 'examples', creating a purposeful spectacle of force and the strategy of the periphery. The power relations do lead to involvement but also to resistance, and this latter leads the central Authorities to develop strategies to remain in power, strategies that are applied with a cunning to match the persistence and power of the resistance. Thus, there is continuous movement and no stability, despite the emphasis that Tunisian authorities always put on this quality as an intrinsic element of the 'regime'. Accommodation does not translate into 'the dreary and stable domination of a homogenising system' but rather into the co-existence of participation and resistance in a 'perpetual, many-shaped struggle' (Foucault 1994c).

However, this negotiated accommodation can also be the result of a much simpler situation that involves a partial, but still real, acceptance of the discipline. This acceptance may derive from the expectation of actual material benefits. Certain segments of the elite subscribe to a pattern of co-optation and differentiation, in the secret hope of being admitted to the 'select', of being 'chosen', even though one of the possible consequences may be disgrace. This active involvement thus cannot be dissociated from the desire to serve ever better, that obscures the constraints and lights up only the improvements and progress. The same can be said for the businessmen who dream of stability and security and would like to have a labour force that is even more disciplined and regimented; of the middle class that worries about delinquency and the 'dangerous elements of society'; of the workers in the tourism sector or in the offshore companies who enjoy a certain level of access to modernity and 'western living'; to the citizens who accept the discipline because it provides them with a certain standard of living, the basics of the infrastructure, and social peace, even if these come at the cost of practices that are much closer to coercion than to persuasion. As de La Boétie (1993, p. 213) said:

> en somme, par les gains et parts de gain que l'on fait avec les tyrans, on arrive à ce point qu'enfin il se trouve presque un si grand nombre de ceux auxquels la tyrannie est profitable, que de ceux auxquels la liberté serait utile

> In all, by profiting with, and sharing in the profits of, tyrants, one can reach the point where there is almost as great a number of those who benefit from tyranny as of those for whom freedom would be useful.

However, the advantages gained through discipline and domination can be the fruit of more subtle playing with ways of life and the construction of subjects. The Tunisian working women of the offshore textile sector are indeed subject to heavy discipline, to demands of time and organisation, but at the same time their work provides them with an undeniable source of revenue and complementary resources, with emancipation and with a transformation of their way of life. The call-operators of the call-centres are certainly 'proletarian, like our fathers, despite our degrees', 'workers of the modern era'[68] where they had dreamed of social mobility made possible by their university studies, but they are also the first to delight in what they consider a first job, a stepping-stone into the world of work, and a source of revenue that gives them some importance within their families. The social status linked to work also provides satisfaction, pleasure, and esteem, which also explains why 'work, even with its negative aspects, is acceptable and accepted' (Durand 2004, p. 311). In contrast to the ideas advanced, from a Marxist perspective, by authors such as E.P. Thompson (2004), or more recently A. Ong (1987), the discipline of capitalism and of urban modernity do not introduce only new social relationships and new power relationships that enhance domination, control, and surveillance. The possibilities for autonomy, for freedom, and for access to material or intangible benefits are also to be clearly seen.[69] Max Weber's works remind us that there is no clear causal relationship between capitalism, the exercise of domination, and the instances and methods of socialisation, while the work of Michel Foucault suggests that the processes of instilling discipline cannot be dissociated from extremely variable and fluid processes of subjectivation (see, particularly, Weber 1996, Foucault 1976). While they may be controlled and watched, the working women of the offshore sector are still able to assemble their dowry and they are still able to share in household costs, for themselves or their parents, in a process that makes them a subject – perhaps an economic subject under disciplines, but still one on the path to emancipation or to a transformation of the social and familial domination, a subject who fulfils herself through some kind of withdrawal or simply by diversifying her social relationships. In the same way, the call-operators can free themselves, can go seek the hand of their beloved, and for those who have job security, can gain access to the world of credit. The social relationships of these young people have indisputably been modernised, even though paternalist behaviour is pervasive and social control, especially as exerted through the family, remains just as weighty.[70]

The multiplicity of the meanings of work and the plurality of the ways in which people live with their work stem from a deep heterogeneity in the perceptions of reality: at the same time discipline and freedom, submission and access to some sorts of freedom, rigidity and new latitude for action. One might make the same observations about social life, the role of the Party, political or administrative actions. This proliferation always, or almost always, makes it possible to find grounds for acceptance, use, and convergence that make the disciplinary power bearable, acceptable, or even desirable. Freedom and obedience appear indissoluble. Both are anchored in the power relationships, and are only expressed in the details of specific situations. Thus, it is easier to understand the meaning of this voluntary servitude that cannot be reduced to a love of domination (de La Boétie 1993). 'Servitude is not the blind and open acceptance of the established order; the opposite of servitude is not purely the revolts that regularly arise to shake the established order' but rather the link and continuous tension between the desire to revolt and the willingness to serve (Abensour and Gauchet 1993, p. 21). It signifies submission and fear of power, but also the appropriation, inflection, the use, the advantages of power.

> The intervention of the political authorities, that in daily relations have no limits, thus becomes not only acceptable and familiar, but deeply desired, but not without also becoming, for the same reason, the grounds for widespread fear ... It becomes an object of desire and the object of seduction; thus desirable, and in the same way in which it is absolutely fearsome. (Foucault 1994b, p. 247)

Notes

1. See also certain analyses by Raid/Attac Tunisie that appeared in their newsletter Raid-Niouz.
2. On this reconciliation of two founding fathers of historical sociology, see Lonsdale (1981), Bayart (1994a), and Colliot-Thélène (2001).
3. This distinction between Marxist works and the works of Karl Marx is particularly well illustrated by Michael Henry; I have drawn inspiration from a reading of his *Le socialisme selon Marx* (Henry 2008).
4. See particularly 'A propos de la situation de la démocratie bourgeoise en Russie' (Weber 2004, pp. 139–179), from which one might cite this extract:

> Si tout dépendait *seulement* des conditions 'matérielles' et des constellation d'intérêts qu'elles 'créent' directement ou indirectement, toute considération devrait dire sobrement: tous les baromètres *économiques* indiquent une tendance orientée vers une 'non liberté' croissante. Il est parfaitement ridicule d'attribuer à l'actuel capitalisme à son apogée, tel qu'il existe en Amérique et tel qu'il est actuellement importé en Russie – phénomène 'inéluctable' de notre évolution économique – une affinité élective avec la 'démocratie' ou même avec la 'liberté' (en *quelque* sens du terme *que ce soit*) alors que la seule question qui se pose est de savoir comment, sous sa domination, toutes choses seront à la longue, 'possibles'. Elles ne le sont effectivement que là où existe durablement pour les appuyer la *volonté* résolue d'une nation de ne pas se laisser gouverner comme un troupeau de moutons. (p. 173)

> If the *only* things that mattered were 'material' conditions and the constellations of interests directory or indirectly 'created' by them, any sober observer would be bound to conclude that all *economic* auguries point in the direction of a growing *loss* of freedom. It is quite ridiculous to attribute to today's high capitalism, as it exists in American and is being

imported into Russia, this 'inevitability' of our economic development, any 'elective affinity' with 'democracy' or indeed 'freedom' (in *any* sense of the word), when the only question one can ask is how all these things can 'possibly' survive at all in the long run under the rule of capitalism. They are in fact only possible if they are supported by the permanent, determined *will* of a nation not to be governed like a flock of sheep. (Weber 1994, p. 69)

5. My references to these interviews are intentionally vague. In a country such as Tunisia, characterised by tight police control, all the tighter because I was a particularly visible foreigner, it would be too dangerous to identify by name the people who were brave enough to grant me the interviews, or even to specify the time and the place of our meetings. For a more detailed explanation of my research methods, see Hibou (2006, esp. pp. 22–26).
6. The offshore sector is extra-territorial in that those rules that apply on national territory are not applied there, particularly in regard to customs duties and taxation. This sector is reserved to companies that are mostly or totally export-driven. Most often, the companies established in the offshore zone are foreign.
7. These figures are averages for the period 1997–2002, and are taken from the Economic and Financial Mission of the Embassy of France in Tunis. Surprisingly, the figures appear exactly the same for the last two years (2006–2007), which raises the very strong suspicion that the figures may be arbitrary and political, intended more to project an order of size and a positive image to the outside world rather than any reflection of an objective reality.
8. This does not occur only in Tunisia; it may be met in China as well. This is the main thesis of Huang (2003), in which he interprets the importance of FDI for China as an indicator of the weakness of the Chinese economy.
9. Also international assistance agencies (interview, Tunis, 1997–2005 and IMF, *Article IV 2003*, Washington, DC, February 2004, p. 20).
10. Interviews, Tunis, January–March 2005.
11. Interviews, Tunis, July 1999, January 2000, January–March 2005, and also Bédoui (2004), World Bank (2004a, 2004b), Casero and Varoudakis (2004).
12. One can specify: physical, linguistic, and cultural proximity to Europe; the relatively low salaries; tax and customs advantages; the efficiency of one-stop administration; assistance from FIPA in purchasing land and obtaining information on applicable laws; the flexibility of the labour force; state assistance for new hires and for training; a pleasant environment for expatriates; the availability of labour. Source: interviews, Tunis, January–March 2005; Bellon and Gouia (1998), Livre blanc sur l'environnement industriel en Tunisie (1999), Barbier and Véron (1991); see also sites such as www.offshore-developpement.com; www.tunisie.com/économie/douanes; www.industrie.web-tunisie.com
13. Interviews and visits to factories, District of Tunis and Nabeul, January–March 2005.
14. Interviews, Paris, December 2004 and February 2005 and in the Districts of Tunis and Nabeul, January–March 2005. The World Bank (2002), Fich Ratings (2004) and Economic Mission of the Embassy of France in Tunisia (2004b).
15. In general, on the perverse effects of the tourist 'zones', see Dehoorne (2002).
16. Interviews and site visits, Tunis and Hammamett, January–March 2005; also Kerrou (2002).
17. Official data from FIPA, February 2008.
18. The expression is taken from Lefebvre (1976).
19. Trainees are paid around 80–100 DT (Tunisian dinars) per month, but occasionally much less (in some cases, 20 DT per month). The length of the training period may extend to three or four years. Contracts for 'Training for professional employment' ('*stages d'insertion à la vie professionelle*': SIVP) are cheap for the employer, as the government finances such jobs and the employers have a minimal contribution. Personnel may be employed partly on the black market, with no record of overtime, and portions of the salary hidden from the tax authorities or the CNSS. Interviews, Tunis, December 2003, January–March 2005.
20. Interviews, Tunis, January–March 2005.
21. An expatriate summarised the situation for me thus: 'In Tunisia, the workshop model operates. There are no managers, no transfer of power within the company; there are only people covering their asses.' Interview, Tunis District, January 2005. This has been demonstrated by Marx in *Capital* or by Marxists such as E.P. Thompson (2004), for example, but equally well by the analyses of Foucault on liberalism (see, for example, Foucault 1994a). See also, for the case of Malaysia, Ong (1987).

22. Interviews, Districts of Tunis, Nabeul, and Monastir, December 1999, January and March 2005.
23. This heading is of course a reference to J. L Rocca's work on China (Rocca 1994 and esp. 2006). For the use of these techniques in Tunisia, interviews in the Districts of Tunis, Nabeul, Sfax and Monastir, 1997–2005, and also H. Yousfi (2005).
24. On the call-centres in general, see Durand (2004); for the Tunisian case, Elbaz (2007).
25. Interviews, Districts of Tunis, Nabeur, and Monastir, January and March 2005.
26. Numerous interviews between 1999 and 2005.
27. All these expressions and quotes are taken from interviews, Districts of Tunis and Nabeul, January–March 2005.
28. This analysis was inspired by Ong (1987) who analyses the possession trances of women workers in the Malaysian textile industry as attempts to reconcile their 'traditional' world and the modern atmosphere of the company.
29. Company owners very often justify the rigour of their controls and discipline by citing employee theft, actual or potential. Various interviews. H. Yousfi *et al.* (2005, p. 39, n. 18) state:

    le mot dérapage revient tout le temps et nos interlocuteurs entendent par dérapage l'ensemble des pratiques frauduleuses ou clientélistes qui peuvent tenter les employés Poulina s'il n'y a pas de contrôle. On part du principe que l'ouvrier va toujours essayer de trouver des 'combines' pour voler ou ne pas faire son travail.
    The word '*derapage*' [going off track] comes up all the time, and our interlocutors understand by it the various fraudulent or nepotistic practices that might tempt the employees of Poulina were there no controls. The starting principle is always that the workers will try to cook up schemes to steal or to avoid doing their jobs.

30. Ben Ali, respectively, from a speech on 3 February 1988 in Carthage, on 7 November 1988 at Le Bardo, and on 31 July 1988 in Tunis.
31. Max Weber's reasoning is recognisable, for instance in his *Ethique protestante et l'esprit du capitalisme* [*The Protestant ethic and the spirit of capitalism*] (Weber 2003). See also Maillard (2004).
32. Interviews, Districts of Tunis and Nabeul, January–March 2005. A comparison is possible here with Taiwan (Guiheux 2002) or with south China where paternalism is even more visible (Lee 1997, 1998).
33. All these examples are drawn from interviews in the Districts of Tunis, Nabeul, and Monastier, January–March 2005, and December 2000, December 2001, and December 2003. This sort of system is limited only to the women who work in textiles, of course. The companies of the tourist sector often act in the same way with their employees (who are mainly men).
34. Interviews, Districts of Tunis and Nabeul, January and March 2005; also Ruiz and Peraldi *et al.* (2003).
35. All these phrases and comments are taken from interviews, Janury–March 2005.
36. This ideology of the 'leader' in the business world pervades the whole society, including many intellectuals, under the guise of a 'culture of allegiance' (Redissi 2004) or of the 'domination of a servile culture' (Chennoufi 2000). On the construction of the 'reformist tradition', see B. Hibou (2006b). On the image of the state as foreign to the society, see Leca (1994). On the culture of riots and sedition, see Camau (1996).
37. Interview, Districts of Nabeul and Tunis, January–March 2005.
38. Speech by Ben Ali, 1 May 1990, Carthage (emphasis added).
39. Interviews, Tunis, January 2005 and March 2005.
40. Interviews, Districts of Tunis and Nabeul, January–March 2005 and Ruiz. This practice is not peculiar to Tunisia, although the methods of control may vary. For China, see Lee (1998) and Chan (2001). For Malaysia, Ong (1987) shows how industrial discipline is allied with family control; besides the practices described for Tunisia, there the families are invited by the company to come see their daughter's work and to get involved in the system of surveillance.
41. Interview, Tunis, March 2005.
42. As expressed, and in other phrasings. Interviews, Paris, December 2004 and Tunis, January 2005.
43. The post of resident customs officer is highly prized, as the work is not very demanding and the rewards in kind can be very large. Corruption in this sector is endemic and widely denounced by businessmen. Interviews, January–March 2005.

44. All these examples are taken from interviews in the Districts of Tunis and Hammamet, January and March 2005.
45. This can certainly be explained by the fact that the whole region is not considered attractive. Still, one cannot avoid noticing the regressive trend that has been operative for ten years or so: whereas up to 1997 Tunisia held about a half of the FDI of the Central Maghreb, now it only attracts about a quarter of the flow. Especially, official statistics never mention the outflows of the FDI, and these are more or less equal to the income (around 650 million Tunisian dinars for payments, as against 700–750 million Tunisian dinars for income), which means that the net FDI is really rather low (FEMISE 2005, Economic and Financial Mission of the Embassy of France in Tunis 2003; Michalet 1992).
46. This is the original result of studies conducted jointly by the Agence Française de Dévelopement (AFD) and the Direction des Relations Extérieures Économiques (DREE) of the Ministry of the Economy: Chaponnière and Perrin (2005) and Chaponnière *et al.* (2004). For Italy, see Lainati (2001), M. Peraldi *et al.* (2003). The cases of France and Italy are particularly revealing, as they represent the two nations most heavily present in Tunisia.
47. See the works of Marx and the Marxians (for example Wallerstein 1979, 1980 or Thompson 1963), but also by Weber (the rereading proposed by C. Colliot-Thélène [2001] also emphasises this dimension), by Polanyi, or by Braudel. For a political rereading, see the various papers in Bayart (1994b).
48. Interview, January 2005, District of Nabeul.
49. Based on very specific cases, these scenarios were presented to me by businessmen, employees, and union representatives: field work, January–March 2005. Casero and Varoudakis (2004) describe how the administrative measures regulating the operations of business have been applied, by those dealing with firings and the closing of companies have proved much more difficult to put into operation.
50. Interviews, January–March 2005; Khiari (2003) and the reports of the LTDH which centre more and more on the topic of Raid/AttacTunisie, which is one of its principal concerns.
51. Employers who do not experience serious conflicts often accuse their counterparts of a 'lack of tact' or not being 'fair', of wanting to 'bulldoze their way' or simply of 'being dishonest'. Interviews, January–March 2005.
52. The phrase 'strategie de pourtour [strategy of the periphery]' is taken from Michel Foucault (1994e), who created it for the workers' protests in Longwy: unlike the workers, the students and the young unemployed people who came to support the workers were severely punished by the French judicial system, for example.
53. I found myself led to this reading of Max Weber through the new French translations and commentaries on the author by Catherine Colliot-Thélène (2001) and by Jean-Pierre Grossein (1996).
54. Interviews, January–March 2005. See also the World Bank (2004b) and the World Bank Operation Evaluation Department (2004), ICFTU (2002, 2003, 2004), World Bank (2002), Fich Ratings (2004), Boltanski and Chiapello (1999), Coutrot (1998), Durand (2004).
55. Interviews, December 2002 and 2003, March 2005.
56. Interview, January–February 2005 and also the World Bank (2002) and Fich Ratings (2004).
57. On this convergence of Foucault with Weber, see C. Colliot-Thélène (2001, esp. pp. 280 ff.)
58. On the importance of internalisation, de La Boétie (1993) or Bentham, as read by Foucault (1975).
59. One might here recall Foucault's phrase: 'rien n'est politique, tout est politisable, tout peut devenir politique. La politique n'est rien de plus rien de moins que ce qui naît avec la résistance à la gouvernementalité, le premier soulèvement, le premier affrontement' [Nothing is political, everything can be made political and can be politicised. Politics are nothing more nor less than that which is born through resistance to governmentism, the first uprising, the first confrontation], unpublished manuscript on governmentality cited by M. Senellart, 'Situation des cours' (pp. 381–411) in Foucault (2004, p. 409).
60. Here we might recall the words of de La Boétie (1993, pp. 195–196): 'Disons donc que, si toutes choses auxquelles l'homme se fait et se façonne lui deviennent naturelles, cependant celui-là seul reste dans sa nature qui ne s'habitue qu'aux choses simples et non altérées: ainsi, la première raison de la servitude volontaire, c'est l'habitude' [Let us say that if all those things to which Man accustoms and adapts himself were to become natural, he alone would remain true to his nature who became accustomed only to simple and unchanged things: in this way, the first principle of voluntary servitude is habit].

61. Interview, Districts of Tunis and Nabeul, January–March 2005.
62. Here we observe what E.P. Thompson (2004) described by the beginning of the nineteenth century. The quotations are taken from interviews.
63. On the ever-renewed permanent preoccupation with morality and maintaining 'proper behaviour', see Kerrou (2002); on the link between moralisation and the Islamisation of society, see Ben Achour (1992), Frégosi (1995) and Bras (2002).
64. Interview, Tunis, March 2005.
65. Interview, Tunis, January 2005.
66. Interviews, Monastir, January 2005 and Tunis, March 2005.
67. This analysis was inspired by Hatzfeld (2002) from whom I have borrowed some of the terms.
68. Phrases used by a Tunisian call-operator interviewed in Paris, October 2007.
69. Interviews, Tunis, January and March 2005, Paris, October 2007; Flamand and Jeudy-Ballini (2002), Parry 2002. On Cambodia, see Bottomley (2002).
70. Interviews, Tunis, Sfax and Nabeul, December 2003, January and March 2005; Ruiz and Elbaz 2007.

References

Abensour, M. and Gauchet, M., 1993. Présentation. Les leçons de la servitude et leur destin. *In*: E. de la Boétie, ed. *Le discours de la servitude volontaire*. Paris Payot.
Azarya, V., 2004. Globalisation and international tourism in developing countries: marginality as a commercial commodity. *Current sociology*, 52 (6), 949–967.
Barbier, J.P. and Véron, J.B., 1991. *Les zones franches industrielles d'exportation (Haïti, Maurice, Sénégal, Tunisie)*. Paris: Karthala.
Bayart, J.F., 1994a. L'invention paradoxale de la modernité économique. *In*: J.F. Bayart, ed. *La réinvention du capitalisme*. Paris: Karthala, 9–43.
Bayart, J.F., ed., 1994b. *La réinvention du capitalisme*. Paris: Karthala.
Bayart, J.F., 2004. *Le gouvernement du monde. Une critique politique de la globalisation*. Paris: Fayard.
Bédoui, A., 2003. La question de l'Etat et la gouvernance en Tunisie. *La lettre de la dilapidation économique et budgétaire en Tunisie*, 5, November.
Bédoui, A., 2004. Spécificités et limites du modèle de développement tunisien. Paper presented at the workshop *Démocratie, développement et dialogue social*, organised by the UGTT (Union Générale des Travailleurs Tunisiens – General Union of Tunisian Workers), Tunis, November.
Bellon, B. and Gouia, R., eds., 1998. *Investissements directs étrangers et développement industriel méditerranéen*. Paris: Economica.
Ben Achour, Y., 1992. *Politique, religion et droit dans le monde arabe*. Tunis: Cérès production-CERP.
Boétie, E. de la, 1993. *Le discours de la servitude volontaire*. Paris: Payot.
Boltanski, B. and Chiapello, E., 1999. *Le nouvel esprit du capitalisme*. Paris: Gallimard.
Bottomley, R., 2002. Contested forests: an analysis of the Highlander response to logging, Rattanakiri Province, Northeast Cambodia. *Critical Asian studies*, 34 (4), 587–606.
Bras, J.P., 2002. L'islam administré: illustrations tunisiennes. *In*: M. Kerrou, ed. *Public et privé en Islam*. Paris: Maisonneuve & Larose, 227–246.
Brown, P., 1998. *Pouvoir et persuasion dans l'Antiquité tardive. Vers un empire chrétien*. Paris: Le Seuil, Collection 'Des travaux'.
Camau, M., 1996. Politique dans le passé, politique aujourd'hui au Maghreb. *In*: J.F. Bayart, ed. *La greffe de l'Etat*. Paris: Karthala, 63–93.
Camau, M. and Geisser, V., 2003. *Le syndrome autoritaire. Politique en Tunisie de Bourguiba à Ben Ali*. Paris: Presses de Sciences Po.
Casero, P.A. and Varoudakis, A., 2004. *Growth, private investment, and the cost of doing business in Tunisia: a comparative perspective*. Discussion paper. Washington, DC: World Bank, January.
Cassarino, J.P., 2000. *Tunisian new entrepreneurs and their past experiences of migration in Europe: resource mobilisation, networks, and hidden disaffection*. Aldershot: Ashgate.
CERES, 1989. Actes du séminaire syndicat et société. Tunis, 1 December 1987. *Les cahiers du CERES*, Série Sociologique,14.
Chaponnière, J-R. and Perrin, S., 2005. *Le textile-habillement tunisien et le défi de la libéralisation. Quel rôle pour l'invetissement direct étranger?* Notes et documents, March. Paris: AFD.

Chaponnière, J-R., Cling, J-P. and Marouani, M.A., 2004. *Les conséquences pour les pays en développement de la suppression des quotas dans le textile-habillement: le cas de la Tunisie.* Document de travail, DT/2004/16. Paris: DIAL.

Chan, A., 2001. *China's workers under assault: the exploitation of labor in a globalising economy.* Armonk, NY: M.E. Sharpe.

Chennoufi, R., 2000. Sujet ou citoyen. *Revue tunisienne de droit.* Tunis: Centre de publication universitaire, 205–550.

Colliot-Thélène, C., 2001. *Etudes wébériennes.* Paris: Presses Universitaires de France.

Coutrot, T., 1998. *L'entreprise néolibérale, nouvelle utopie capitaliste.* Paris: La Découverte.

Coutrot, T., 2002. Néolibération du travail et autogestion. *La pensée*, 330 (April–June), 5–20.

Dehoorne, O., 2002. Tourisme, travail et migration: interrelations et logique mobilitaires. *Revue européenne des migrations internationales*, 18 (1), 7–36.

Denieul, P.N., 1992. *Les entrepreneurs du développement. L'ethno-industrialisation en Tunisie. La dynamique de Sfax.* Paris: L'Harmattan.

Dimassi, H. and Zaïem, H., 1987. L'industrie: mythe et strategies. *In*: M. Camau, ed. *Tunisie au présent. Une modernité au-dessus de tout soupçon?* Paris: Editions du CNRS, 161–179.

Durand, J.P., 2004. *La chaîne invisible. Travailler aujourd'hui: flux tendu et servitude volontaire.* Paris: Le Seuil.

DREE, 2002. *Le textile-habillement dans les pays méditerranéens et d'Europe centrale: l'enjeu de la compétitivité.* December. Paris: Ministry of the Economy, Finance, and Industry.

Economic and Financial Mission of the Embassy of France in Tunis, 2003. *Les investissements directs étrangers en Tunisie (Foreign direct investment in Tunisia).* Briefing note, December.

Economic and Financial Mission of the Embassy of France in Tunis, 2004a. *Les investissements directs étrangers en Tunisie (Foreign direct investment in Tunisia).* Briefing note, November.

Economic Mission of the Embassy of France in Tunisia, 2004b. *Le secteur du tourisme en Tunisie.* Briefing note, 13 December.

Elbaz, S., 2007. *Tunisie, pays émergent?* December. Paris: FASOPO.

Elbaz, S., 2008. *Les ambivalences de la politique migratoire en Tunisie.* December. Paris: FASOPO.

Fehri, H., 1998. Economie politique de la réforme: de la tyrannie du *statu quo* à l'ajustement structurel. *Annales d'économie et de gestion*, 5 (10).

FEMISE, 2005. *Le partenariat euro-méditerranéen, 10 ans après Barcelone. Acquis et perspectives,* coordinated by S. Radwan and J.L. Reiffers, February.

Ferguene, A. and Ben Hamida, E., 1998. Les implantations d'entreprises offshore en Tunisie: quelles retombées sur l'économie? *Monde arabe Maghreb-Machrek*, 160 (April–June), 50–68.

Fich Ratings, 2004. *L'Industrie touristique tunisienne.* 24 June. New York and Tunis: Fich Ratings-Corporate Finance.

Flamand, N. and Jeudy-Ballini, M., 2002. Le charme discret des entreprises. L'ethnologie en milieu industriel. *Terrain*, 39 (September).

Foucault, M., 1975. *Surveiller et punir. Naissance de la prison.* Paris: Gallimard.

Foucault, M., 1976. *Histoire de la sexualité. 1. La volonté de savoir.* Paris: Gallimard.

Foucault, M., 1994a. L'œil du pouvoir. *In*: *Dit et ecrits. Vol. 3, 1976–1979.* Paris: Gallimard, 190–207.

Foucault, M., 1994b. La vie des hommes infâmes. *In*: *Dits et ecrits. Vol. 3, 1976–1979.* No. 198. Paris: Gallimard, 247.

Foucault, M., 1994c. Pouvoir et savoir. *In*: *Dits et ecrits. Vol. 3, 1976–1979.* No. 219. Paris: Gallimard, 407.

Foucault, M., 1994d. Pouvoirs et stratégies. *In*: *Dits et ecrits. Vol. 3, 1976–1979.* Paris: Gallimard, 418–428.

Foucault, M., 1994e. La stratégie du pourtour. *In*: *Dit et ecrits. Vol. 3, 1976–1979.* Paris: Gallimard, 794–797.

Foucault, M., 2004. *Sécurité, territoire, population. Cours au Collège de France, 1977–1978.* Paris: Gallimard and Le Seuil, Hautes Etudes.

Frégosi, F., 1995. Les rapports entre l'islam et l'Etat en Algérie et en Tunisie: de leur revalorisation à leur contestation. *Annuaire de l'Afrique du Nord*, 34, 103–123.

Gentile, E., 2004. *Qu'est-ce que le fascisme? Histoire et interprétation.* Paris: Gallimard Folio Histoire.

Grossein, J.-P., 1996. Présentation. *In*: Max Weber, *Sociologie des religions.* Paris: NRF-Gallimard, 51–129.

Guiheux, G., 2002. *Les grands entrepreneurs privés à Taiwan, la main visible de la prospérité*. Paris: CNRS Editions.

Halperin, C.J., 1985. *Russia and the golden horde. The Mongol impact on Russian history*. London: Tauris.

Hamzaoui, S., 1999. Champ politique et syndicalisme. *Annuaire de l'Afrique du Nord*, 37, 369–380.

Hatzfeld, N., 2002. La pause casse-croûte. Quand les chaînes s'arrêtent à Peugeot-Sochaux. *Terrain*, 39 (September), 33–48.

Henry, M., 2008. *Le socialisme selon Marx*. Paris: Sulliver.

Hibou, B., 2006a. *La force de l'obéissance. Economie politique de la répression en Tunisie*. Paris: La Découverte.

Hibou, B., 2006b. Tunisie, d'un réformisme à l'autre. *In*: FASOPO, *Legs colonial et gouvernance européenne*, vol. 1, December. Available from: http://www.fasopo.org/publications/legscolonial_bh_1205.pdf.

Huang, Y.S., 2003. *Selling China: direct investment during the reform era*. New York: Cambridge University Press.

International Confederation of Free Trade Unions (ICFTU), 2002. *Tunisia, annual survey of violations of trade unions rights*. Brussels: ICFTU.

International Confederation of Free Trade Unions (ICFTU), 2003. *Tunisia, annual survey of violations of trade unions rights*. Brussels: ICFTU.

International Confederation of Free Trade Unions (ICFTU), 2004. *Tunisia, annual survey of violations of trade unions rights*. Brussels: ICFTU.

Kerrou, M., 2002. Le mezwâr ou le censeur des mœurs au Maghreb. *In*: M. Kerrou, ed. *Public et privé en Islam*. Paris: Maisonneuve & Larose, 313–343.

Khiari, S., 2000. Reclassement et recompositions au sein de la bureaucratie syndicale depuis l'Indépendance. La place de l'UGTT dans le système politique tunisien. *La Tunisie sous Ben Ali* du site du CERI. Available from: www.ceri-sciences-po.org/kiosque/archives/déc.2000.

Khiari, S., 2003. *Tunisie, le délitement de la cité. Coercition, consentement, résistance*. Paris, Karthala.

Lainati, C., 2001. Le imprese straniere in Tunisia. Nascita e sviluppo dei circuiti produttivi: gli italiani nel tessile-abbigliamento. Research report, mimeo. October–December.

Lallement, M., 2003. *Temps, travail et modes de vie*. Paris: PUF.

Le Saout, D. and Rollinde, M., eds., 1999. *Emeutes et mouvements sociaux au Maghreb*. Paris: Karthala, 1999.

Leca, J., 1994. La démocratie dans le monde arabe: incertitude, vulnérabilité et légitimité. *In*: G. Salamé, ed. *Démocratie sans democrats*. Paris: Fayard, 35–93.

Lee, C.K., 1997. Factory regimes of China capitalism: different cultural logics in labor control. *In*: A. Ong and D. Nonini, eds. *Undergrounded empires: the cultural politics of modern Chinese transnationalism*. New York: Routledge, 115–142.

Lee, C.K., 1998. *Gender and the south China miracle: two worlds of factory women*. Berkeley, Los Angeles and London: University of California Press.

Lefebvre, H., 1976. *De l'Etat*. Tome 2, *Théorie marxiste de l'Etat: de Hegel à Mao*. Paris: UGE.

Livre blanc sur l'environnement industriel en Tunisie, 1999. *Les cahiers du CEPI*, no. 1. Final Report, December.

Lonsdale, J., 1981. States and social processes: a historical survey. *African studies review*, 24 (2–3), 140.

Lüdtke, A., 2000. *Des ouvriers dans l'Allemagne du XXème siècle. Le quotidien des dictatures*. Paris: L'Harmattan.

Maillard, A., 2004. E.P. Thompson. La quête d'une autre expérience des temps. *In*: E.P. Thompson, ed. *Temps, discipline du travail et capitalisme industriel*. Paris: La Fabrique Editions, 7–28.

Marx, K., 1972. *La première critique de l'économie politique. Les manuscrits de 1844*. Paris: UGE.

Meddeb, R., 2003. Le tourisme en Tunisie. Presentation at Club Bochra El Khair, 10 January.

Melliti, I. Observatoire de la condition de la femme en Tunisie. *Correspondances*, 26. Tunis: IRMC.

Michalet, C.A., 1992. Investissements étrangers: les économies du sud de la Méditerranée sont-elles attractives? *Monde arabe Maghreb-Machrek*, December, 3–82.

Miossec, J.M., 1997. Le tourisme en Tunisie: acteurs et enjeux. *Bulletin de l'Association des Géographes Français*, 1 (March), 56–69.

Ong, A., 1987. *Spirits of resistance and capitalist discipline*. New York: State University of New York Press.

Parry, J.P., 2002. Du bagne des champs aux riantes usines. Le travail dans une entreprise sidérurgique indienne. *Terrain*, 39 (September), 121–140.

Peraldi, M., with Bettaieb, H. and Lainati, C., 2003. Affranchissement et protection: les petits mondes de la confection en Tunisie. Paper presented at the Colloquium of Sousse, Tunisie.

Redissi, H., 2004. *L'Exception islamique*. Paris: Le Seuil.

Rocca, J.L., 1994. La 'mise au travail' capitaliste des Chinois. *In*: J.F. Bayart, ed. *La réinvention du capitalisme*. Paris: Karthala, 47–72.

Rocca, J.L., 2006. *La condition chinoise. Capitalisme, mise au travail et résistances dans la Chine des réformes*. Paris: Karthala.

Roitman, J. and Roso, G., 2001. Guinée Equatoriale: être 'offshore' pour rester national. *Politique africaine*, 81 (March), 121–142.

Ruiz, I. Du rural à l'urbain. Travail féminin et mutations sociales dans une petite ville du Sahel tunisien. *Correspondances*, 25. Tunis: IRMC.

Sahli, M., 1990. Tourisme et développement en Tunisie. *Bulletin du groupe de recherche et d'étude en économie du développement*, 15 (December), 37–50.

Signoles, P., 1985a. *L'espace tunisien: capitale et Etat-région*. 2 vols. Tours: URBAMA.

Signoles, P., 1985b. Industrialisation, urbanisation et mutations de l'espace tunisien. *In*: R. Baduel, ed. *Etats, territoires et terroirs au Maghreb*. Paris: Editions du CNRS, 277–306.

Thompson, E.P., 1963. *The making of the English working class*. New York: Vintage Books.

Thompson, E.P., 2004. *Temps, discipline du travail et capitalisme industriel*. Paris: La Fabrique Editions.

Valente, J.C., 1999. *Estado novo e alegria no trabalho. Uma historia politica da FNAT (1935–1958)*. Lisboa: Edições Colibri.

Wallerstein, I., 1979. *The capitalist world economy*. Cambridge: Cambridge University Press.

Wallerstein, I., 1980. *The modern world system II. Mercantilism and the consolidation of the European world-economy, 1600–1750*. New York: Academic Press.

Weber, M., 1994. *Political writings*. Ed. and trans. P. Lassman and R. Speirs. Cambridge: Cambridge University Press.

Weber, M., 1996. *Sociologie des religions*. Paris: NRF-Gallimard.

Weber, M., 2004. *Œuvres politiques (1895–1919)*. Paris: Albin Michel, Bibliothèque Idées.

Weber, M., 2003. *Ethique protestante et l'esprit du capitalisme*. Paris: Gallimard.

World Bank, 2002. *Stratégie de développement touristique en Tunisie. Rapport de phase 1*. UP'Management, KPMG THL Consulting, JC Consultants, KA02R20. 13 juillet. Washington, DC: World Bank.

World Bank, 2003. *Tunisia. Economic monitoring update*. MENA Region. September. Washington, DC: World Bank.

World Bank, 2004a. *Republic of Tunisia. Development policy review. Making deeper trade integration work for growth and jobs*. Report 29847-TN. Washington, DC: World Bank, October.

World Bank, 2004b. *Stratégie de coopération, République Tunisienne – Banque mondiale, 2005–2004*. December. Washington, DC: World Bank.

World Bank Operation Evaluation Department, 2004. *Republic of Tunisia. Country Assistance Evaluation, advance copy*. Washington, DC: World Bank.

Yousfi, H., Filipiak, E. and Bougault, H., 2005. *Poulina, un management tunisien*. Notes et Documents, 17, May. Paris: AFD.

Zeghidi, S., 1997. L'UGTT, pôle central de la contestation sociale et politique. *In*: M. Ben Romdhane, ed. *Tunisie: mouvements sociaux et modernité*. Dakar: CODESRIA, 13–61.

Zghal, R., 1992. Postface. *In*: *Les entrepreneurs du développement. L'ethno-industrialisation en Tunisie. La dynamique de Sfax*. Paris: L'Harmattan.

Zghal, R., 1998. Nouvelles orientations du syndicalisme tunisien. *Monde arabe, Maghreb-Machrek*, 162 (October–December), 6–17.

Migration for 'white man's work': an empirical rebuttal to Marxist theory

Isaie Dougnon

Faculté des Lettres, Langues, Art et Sciences Humaines (FLASH), Department of Social Sciences, University of Bamako, Mali

Enlisted between 1920 and 1960 for mines in Ghana and and for the construction of the Markala dam in Mali, migrant Dogon workers offer a definition of colonial work that runs counter to that of Marxist intellectuals who have denounced it in all its forms. Within the colonial towns, the migrant workers established a hierarchy of tasks according to the amount of labour and the technical and social organisation required to accomplish them. This article analyses why the Dogon migrant workers glorified colonial work in these different dimensions (time, organisation, discipline). This new hierarchisation of activities places 'white man's work' at the top, and other activities at the bottom, of the scale. The following questions lie at the heart of this article: (1) In what manner does the discourse of Africanist researchers reflect the practices, the experiences, and the minds of those people who migrated and worked in colonial centres? (2) Does the 'ancestral' system of work have any influence on the differentiation and evaluation of the 'white man's work'? (3) Does the local classification of village activities have any effect upon the classification of the colonial world?

'White man's work': colonialism and a redefinition of the concept of work

To examine colonial work from the perspective of the migrant workers shows that the latter entered into it with their own social, cultural, and economic backgrounds, and that these, in turn, influenced their perception of work. An analysis of the testimony produced by Dogon migrant workers on the glorification of the 'white man's work' reveals a contradiction between studies inspired by Marxism and the conception of work encountered in the field. François Manchuelle faced just such a contradiction when he tried to analyse the migration of the Soninke to France as the result of French imperialism in Africa:

> I wish to show that the migration of the Black African workers to France was the result of Africa's exploitation by France, thus, in keeping with Marxist theory, that it was the result of economic factors. However, historical evidence pointed to the fact that Soninke migration pre-dated the domination of Western capitalism and may have been related to cultural factors. (Manchuelle 1997, 3)

While Manchuelle resolved this 'Marxist' contradiction by turning resolutely to cultural factors, this was not the case for a considerable number of French-speaking Marxist anthropologists who literally dominated labour studies for black Africa. Their analyses were premised upon the forms of forced labour[1] and the displacement of workers within the former French colonies (Meillassoux 1964, Coquery-Vidrovitch 1988, Ouedraogo 1989, Agiers *et al.* 1987). In their analyses of the modes of production and the stages of development of African economies, they denounced and condemned the forms of labour organisation and their diffusion in the countries of the Third World (Lakroum 2003). Denouncing, in the name of African workers, the worst forms of colonial exploitation remains the central theme of these authors' works. They gave no room to the perspective of the workers, to the perceptions born from their collective and individual experiences in the 'white man's work'. However, the accounts of many African migrant workers in the colonial workplaces, in Ghana and at the Office du Niger in Mali, show that one cannot evaluate or understand the meaning of colonial work in Africa in its totality without taking into account the perspective of those very workers.

Colonialism introduced to Africa methods of work that were totally different from those which the migrant workers had known in their home villages. New social models and new types of consumption fuelled by work were introduced. Leaves, salaries, retirement, the professional hierarchy, dues and unions proved that they belonged to a new type of labour. This break had a profound influence on their perceptions of work in the colonial service (Dougnon 2003).[2]

It was in this context, in the 1920s, that a redefinition of labour was born, articulated by the concept of *anasara bire*,[3] literally 'white man's work': *anasara*, the white man, and *bire*, work. According to our informants, the term *anasara*[4] was introduced to the Dogon language by veteran soldiers who returned home between 1914 and 1918. In their accounts of the war, the former *tirailleurs sénégalais* (Senegalese sharpshooters) told how the whites worked with specialised machines (Caterpillars, earth-movers). They also spoke of the modern means of transportation (planes, boats, cars). But it was mostly through migration to Ghana and to the Office du Niger[5] that many young Dogon were able with their own eyes to see these machines, and later, especially to learn to use them. In Ghana, the concept of 'white man's work' referred to two sorts of activity: public works and the mines. The migrant worker employed in those fields was called a labourer.[6] In the Office du Niger, it refers to the construction of the dam and bridge at Markala and to the irrigation canals, but also to the workshops and to the administration. Between 1920 and 1960, the Dogon rated jobs according to the amount of labour involved, or the technical or social organisation required to complete them. This new hierarchy of activities placed 'white man's work' at the top and local activities at the bottom of the scale. How to explain this attitude towards 'white man's work'?

In terms of methodology, this article looks at the problem raised some years back by the Amsterdam Work-group for Marxist Anthropology, which was: 'how to relate the data gathered at a local or regional level to broader historical development?' The central question of the work was to study how French anthropologists in particular applied Marx's concepts to their analysis of African modes of production and their articulation with European capitalism (Van Binsbergen and Geschiere 1985, 1–37).

The conclusions of the Marxist anthropologists lead to the view that the Dogon migrant workers' positive appreciation of colonial work – considered as one of the most inhuman forms of capitalism – must be seen as anomalous and due to a lack of awareness or to the irrational. However, there is no anomaly if we link the characteristics of white man's work to those of their ancestors' work (cultural factors); also if we compare white man's work to that of Africans (technical and organisational factors), and, finally, the system of the French colonisers with that of the British.

If Marxism is not to be a dogma, one must accept that the workers' notions, based upon their own experience, represent their cultural interpretation of the colonial fact (Gluckman 1974, Burguière 1971).

Why certain communities work more than others, why the Dogon celebrate colonial work over local activities: these are not the questions of structure exposed in Marxist studies, but questions of values and work ethic which require anthropological methods of inquiry.[7] For example, the seasonal organisation of work in Dogon country explains why the Dogon migrant workers did not like the 'daily job'. The regular work habits and sustained effort of the Dogon homeland are parameters to consider in analysing their view of 'white man's work'. Simone Weil never believed that one might enter into the relations of work and workers except by working oneself.[8]

In Ghana, while conducting our research, we met retired former workers who live, generally, under difficult conditions. In the town neighbourhoods, *zongo*,[9] there is no need to describe from the outside – given the shanties and the *banco* houses overrun with uneducated and unemployed children – the disastrous consequences of colonial work on these former labourers. Many of these families only survive thanks to their children who emigrated to Europe or Asia. One might well ask, then, why they hold such a high opinion of colonial work? The lines which follow, thanks to their accounts, may help to perceive the problem differently: how can we condemn colonial labour in the name of these migrant workers without clearly understanding what it meant to them?

An analysis of their testimony shows that the new significance accorded to white man's work was based on four principal elements: the influence of local notions of work, white man's work as the source of a new identity for the migrant labourer, access to a 'professional career,' and finally nostalgia for colonial work following the fall in the demand for work in the post-colonial era.

Before our analysis of these four elements, which endow the white man's work with its prestige, let us briefly discuss the state of research on labour in Africa.

On the anthopology of work in Africa

The historiography of migration and labour in Africa has been dominated for several decades by the South African paradigm of the 'Kraal-to-compound' model, itself influenced by a materialist interpretation of modes of production (Thaddeus 1996). In Francophone West Africa, research has focused particularly on zones such as Senegal and Côte-d'Ivoire; both areas were marked, during the colonial period, by the immigration of Malians and Burkinabé drawn by the cocoa, coffee, and peanut crops (Amin 1974, Lakroum 1982). Claude Meillassoux has analysed the migration between African villages and homes in Paris as the consequence of the over-exploitation which victimised the countries of the Third World after the end of the Second World War (Meillassoux 1991).

While numerous, anthropological studies have not gone beyond the description and documentation of models and trends in labour migration and its economics and social effects (Gupta and Ferguson 1997). All these studies have neglected the specifically cultural questions which lie at the heart of the discourse of the migrant workers on work and its value.

Beyond the discourse of researchers, centres on urban–rural relationships or those of wages and work, the migrant workers have developed their own perceptions and definitions of work in the colonial era, of its value and its ethos. It is only recently that historians and anthropologists have begun to explore the mindset, the culture, and the identity of migrant workers (Atkins 1993, Moodie and Ndatshe 1994). Patrick Harris has contributed to this anthropological perspective through his description of the role of evangelical pastors in the adoption by African migrants of the values and norms of industrial labour in South Africa (Harries 1994).

A few years ago, Gerd Spittler, who established the school of labour anthropology at Bayreuth University in Germany, was wondering about the state of social science research on labour in Africa.[10] The conclusion of his analysis is devastating:

> Si nous essayons, en guise de conclusion, de résumer les résultats de la recherche ethnologique du travail sur l'Afrique, nous retiendrons tout d'abord que le sujet a été peu traité. À l'époque coloniale, l'ethnologie des sociétés africaines a connu sa gloire mais le sujet de travail a été quasiment absent... À chaque fois que l'on a abordé le sujet du travail, c'était toujours pour parler de sa division. (Spittler 2003)

> If we attempt, as some sort of conclusion, to sum up the results of ethnographic research on labour in Africa, the first observation is that the subject has received little attention. During the colonial period, the ethnology of African societies was in its heyday, but the subject of labour was almost entirely neglected... Whenever the subject of labour was raised, it was only to discuss how it was divided.

He does, however, point to one essay, 'Le travail en Afrique Noire' (Work in Black Africa), published in 1952 in the magazine, *Présence Africaine*, as one which tried to answer anthropological questions on labour.[11] The authors of this essay did in fact try to answer Pierre Naville's question: what might Africans think of European work? We do not have the space here to go over this essay in detail.

However, in the context of this article, we should discuss the ideas of one of the authors of this edited work, as presented in Jean Jacques Pauvert's 1952 article which addresses quite specifically the question of the relationship of labour and colonialism. In Africa, according to his view, when one leaves the traditional labour setting, one enters into the setting of the paid employee's individual work. In the colonial centres, the African male was paid wages (as labourer, house-boy, trade or office worker) while the woman maintained a plantation of manioc and bananas or engaged in trade with cigarettes or dried fish, while their relatives often remained in their village of origin. In this context, according to Pauvert, the notion of labour becomes heterogeneous and does not correspond exactly with either the traditional economy or the Western type of economy (Pauvert 1952, 103–104).

As Pauvert saw it, the central element in the notion of labour during the colonial period was the white man, as director of the site or workshop, head of the office, foreman, and owner. The black lived in a situation of dependence towards the white, and it is through that situation that one must analyse his understanding of labour. Basically, Pauvert writes:

> Les professions les plus recherchées sont celles qui ont paru longtemps être l'apanage du Blanc: les activités techniques (mécaniciens, chauffeurs) et les travaux de bureau (dactylographes, écrivains, secrétaires). Peu à peu ainsi la notion de travail se transforme. ... Mais il ne faut pas perdre de vue qu'un des facteurs les plus importants, c'est la référence au travail du Blanc, la comparaison avec le Blanc. Un Noir pense toujours son travail en fonction du Blanc. (Pauvert 1952, 106)

> The most sought-after professions are those which seemed for a long time to be the prerogative of the White: technical activities (mechanic, driver) and office-work (typists,

scribes, secretaries). Little by little, thus, the notion of work is transformed … But one should not lose sight of the point that one of the most important factors is the reference to the White man's work, the comparison with the White man. A Black always sees his work in relation to that of the White man.

Pauvert did indeed offer an objective analysis of the 'colonial situation' as a crucial factor in the new definition of labour reached by Africans, but his conclusion seems too simplistic, and does not reflect the argument that will be developed in this article. His Eurocentrism prevented him from making the link between the worker's culture of origin and the labour values imported by colonisation. The African emigrates freely to seek the white man's work, and not to imitate his European employer for pleasure. Constraints did exist, but they did not prevent the African from forming a clear idea of the values linked to white man's labour and a comparison with the activities he engaged in at home. At the Office du Niger, the (forced) labourers of the Deuxième Portion[12] and free migrant workers shared the same idea on white man's work as the two groups worked on the same colonial workshops and had the same European and African staffs (Bogosian 2004).

European colonisation in African made work secular. Over the course of more than a century, many hundreds of new jobs were created. To emigrate to the colonial centres – which later became the great cities of Africa – meant that the African could do any job.[13]

The upheavals associated with transportation, methods of production, and the extension of borders for work (French subjects found work in English colonies, and vice versa) were violent disruptions of the local traditions of labour in which status and occupations were hereditary.

We need, today, to give a new dynamic to the anthropology of labour in Africa. We suggest that it involves the study of the process which moves Africans from the systems in which occupations were hereditary to the colonial or post-colonial situation which sees labour becoming entirely secularised.[14]

Colonial towns seen as the locus for reinterpreting the notion of work

At the end of the nineteenth century, the Gold Coast (now Ghana) was one of the most prosperous British colonies in West Africa. Thousands of peasants from the neighbouring French colonies made their way there. Jean Rouch, during his investigations in 1953–55, estimated that 300–400,000 migrant workers from northern Upper Volta (now Burkina Faso), the French Sudan (now Mali), Niger, the north of Dahomey (now Benin), Togo, the Northern Territories of Ghana, and Côte d'Ivoire, found work each year in the Gold Coast.[15]

Even though a large part of the population was engaged in agriculture, several thousands were employed in offices or as craftsmen. Many young migrant workers across the country sold their services to the stage, to the mining companies extracting gold, diamonds, or magnesium, to the fisheries, to the builders, to banks, to chambers of commerce, in short to the colonial enterprise. Each community of migrant workers sought out the work for which it felt qualified. The consequences were an ethnic division of labour as described by Rouch:

> Ce tableau fait apparaître les tendances suivantes: les Mossi sont bons à tout, ils se repartissent à peu près également partout. Les Busanga sont spécialistes dans les Travaux Publics et les services municipaux. Les Wangara et les Dogon sont spécialisés dans les mines et services municipaux. Rouch 1957, 104)

> This table brings out the following trends: the Mossi can do anything, and are to be found in equal numbers almost anywhere. The Busanga specialize in Public Works and municipal services. The Wangara and the Dogon specialize in mines and municipal services.

Except for the members of the Deuxième Portion, migrants coming to work at the Office du Niger were young men from rural areas who had freely left the Dogon villages for the new urban centres and the townships of workers.

At that time (1920–60), every young Dogon wished to travel at least once in his life to Kumasi. It was for him a sort of renaissance (Dougnon 2006). Getting to the colonial town of Ghana required at least 35 days walking. The trips were often dangerous. The peasants passed through several villages in which they encountered different peoples. Some of them were considered dangerous, having a reputation as sorcerers, or cannibals, or for practising human sacrifice. The migrants braved the wild animals, hunger and thirst, and servitude. Later, during the period 1950–60, the peasants used trucks and trains to reach the industrial cities. The train stations, the car parks and the ports were important factors in the way they reconfigured their new understanding of labour.

In Ghana, the quest for work cannot be separated from the attraction of the city of Kumasi. It was perceived as a land of prosperity where the Francophone migrant worker was freed from the fear of forced labour, military service, forced contributions, and the abuses of the canton chiefs in the French Sudan. Another factor was the prestige of English merchandise, far beyond that which might be found in the French Sudan or in Upper Volta (now Burkina Faso). In Dogon villages one can still find stored away in the houses sundry objects imported from Ghana: old shoes, spears, sabres, knives, suits, and photographs of the migrant labourers wearing uniforms, and trunks of varying size, depending on whether the owner returned on foot or by car.

Besides access to luxury objects, the migrant workers enjoyed two other important working conditions: voluntary employment, and the existence of a contract. They were fleeing forced labour in the French Sudan, and in Ghana they tasted the pleasure of free work. In Kumasi and in Accra, the migrants met countrymen who supplied them on arrival with food, clothing, and often an employer, preferably a white man.

In the Office du Niger, a large number of young Dogon migrant workers were employed in the preparatory work for large projects such as the bridge-dam of Markala, the navigation canal, the supply canal, the canal of the Sahel, the Macina canal, etc. Besides these large workplaces, there was also employment in the workshops (agricultural machinery), the rice-plantations, the garages, and in administration which hired many migrant workers.

Analysis of the concept of 'white man's work' in the colonial context requires us to consider the notion of labour in the Dogon country, which defines labour according to the amount of effort required for execution.

The Dogon notion of work: work is a function of the mass of effort

We noted above that the Dogon entered into the colonial enterprise with their own notions of work.[16] The characteristics of white man's work (rigour, difficulty, sweat, colossal effort, the personality of the work-leader) are those which prevail in their own occupations at the village (millet cultivation and commercial gardening).

During the years 1970–80, the Dogon quickly gained the reputation in the cities of Mali for being heavy workers who were not inclined to theft or laziness. They were sought after for household work and in other sectors. Further, their tendency to work more than their compensation required gave them the image, in the eyes of the city-dwellers, of somewhat backward, uncivilised people who had no taste for luxury or personal enrichment. This image is disappearing gradually because of the growing number of young rural Dogon incarcerated in the main prison of Bamako.

The Dogon language has a single word for work, *bire*.[17] However, the Dogon do distinguish three principal activities that are classified according to the amount of labour required to accomplish them. If the value of work is determined according to the sweat expended, first comes agriculture, then crafts (smithying and leather-working) and finally raising household livestock. The first occupation is the domain of the farming Dogon, the second of the smiths and leather-workers (caste groups), and the third is reserved for children.[18]

Agriculture essentially involves field labour: tilling the earth and the harvest. The tool involved is the *daba* (a kind of hoe) that is hard to handle. It is the activity that evokes ideas of toil, effort, and courage. The product, grain-crops, is the staple of human life. It is because of its vital essence that the activity required to produce it is the queen of all activities.[19]

The rigours of agriculture are linked to the physical environment. Levelling or cutting into a cliff to create fields and houses requires huge effort. The Dogon cultivate small plots on the Plateau, holding the soil back with little retaining walls made of stones piled one on top of the other. They raise millet, sorghum, fonio (a variety of millet), beans, and rice. There is also a season to this work. It involves at least six months of work during the year: from the preparation of the fields to the harvest. Besides growing cereal crops, the Dogon also grow onions, and this culture has developed greatly in recent years, almost exclusively as a cash crop (Paulme 1988).

Artisanal work is called *numo-bire*, from *numo*, the hand, and *bire*, work: it is the occupation of the *irine*, blacksmiths, and the *dyam*, leather-workers. These two castes are endogamous and live on the outskirts of the villages because of the many prohibitions which affect them.

Blacksmiths do not farm. They make the tools for the Dogon farmers: the hoe, the axe, the pick, and knives. The latter must offer them millet and other cereals after the harvest. The blacksmiths are also good sculptors. Their art, at a certain time, has attained a remarkable degree of development, as witnessed still by shutters made up of carved anthropomorphic or geometric figures and many locks (Paulme 1988, 183–184).

Smithying, although placed below the growing of millet, enjoys a certain respectability because of the mystery surrounding mastery over fire and iron. The smith is in fact the demiurge, a producer of knowledge in the broadest sense, as Marcel Griaule (1994, 48–50) described in his work, *Masques Dogons*. This knowledge endows him with an important position in society.

On the other hand, it is the universal opinion, among the Dogon, that leather-workers engage in easy work which does not demand great efforts. One way of saying that someone does not like work is to call him 'as lazy as a leather-worker'. Leather-workers work without having to bend over. They sit all the time when at their jobs. They work with leather and are also tanners; their tools include small knives, scrapers, awls – tools made by the smiths.

Unlike smiths, leather-workers may farm. All they need to do is ask for a parcel of land from the Dogon. Although they do not farm, leather-workers constitute the best-off social category of the Dogon (Paulme 1988).

Finally, herding or livestock-raising falls in the category of non-work. The staff of the herdsman is not a tool comparable to the *daba* or the sickle. The herdsman depends on the farmer for his food.[20] Herding, as a secondary activity, is entrusted to children until they become strong enough to engage in millet-farming. Hannah Arendt describes the same criteria of classification among the Greeks at the time of Aristotle (Arendt 1958, 82).

From what has been said, one can easily make out the criteria for the classification of work in Dogon country: effort, rigour, courage, regularity are the most important determinants. The community's opinion is by far the most important factor for a young man starting work. Concern, also, for the family or individual reward is also important. The difficult natural conditions for raising crops, either for subsistence (millet, fonio) or for cash (onions), are the same that the worker will face in the coloniser's jobs. But one difference between work in Dogon country, where the farmer relies on his physical strength, and work in the colonial system is that in the latter, the worker has access to modern equipment, the mastery of which gives him pride and self-esteem. He then acquires a new work identity which will determine his discourse on colonial work.

White man's work as a response to the desire to travel

Thanks to his travels, the Dogon migrant worker finds himself earning something more than just his living in work which was unheard of for himself or his relatives who remained in the village (Hughes 1958). For the migrants who settled in Ghana, colonial work was a new activity which furnished a satisfactory response to their migratory hopes. They were not forced into this. The young peasants chose to walk thousands of kilometers to engage in this. At first, the work was not a necessity for them, not required for their living. The goal was to make a bit of money and to return to the village with European things.

The valorisation of European objects expressed by the maidens through song and dance, the attractions of the colonial cities, of imported products, the expectations of the village community, and a competition between age-mates who share the desire to gain universal knowledge – in other words, to fight ignorance – are the principal factors determining the migratory aspirations which can only be fulfilled through paid labour for the whites.

White man's work could not make them slaves, because they did not find themselves forced into it. According to Simone Weil, the servile character of labour derives from the fact that it is governed by necessity. Those who spend their lives in it say it is because 'one must earn one's living' (Weil 1951, 355). Besides the desire for luxury objects, the peasant migrations towards the colonial towns was motivated, in the village of the Sahel, by the Francophone-area peasant's desire to sell his work rather than his livestock to get the cash he needed to pay his taxes. Nor should this desire be separated from the desire to work for wages in Ghana rather than to stagnate in the French territories, caught in forced labour. A person who freely found a paid job felt a constant source of pride.

They did not feel that they were being directed by the British, but rather by the demands of the job. Socially and in terms of their identity, they formed a group of migrants from the same ethnic group working in the same sector (mines and public works). Cooperation and mutual respect were more a part of their collective experience than in the impersonal empire of the classic factory. They never lost the feeling of being free men who might return to their villages whenever they wished.

Moreover, all the accounts and the colonial archives testify that the majority of these migrant workers returned to their villages of origin after a three-year stay.[21] Men from the Northern Territories or from Upper Volta returned in the April of the following year, to have enough time to work on the family fields. Another specific feature of colonial labour is that it developed among the African migrant worker the idea of working for oneself. In contrast to the alienated worker of the Marxists, the Dogon migrant seems to have developed a self-image as a worker who, unlike his fellows caught in ancestral activities, has learned a trade.

Upon his return to the village of his birth, the migrant worker takes great pleasure in an ostentatious display of the treasures he has brought back. Nor does he stint the stories about the great people he met and the thousand-and-one details of the travels. These tales, from someone who travelled far away, have a decisive effect on the young men of the village. Later they will note that the returnee has married a beautiful girl who was the fiancée (betrothed) of some old man in the village. His fellows will also note that the migrant workers show a spirit of independence and initiative. Finally, they will note that the migrant worker also allows himself more time to work on his own field, rather than that of his extended family.[22]

Despite the many years spent at work, Dogon migrants did not become a working class in the Marxist sense of the term. On the contrary, they thought that the colonial methods of managing work were ones which African cadres should pursue (rigour, efficiency, promotion of the good workers). What they liked was the fact that in a few years, through his works, the white man transformed parts of nature that had been considered untouchable, being the habitat of hostile spirits. The great machines of the whites overcame the power of nature. It was the creative power of white man's work which mobilised the emotional energies of the migrants.

For the Dogon, it is sweat: the *sine qua non* of 'white man's work'

To understand in what way the Dogon notions of effort and of time of work (the fundamental criterion of work) were transposed in their definition of 'white man's work', let us consider the account of this old migrant worker, who emphasises the notion of sweat:

> Il y a travail, lorsque la terre mange la sueur du travailleur. L'homme doit travailler jusqu'à ce que sa sueur tombe abondamment sur la terre. Lorsque la terre en aura suffisamment mangé, elle s'adresse à Amma (Dieu) et dit: Ha! J'ai assez mangé la sueur de cet homme, je te demande de lui donner beaucoup de fruits. La terre adresse la prière à Dieu, car c'est lui qui récompense.

> It is work, when the earth eats the worker's sweat. A man must work until his sweat falls copiously onto the earth. When the earth will have had enough of it, she speaks to Amma (God) and says, 'Ha! I have eaten enough of the sweat of this man, I ask you to give him lots of fruits.' The earth addresses the prayer to God, because he is the one who rewards.

This narratives brings us straight back to our central question, which is the meaning of work in Dogon country. It focuses on the role of man through the notion of sweat. Here, work implies ardour, in the literal sense of doing something difficult, hard. The earth is a form of matter that is difficult to work, and it demands of the one who wishes to work it enormous effort and courage.

In studies by leftist intellectuals, and particularly in Marx's chapter on 'A day's work,' one finds a constant opposition between capital, thirsting for overtime labour, and the worker who wants to sell his labour as a commodity and asks for a normal-length working day (Marx 1982, 228).

The voice of this abstract worker is the opposite of that of the Dogon migrant who spends his life in paid employment in a colonial town. Let us listen to him:

> ... J'ai trouvé les ouvriers en train d'abattre un gros karité à la cité des Blancs. C'était mon premier travail salarié chez un Blanc. Je me suis mis aussi à le couper. Lorsque la sirène a sonné, les manœuvres ont immédiatement déposé leurs haches et sont rentrés à la maison. Quant-à-moi, j'ai continué à cogner. Le Blanc est rentré de son travail. Il a mangé et s'est couché. Entre temps, je suis allé manger et je suis revenu aussitôt pour continuer. Le soir, j'ai continué à couper le plus longtemps que possible. Le lendemain, le Blanc a appelé Moussa Guindo, le surveillant, pour lui demander 'Pourquoi celui-ci travaille sans arrêt? Quelle sorte

de personne est-elle?' Moussa lui répond: 'C'est un Dogon, un frère. Au Pays Dogon, on n'arrête le travail que lorsqu'on est fatigué. Il n'existe pas un temps indiqué pour arrêter le travail.' [El Hadj Abdoulaye Sagara, migrant Dogon à Markala depuis 1930]

> I found the workers cutting down a large *karite* tree [also known as shea: trans.] in the White man's city. It was my first paid job with a White man. I began to help cut it as well. When the whistle blew, the laborers immediately put down their axes and went home. But I continued to whack at it. The white man came back from his job. He ate and went to bed. Meantimes, I went to eat, and I came back immediately to continue. That evening, I continued cutting as long as possible. The next morning, the White man called Moussa Guindo, the supervisor, to ask him, 'Why does this man work without stopping? What sort of a person is he?' Moussa answered him, 'He is a Dogon, a brother. In Dogon country, you only stop working when you get tired. There are no fixed times to stop work.'

How to calculate and interpret the work-time of this labourer? The worker makes no distinction between his 'personal time' and that of his employer. The latter, stupefied, cries out: 'How can he keep working after the whistle has blown?' We see clearly that the time in working does not have the same value for the Dogon worker as for his white employer.[23] The Dogon does not reduce time to its fair monetary value. This brings us back to the issue raised by Frederick Cooper – that Africans did not enter into capitalism as 'anonymous sellers of labour power'. 'Can a category of people made to enter production with nothing to offer but their labour power?'[24]

In the Office du Niger, the migrant workers claimed that the difficult jobs of the whites were for the bravest; their countrymen in the Gold Coast maintained that they engaged in these activities because they were qualified for them, as seen in this account:

> En dehors du travail qui appelle la sueur nous, nous n'en connaissons pas d'autre. Chaque groupe ethnique a son travail. Nous les Dogon, c'est la culture. Même au village, manger [le mil] de son grenier et manger celui du marché sont différents, ils n'ont pas la même valeur. Nous, nous refusons tout autre travail, excepté les travaux pénibles des Blancs.

> We do not know of any kind of work except that which demands sweat. Every ethnic group has its own work. For us Dogon, it is farming. Even in the village, eating [the millet] out of one's granary and eating that from the market are different things, they don't have the same value. We, we refuse all other sorts of work except the demanding work of the Whites.

What emerges from this account, as from others, is that demanding work was, by definition, a Dogon activity; the whites had jobs that corresponded to their disposition. 'White man's work' was very hard, because from dawn to dusk it involved cutting down trees to build roads or houses, said the migrant workers.

From the preceding discussion, one can see the difference between Marx's abstract worker[25] and a worker belonging to a given culture. For the migrant worker from Dogon country, the greater the demands in time and effort required, the greater the prestige accorded to the job involved.[26] In his own village, that task which he perceived as being work, i.e. the cultivation of millet, involved a work period going from dawn to dusk. Getting up early to work in the millet-fields is called 'waking up the rooster', and one comes back after the sun has set, when you cannot tell from a distance of a hundred yards whether the person you see is male or female.

In *Work and human behavior* (1977), Neff shows that the meaning of the idea of work derives from social and cultural determinants. In the United States, as he sees it, notions of work are linked with the settling of migrants who had come from Europe. Their ideas are based on the notion of work as a hard activity, recalling the idea of sweat among the Dogon. This new meaning can be explained by several factors: a political situation which was not propitious to the development of feudalism, an abundance of land, an extreme scarcity of labour, a strong tendency to manufacturing, and anti-aristocratic ideas. 'Except for the slave-owning areas of the American South, no country has been as work-oriented as the United States' (Neff 1977, 87–88).

In Europe, by contrast, with its strong aristocratic traditions, we note the distinction between manual and intellectual labour, whereas any American, whatever the social class, is expected to be able to work with head or hands, even where there might exist a preference for 'white-collar' work to 'blue-collar' work (Neff 1977, 88–89).

In a noteworthy article, 'Time, work-discipline, and industrial capitalism', E.P. Thompson illustrates the difference in concepts of time through history and across societies. He opposes natural time to the measured time of capitalist production. As he sees it, a work period going from dawn to dusk would seem to be a 'natural' time, one that is 'task-oriented'. Thompson (1967, 56–99) holds that 'task-oriented' time ends where paid time begins. However, we have just seen that the transition is not so easily generalised as Thompson believes.

White man's work and the professional advancement of the migrant

Dogon migrant workers valorised colonial work by insisting on the qualities of their white leaders. In this valorisation, they set up a detailed comparison between the varying task managers. For instance, they would compare the oversight of work by an African boss and a white boss. To have a white boss was to be on the path to success in work. By contrast, the African overseer will do anything to impede his workers. Social and professional advancement was a major goal for the work-oriented migrants. In their accounts, a worker only advanced when he had a white man as a boss. Their comparisons of white bosses and African bosses are illustrated by this passage:

> Si le colon blanc te prend au travail, il n'y met pas de 'tricherie', mais le Noir triche fatalement. Il y avait un moment, où les commis Noirs renvoyaient arbitrairement les ouvriers. Alors les Blancs ont pris une loi qui interdit aux commis de renvoyer un ouvrier qui a deux ans d'expérience.

> When a white man takes you on, he won't 'cheat' you, but a Black will always do so. At one time, the Black overseers fired workers arbitrarily. Then the Whites made a law which prevented the overseers from firing a worker who had two years of experience.

In their accounts, they compare different types of bosses: the French boss with the English boss, and either of them with local bosses. The comparison also occurs within the same establishment: between African and white overseers. Consider the voice of this migrant worker:

> Pendant la période coloniale, j'avançais plus en grade que pendant la période post-coloniale. Le Noir recrute suivant la parenté, le Blanc embauche suivant la capacité. J'ai vu de nombreux cas, même dans l'administration. Partout c'est comme ça. Lorsqu'il y a du travail, les commis appellent leurs parents du village: 'viens vite il y a un recrutement'. Même si, ceux-ci n'ont pas la compétence exigée.

> During the colonial period I was promoted more readily than in the post-colonial period. A Black recruits according to kinship, a White will hire according to ability. I saw this quite often, even in the administration. It was like that everywhere. When a job opens up, the clerks would call their relatives from the village, 'Come quickly, they're hiring.' Even if these people don't have the skills that are needed.

An analysis of the accounts by Dogon migrant workers shows a different way to see the rigours of 'white man's work'. They speak of work in terms of the worker's abilities. As they saw it, to enter into the white man's system was a question of courage. Lazy people go into the system that is not so hard, that of the blacks. An old migrant worker explains the difference between the two systems:

'Le travail de Blanc' était dur, les courageux restaient, mais les paresseux s'enfuyaient, ils se faisaient employer par les Noirs. Chez les Noirs on travaille peu et on mange à sa faim. Par contre les Blancs, en dehors du salaire, ne donnent pas à manger ou en petite quantité.

'White man's work' was hard, and the brave would stay but the lazy ran away. They would get jobs with the Blacks. With the Blacks you don't work very much and you eat as much as you want. But the Whites, on the other hand, besides the salary, don't give you anything to eat, or else very little.

Some emphasised courage, as expressed by this informant:

Le travail c'est le cœur, le courage, ça dépend de la manière dont tu as été élevé, le jour où je me suis présenté au travail, on a dit que j'étais trop petit. Le commis, un Peul de Djenné a dit: c'est un Dogon, il est capable de déployer de gros efforts.

Work – it's the heart, it's courage. It depends on how you were brought up. The day I came to work, I was told I was too small. But the foreman, a Peul from Djenne, said, 'He's a Dogon, he can work very hard.'

According to many migrant workers, 'white man's work' was hard, and so some people found jobs with blacks before they gained the strength and courage needed to get back to white man's work.

Several life stories show that time, grades, and transfers are important notions. 'White man's work' was full-time work. Peasants had a favourable idea of it, because it was the condition to aquire skills and a trade. Mastering a trade became, for those who chose to work at the Office du Niger, a challenge to undertake. It was the condition for social and professional advancement. A career became a central concern for those workers. Certain peasants believed that 'white man's work' was not the path to amassing wealth, but to gaining mastery of some trade. Transfers, meaning changes in the workplace, were a specific feature of 'white man's work,' and one emphasised by peasants. It contrasts with the peasant's life in his home village, where he was born, grows up, and will die. Transfers are associated with the rich progression of the worker.

Conclusion – the collapse of labour in post-colonial Africa and the awakening of nostalgia for colonial-era work

What lessons can we draw from all the accounts by migrant workers on colonial work in Africa? They refute the ideas of Marxist anthropologists who saw the relations between a white employer and a black worker as adversarial and constantly oppositional.[27] Their discourse also runs counter to that of the African and European intellectual elites of the 1960–70s. Here is how a migrant describes work after the departure of the whites:

Au temps des Blancs, le travail était chaud à l'Office du Niger. Avec cinq minutes de retard le travailleur était renvoyé à la maison. Aujourd'hui, dans les lieux du travail les gens font du thé, font griller de la viande, tandis qu'à notre époque [1920–60, c'est ID qui souligne] nous n'avions même pas le temps de prendre le petit déjeuner.

At the time of the whites, work was demanding at the Office du Niger. If he was five minutes late, a worker could be fired and sent home. But now people make tea or grill meat at the workplace, while in my time [1920–60, the four decades of colonial work] we didn't even have time to have breakfast.

Marx called the Factory Act of 1850 a victory of the working class over the capitalist class for English labourers: the establishment of a standard working day of 10 hours. In Africa, the independences of the 1960s should have played the same role, freeing Africans from colonial labour and establishing a standard working day. But people were disappointed. Monsieur Traoré voices the feelings of all the former workers:

> Quand je vais dans les centres, et que je vois dans quel état ils se trouvent mes yeux se chargent de larmes. Pourquoi enlèvent-ils les tôles de ces ateliers? Ces bâtiments ne pourraient-ils pas un jour servir l'Office du Niger? Les fils de la Nation sont là, ils peuvent toujours utiliser ces ateliers. Les Blancs nous ont appris à faire le travail. Quand ils sont partis, la mauvaise gestion a tout gâché. Qu'est-ce que l'encadrement fait maintenant? Les canaux sont bouchés. C'est une trahison contre la Nation.

> When I go to the work centres and I see what shape they are in, tears come to my eyes. Why are they taking the sheets of corrugated iron [used for roofs: trans.] from those workshops? Won't the buildings be useful to the Office du Niger some day? The sons of the nation are there, they will always be able to use those workshops. The Whites taught us to work. After they left, bad management spoiled everthing. What does the management do now? The canals have clogged up. It's the betrayal of the Nation.

Migrants felt that African managers were responsible for the collapse and devalorisation of labour. Lynn Schler (2009) reached the same conclusion in her study on 'Transnationalism and nationalism in the Nigerian Seamen's Union' (in this issue). She describes how Nigerian sailors assessed decolonisation through the prism of their work on the high seas. According to their testimony, the politicisation of work led to ruin, to bad management, and the destruction of the transnational alliances, and so also of work as a creative value.

Let us recall that the individual goals in the migration of the young peasants in the colonial period was a quest for cash, for European clothing, and learning foreign languages such as English or Bamana, and that these things were made possible by the colonial workplaces. Unlike the workers of the Marxist school, these workers were not independent labourers, owners of merchandise, making a deal with the capitalist. They would be hired thanks to a network of countrymen. The migrant worker would go to the headman of his ethnic group, who would introduce him to the white man. The headman was responsible for his behaviour at work.

In our historical and anthopological sketch, we have described the conception of work and the criteria for the classification of productive activities in Dogon country. The following points emerge from our exposition:

- First, the glorification of white man's work is not the consequence of the internal structures of the colonial system, but of a comparison of this system with others. At the Office du Niger, it was workshops as opposed to farming; in Ghana, work in the mines or on public works as opposed to cocoa-plantations, and finally the English system against the French system. Marx recognises that France was slowly following the English footsteps. The Dogon migrant workers provide an excellent description of the difference between these two empires in terms of the organisation of work. Among the French, said the migrants, they beat too much and paid too badly. Hamidou Magassa (1978) has devoted a work to the condition of the forced labourers in the Office du Niger. He has collected devastating testimony on the inhuman conditions in which the French forced their subjects to work in the colonies.
- Second, the history of labour migration towards Ghana illustrates an ethnicisation of work (the Dogon say that they are qualified for the mines and the Public Works, which demand hard labour, while the Sonrai [or Songhai: trans.] specialise in trade in the market of Kumasi). In analysing the work concept of Dogon immigrants

in colonial workplaces we cannot refer to Marx's theory of the free labourer who sells his labour-power, nor to his theory of the clash between the working class and employers, because of the fact that the Dogon migrant enters into white man's work through his ethnic network.

- Third, the migrant workers of the colonial period left the white man's work as poor as they entered into it. But what bothers them is not their poverty, but the catastrophic collapse of the pace of work after the departure of the white. Here a migrant worker explains why work fell apart in the company where he had worked all his life:

> L'Office du Niger a commencé à chuter lorsque les autorités nationales ont demandé l'africanisation des cadres après l'indépendance. Certains Blancs qui travaillaient avec nous; disaient que, vu l'importance de l'Office du Niger, le Mali ne va pas les chasser. Mais ce fut le contraire. La France s'est désengagée. Le Mali devait faire les travaux avec ses propres moyens. Voilà la cause de la chute de l'Office du Niger. Nous avons voulu tout diriger. La France ne nous donnera pas son argent pour que nous le gérions à notre guise.

> The Office du Niger began to fall apart after the national authority asked for the managers to be Africans after independence. Certain of the Whites who worked with us would say, 'Given how important the Office du Niger is, Mali is not going to kick out the Whites.' But the opposite happened. France got out of it. Mali had to undertake the work by itself. That is why the Office du Niger collapsed. We wanted to manage everything. France won't give us money for us to manage it as we wish.

The role of a head at whatever level of work is central in 'white man's work'. Peasants perceived and judged their work according to the black or white heads who supervised them. Work was seen in terms of personality traits. Rigour, severity, ubiquity are mentioned as the managers of the works of the whites.[28] Formerly, the migrant workers felt, the white masters had no time for anything but work. Nowadays the black masters only make time for quick money without shedding any sweat.

We have considered the cultural and economic factors which permitted Dogon migrant workers to devise new conceptions of colonial work. From these new conceptions, they made themselves a new identity as workers. Marxist studies might see these migrant workers as people who had broken with their environment and their local views of work. Our ethnographic materials show the opposite. These migrant workers gave meaning to colonial work through establishing the similarities and the differences between colonial work and their local activities.

This new view of labour can only be grasped by collecting the autobiographies of the workers and their stories, which means that a study of the definition of work must be based on oral interviews. This method allows us to follow the changing configuration of the migrant worker's view of work from his village to his new work location.

Forty years after the end of the 'white man's work', object of their memories and conversation, we have collected their testimony in narrative form. Such a method remains rare, even nowadays. The sources underlying current work on labour come as much from the depositions of the union leaders and the reports of the commissioners of the International Labour Organisation (ILO) as from the words of the workers themselves, not omitting the reports of many non-governmental organisations which made issues such as child-trafficking or child-labour their rallying cry for work in Africa. Going hastily over these reports, readers draw conclusions on the greed of the children's parents or employers to explain how these young Africans or Asians have become embroiled in laborious and poorly paid work. The poor workers themselves are never given the opportunity to express their own opinions of their work and how they got there.

Acknowledgements

Translated by Stephen Belcher. This article owes a great deal to my discussions with Frederick Cooper of New York University. I remain, however, solely responsible for any errors of fact or of judgment.

Notes

1. The suppression of forced labour throughout the colonies was the theme of the 14th session of the International Labour Organisation (ILO), held in Geneva in June 1930. Following this session, a convention was ratified by the member nations. Article 1 of this convention stipulates that obligatory or forced labour should be suppressed in all its forms within the shortest time possible (five years). The Convention also specifies that with the aim of total suppression, forced or obligatory labour might be used only for public purposes during the period of transition. For further details, see Volume 1 of the International Labour Conference of the League of Nations (Conference International du Travail 1930). In Francophone Africa, this period of transition lasted far more than five years, for forced labour was only finally stopped in 1946, i.e. 16 years after France ratified the Convention. On this point, see Fall (1993). This work presents the process of forced labour as an extension of slavery.
2. On this point, see my article (Dougnon 2003).
3. The opposite concept would be *ine genu bire*, literally 'black man's work'. This concept was created by the migrant workers because of the opportunities for wage labour offered by blacks besides those offered by the whites. We have here a definition of work as defined by the offerer. 'Black man's work' included the cocoa or coffee plantations in Ghana; in the Office du Niger it indicated rice-growing and gardening and many other local activities offered to the migrant workers by Africans. For further details, see our previous work. (Dougnon 2002, 2003, 2007).
4. *Anasara* is from the Arabic *nasara* which means 'people who help Jesus' [actually, Nazarene: trans.]. In Bamana, which has many Arabic terms, it denotes, by extension, European whites in general.
5. Located in the western part of the central Niger delta, the Office du Niger was created in 1932 by French colonial authority. It became a large hydro-agricultural company, engaging in irrigated farming on a large scale (rice, gardening, livestock). Currently, their developed lands cover an area of over 82,000 hectares, with 28,573 families settled as farmers, for a population of 300,000. On the economic and social evolution of the Office du Niger, see Dougnon and Coulibaly (2007).
6. The word 'labourer' here is used not in the sense current for political economy, but to mean 'a white man's worker' according to the new definition which the emigrants gave to the word 'work'.
7. See Walter Elkan's (1979) article, where he clearly demonstrates the importance of a sociological approach when one is trying to understand the concept of work among different peoples. 'Most economists are frightened to say outright that the reasons why the Germans produce more than the British are that they work harder and likewise that the Chinese in Hong-Kong, Singapore and Taiwan are making much greater progress than Indian and or Bangladesh, because the former are more hard-working. That is either a racialism and therefore not kosher or it is a "sociological factor" requiring sociological or anthropological methods of investigation' (Elkan 1979, p. 21).
8. On this topic, see the preface by Albertine Thévenon (1951). However, it does seem strange that Simone Weil should be so cautious about the ideas that workers themselves might have of their own work. She writes:

   > ... Les ouvriers quand ils parlent de leur propre sort, répètent-ils le plus souvent des mots de propagande faits par des gens qui ne sont pas ouvriers. La difficulté est au moins aussi grande pour un ancien ouvrier; il lui est facile de parler de sa condition première, mais très difficile d'y penser réellement, car rien n'est plus vite recouvert par l'oubli que le malheur passé. (Weil 1951, 9)

   > ... Workers, when discussing their own lot, most often repeat the propaganda phrases of people who are not workers. The difficulty as at least equally great for a former worker; it is very easy for him to speak about his initial conditions, but very difficult to think clearly about it, for nothing is so quickly covered over by forgetfulness than past unhappiness.

9. In Hausa, *zongo* means the neighbourhood of people who have come from elsewhere, the immigrants. Having been the first immigrants to Ghana with the British coloniser, the Hausa left their traces in the *zongon*, their language, and their religion, Islam.

10. In *The African worker* (1988), Bill Freund performs a critical analysis of the study of work in Africa. He raises the question of the simplistic views of work in the pre-colonial era and of the 'class analysis' inherited from Karl Marx which was much in style after the 1950s. He notes pertinently that very little work has been done to identify the specific character of proletarisation in Africa (Freund 1988, 22). The most innovative criticism of Marxist analyses of work in African has been recently made by Frederick Cooper (2000).

11. Spittler (2003, 2008) recognises the great unparalleled contributions of British anthropology to the study of work in Africa, and cites specifically Audrey Richards who published two pioneering studies: *Hunger and work in a savage tribe* (1932) and later *Land, labour and diet in Northern Rhodesia: an economic study of the Bemba tribe* (1939) and also Sandra Wallman, *Social anthropology of work* (1979). To this list should be added the work of Henrietta L. Moore and Meghan Vaughan, *Cutting down trees – gender, nutrition and agriculture change in the North Province of Zambia 1890–1990* (Oxford, 1994).

12. The French colonial recruitment system divided the young recruits into two groups (Magassa 1978). The first, the Première Portion [first division], was engaged in military service, and the members of the second group, called the Deuxième Portion [second division] were sent to forced labour. Emil Schreyger (1984, 69–70) gives a figure of 2000–2500 recruits per year in his study *L'Office du Niger au Mali*.

13. In his work on the social division of labour, Emile Durkheim speaks of migration as the major path for rural people to learn a trade in the town. As he sees it, a trade more or less implies a town, and the towns are always formed by the recruitment of immigrants who must leave their natural environment. See the 'Preface' to the second edition of *De la division du travail social* (Durkheim 1902, 30–34).

14. In the view of Florent Valère Adegbidi, the African's encounter with wage labour was a culture shock. He emphasises particularly:

    > De fait, il n'y aurait aucune exagération à souligner le véritable choc (culturel) qu'a pu constituer pour le travailleur Africain sa présence formelle dans un univers, sinon étranger du moins étrange, puisqu'on a pris soin d'y transférer aussi bien les machines, la technologie occidentale que les méthodes de gestion et d'organisation tayloriennes du travail. (Adegbidi 1998, 13)

    > In fact, it would scarcely be an exaggeration to underline the real (culture) shock caused to the African worker by his formal presence in a universe which, if not foreign, was certainly strange, since care was taken to transfer into it not only the machines, the western technology, but also management methods and the Taylorian methods of work organisation.

15. Mansell Prothero (1957) reports the results of investigations run by the University College of the Gold Coast in collaboration with the Ministry of Labour in March 1954. The results show that 70% of the migrants to the southern Gold Coast came from the neighbouring French colonies: Upper Volta (Burkina Faso), French Sudan (Mali), and Niger.

16. See Murray (1979). His stimulating notion of the *political economy of migrant labour* based on the investments made by migrant workers in traditional ceremonies is the challenge thrown down by the anthropology of labour to Marxist theory. See also Dougnon 2006).

17. For a detailed linguistic study of the notion of *bire*, see Leiris (1952). See also Arendt (1954, 80) on the etymological difference between the words 'labour' and 'work'. 'Thus, the Greek language distinguishes between *ponein* and *ergazesthai,* the Latin between *laborare* and *facere* or *fabricare,* the French between *travailler* et *ouvrer* the German between *arbeiten* and *werken.*'

18. Besides these three activities, the language also differentiates *guno bire*, slave labour, and *giri bire*, domestic work.

19. Hannah Arendt's discussion (see note 17 above) of the concepts of 'labour' and 'work' among the Greek philosophers of antiquity and thinkers of the modern period (Locke, Smith, Marx) illustrates the different assessments of work in time and space. For instance, agriculture, considered noble work by the Dogon, is seen as an evil and a punishment from the gods by the Greeks. The peasants who produced life's necessities are categorised by Plato and Aristotle as slaves.

20. Hannah Arendt refers to Aristotle's *Politics*, when she mentions how herding is excluded from the notion of work: 'that the Greek public opinion in the city-states judged occupations according to the effort required and the time consumed is supported by a remark of Aristotle about the life of shepherd' (1958, pp. 82-83). She quotes: 'There are great differences in human ways of life. The laziest are shepherds; for they get their food without labor [*ponos*] from tame animals and have leisure [*skholazousin*]' (1958, p. 83) It is interesting to note that the main reason why the Dogon believe that their neighbours, the Peuls, don't work is that the latter cannot live by the products of their herding (milk and meat) alone.

21. Three years (three is the male number in Dogon cosmology) was the cut-off date for young Dogon to return to their home village. Beyond that period of time, if the migrant worker had not sent a letter to explain why he was delayed, he might be treated as someone who has chosen the life of a vagabond.

22. See the file, 'The annual invasion of the Gold Coast by French and Northern Territories subjects in search of labour', *ADM 11/1076*, Archives of Accra.

23. In Dogon country, every adult is considered to be someone who works all the time, without stopping. The youngest must greet them with the term *u bire* (you and work). To greet them by saying *po*, which means hello, would be impolite, because even while resting, the adult is expected to be working. This Dogon notion of the worker meets Marx's idea in which the worker is nothing other than the work period personnified (Marx 1982, 237).

24. On this topic, Cooper (2000, 26) draws the following conclusion: 'capitalism's spread has a discursive and political as well as a market element to it: colonisers had to define and enforce categories like private property and alter notions of time and discipline. Africans were meanwhile trying to give such categories their own meanings.'

25. See Lakroum (2003, p. 42). She specifically aims at Marxist influence in this area when she writes:

> Voilà l'interrogation qui ressort de l'analyse des publications de ces trente dernières années. Le travail ne devient un objet d'étude scientifique que s'il peut être isolé de son contexte socio-économique, s'il se distingue des pratiques culturelles et apparaît comme une valeur autonome.

> This is the question that emerges from an analysis of the last thirty year's publications. Work only becomes the object of scientific study when it can be isolated from it socio-economic context, if it is distinguished from cultural practices and is presented as an autonomous value.

26. Here we take the concept of work, meaning any productive activity, as the equivalent of 'labour' in English or *Arbeit* in German. For an etymological analysis of these concepts, see Arendt (1958, 80).

27. Some of the former workers from the workshop at Diabali told how painful it was to separate from 'their whites'. At the end of 1959, the general topic of conversation in the workshops and the garages was the fact that the French engineers were leaving for good. Some of the engineers told the workers that they were going back to France unwillingly. They wanted to stay in Markala or Diabaly and to continue working for the Office du Niger. But return to the capital was unavoidable. Some of the West African workers decided to pay them a last visit and to say goodbye to them. But this gesture was forbidden by the Union Soudanaise: Rossemblement Démocratique Africa (US-RDA) Party, which threatened to fire any worker who went to the area where the whites lived to say goodbye or to express friendship. According to one of our informants, the Party of Independence had appointed people to watch the workers who might display friendly feelings towards the Europeans.

28. For the post-colonial history of the Office du Niger, Issa Ongoïba is the sole reference on the topic of work. Everything said by peasants and former workers of the Office du Niger after 1960 involves his name. According to the peasants, Issa Ongoïba is the director who forced people to change their work-habits in the offices, in the rice fields, and in the workshops.

References

Adegbidi, F.V., 1998. *Susciter l'engagement au travail en Afrique*. Paris: L'Harmattan.
Agiers, A., Copans, J. and Morice, A., 1987. *Classes ouvrières d'Afrique Noire*. Paris: Karthala.
Amin, S., 1974. *Les migrations contemporaines en Afrique de l'Ouest*. Dakar: IDEP.
Arendt, H., 1958. *The human condition*. Chicago: University of Chicago Press.
Atkins, K., 1993. *The moon is dead! Give us our money! Cultural origins of an African work ethic, Natal, South Africa, 1843–1900*. London and Portsmouth, NH: Heinemann.
Van Binsbergen, V. and Geschiere, P., 1985. *Old modes of production and capitalist encroachment: anthropological explorations in Africa*. London: Kegan Paul.
Bogosian, C., 2004. The little farming soldiers: the evolution of a labor army in post-colonial Mali. *Mande studies*, 5, 85–100.
Burguière, A., 1971. Histoire et structure. *Annales*, 3 and 4, 1–6.
Cooper, F., 2000. African labor history. Communication présentée au Colloque *Global labour history in the 21st century*. International Institute of Social History, 23–25.
Coquery-Vidrovitch, C., 1988. *Africa, endurance and change south of the Sahara*. London: University of California Press.
Conférence Internationale du Travail, 1930. 14th session, Geneva. Vol. 1: Bureau Internationale du Travail.
Dougnon, I., 2002. Peasant migration and labour codification in the colonial era: emigrants from Dogon Country in the Gold Coast, 1910–1950. *In:* K.S. Jomo and K.K. Jin, eds. *Globalization and its discontents, revisited*. New Delhi: Tulika Books, 73–83.
Dougnon, I., 2003. Migration paysanne, redéfinition du concept du travail et relations sociales entre 'colons' et 'travailleurs' à l'Office du Niger, 1930–1980. *In:* H. d'Almeida Topor, M. Lakroum and G. Spittler, eds. *Le travail en Afrique noire: représentation et pratique à l'époque contemporaine*. Paris: Karthala, 166–176.
Dougnon, I., 2006. 'Ghana boys and the glamour': European clothing among the Dogon, 1920–1960. Paper presented at the Cadbury Conference: Social Aspiration and Personal Lives, 19–20 May, Centre of West African Studies, University of Birmingham.
Dougnon, I., 2007. *Travail de blanc, travail de noir: la migration des paysans dogons vers l'Office du Niger et au Ghana 1910–1980*. Paris: Karthala.
Dougnon, I. and Coulibaly, B., 2007. Institutional architecture and pro-poor growth in Office du Niger: responses from farmer organisations. University of Manchester. Available from: http://www.ippg.org.uk
Durkheim, E., 1902. *De la division du travail social*. Paris: PUF.
Elkan, W., 1979. Views from three other disciplines: (1) Economics. *In:* S. Wallman, ed. *Social anthropology of work*. London: Academy Press, 26–30.
Fall, B., 1993. *Le travail forcé en Afrique Occidentale française 1900–1946*. Paris: Karthala.
Freund, B., 1988. *The African worker*. Cambridge: Cambridge University Press.
Gluckman, M., 1974. *Structuralist analysis in contemporary social thought: a comparison of the theories of Claude Lévi-Strauss and Louis Althusser*. London: Routledge.
Griaule, M., 1994. *Masques Dogons*. Paris: Institut d'Ethnologie.
Gupta, A. and Ferguson, J., 1997. *Culture, power and place*. Durham, NC: Duke University Press.
Harries, P., 1994. *Work, culture, and identity: migrant laborers in Mozambique and South Africa, c. 1860–1910*. Johannesburg and Postmounth, NH: Heinemann.
Hughes, C.E., 1958. *Men and their work*. IL: Illinois University Press.
Lakroum, M., 1982. *Le travail inégal. Paysans et salariés sénégalais face à la crise des années trente*. Paris: L'Harmattan.
Lakroum, M., 2003. Le travail en Afrique Noire peut-il être un objet d'étude scientifique? *In:* H. d'Almeida Topor, M. Lakroum and G. Spittler, eds. *Le travail en Afrique noire: représentation et pratique à l'époque contemporaine*. Paris: Karthala, 43–64.

Leiris, M., 1952. L'expression de l'idée de travail dans une langue d'initiés soudanais. *Présence africaine*, 13, 69–81.

Magassa, H., 1978. *Papa Commandant a jeté un grand filet devant nous les exploités des rives du Niger 1902–1962*. Paris: Maspéro.

Manchuelle, F., 1997. *Willing migrants Soninke labor diaspora, 1845–1960*. London: Ohio University Press.

Marx, K., 1982. *Le Capital,* I. Moscow: Éditions du Progrès.

Meillassoux, C., 1964. *Anthropologie économique des Gouros de la Côte d' Ivoire: de l'économie de subsistance à l'agriculture commerciale*. Paris: Mouton.

Meillassoux, C., 1991. *Femmes greniers et capitaux*. Paris: Maspero.

Moodie, D. and Ndatshe, V., 1994. *Going for gold: men, mines, and migration*. London: University of California Press.

Murray, C., 1979. The work of men, women and the ancestor: social reproduction in the periphery of Southern Africa. *In:* S. Wallman, ed. *Social anthropology of work*. London: Academy Press, 337–363.

Neff, S.W., 1977. *Work and human behaviour*. Chicago: Chicago University Press.

Ouedraogo, J.B., 1989. *Formation de la classe ouvrière en Afrique Noire: l'exemple du Burkina Faso*. Paris: L'Harmattan.

Paulme, D., 1988. *Organisation sociale des Dogon*. Paris: Editions Jean-Michel Place.

Pauvert, J.C., 1952. La notion du travail en Afrique Noire. *Présence Africaine*, 13, 93–107.

Prothero, M.R., 1957. Labour migration in British West Africa. *Corona*, 9 (5), 169–172.

Rouch, J., 1957. Migration au Ghana 'Gold Coast' (enquête 1953–1955). *Journal de la Société des Africanistes*, 26 (1–2), 1–3, 33–196.

Rouch, J., 1961. Note sur l'importance des migrations au Ghana. Communication présentée au *Colloque de Niamey*, 13–25 February.

Schler, L., 2009. Transnationalism and nationalism in the Nigerian Seamen's Union. *African identities*, 7 (3) 387–398.

Schreyger, E., 1984. *L'Office du Niger au Mali: la problématique d'une grande entreprise agricole dans la zone du Sahel*. Wiesbaden: Steiner.

Spittler, G., 2003. L'anthropologie du travail en Afrique traditions allemandes et françaises. *In:* H. d'Almeida-Topor, M. Lakroum and G. Spittler, eds. *Le travail en Afrique noire: représentation et pratiques à l'époque contemporaine*. Paris: Karthala, 8–29.

Spittler, G., 2008. *Founders of the anthropology of work, German social scientists of the 19th and early 20th centuries and the first ethnographers*. LIT.

Thaddeus, S., 1996. Labour migration in colonial Tanzania and the hegemony of South African historiography. *African affairs*, 95 (381), 581–595.

Thévenon, A., 1951. Preface. *La condition ouvrière*. Paris: Gallimard.

Thompson, E.P., 1967. Time, work-discipline, and industrial capitalism. *Past and present*, 38, 56–97.

Weil, S., 1951. *La condition ouvrière*. Paris: Galimard.

Casting aluminium cooking pots: labour, migration and artisan production in West Africa's informal sector, 1945–2005

Emily Lynn Osborn

Department of History, University of Chicago, Chicago IL, USA

This article investigates the history of aluminium casting, a sector of the informal economy devoted to recycling scrap aluminium. Artisans who cast aluminium make a variety of products out of scrap, including various utensils and receptacles for food preparation, such as cooking pots. While labour and its history in West Africa has garnered much historical research, as has the work of artisans who specialise in working other types of metal, especially iron, little attention has been paid to aluminium casting. The oversight is significant, because the diffusion of aluminium casting opens up a history on the transnational movement of labour and artisan production in late colonial and post-colonial Africa.

Today in West Africa, a dynamic sector of the informal economy is managed by artisans who specialise in taking scrap aluminium and recycling it into shiny new aluminium goods. These artisans use a labour-intensive process called sand-cast moulding, or sand-casting, to transform scrap aluminium – used aluminium, drinking cans, automobile gear boxes, even airplane fuselages – into an array of household goods and mechanical parts. Typically working without electricity, running water, or industrialised furnaces or tools, casters mould scrap into spoons, teapots, platters, plumbing pipes, and parts for bicycles, motorcycles, and cars. The mainstay of the aluminium casting market is, however, cooking pots. These cooking pots can be found in just about any context where cooking takes place: in the central compounds and open-air cooking areas of urban and rural dwellers; in the food stalls run by street vendors; in restaurants, bars, and *maquis*; and in the kitchens of middle-class and elite families.

While products made by aluminium casters are today ubiquitous in West Africa – it is almost impossible to find a household, food stall, or restaurant that is not home to a locally-made cast aluminium cooking pot – such was not the case in the mid-twentieth century. At that time, it was difficult to find cast aluminium goods and only a few artisans, living mostly in coastal capital cities, knew how to transform scrap into products with local market appeal. That aluminium casting went from being rare to commonplace in less than half a century opens up a story about technology, training, and migration which takes in new directions our understanding of labour and its history in Africa. Focusing on aluminium casters moves African labour history beyond its traditional focus on wage labour and formal-sector employment, while it enriches a growing body of literature devoted to migration and to the ways that social and economic transformations transcend national boundaries and operate outside of state mandates. In effect, the aluminium casting sector unveils a fresh perspective on colonial and post-colonial experiences of work and mobility in Africa and to the ways that members of the informal sector respond to and manage the complex political, social, and economic forces that have shaped Africa over the second half of the twentieth century.

Labour history in Africa

Labour has proved to be a rich and fruitful topic of study in African history. Starting in the 1970s, labour history drew a great deal of attention from academics, and studies of different parts of Africa focused on labour in various industrial and urban contexts. Research on mining in Southern Africa explores the experience of migrant labourers, who often came from neighbouring colonies to fulfil extended labour contracts, taking up residence in socially and culturally complex all-male mining compounds (Harries 1994, Moodie 1994, Van Onselen 1976). Other studies have focused on the efforts by the colonial state to create a stabilised, regularised pool of (male) wage labourers (Cooper 1987, 1996, Jones 2002). So too have historians illustrated the often unintended and unanticipated political consequences of labour movements, particularly the effect of labour strikes on the decolonisation and independence movements of the 1950s and 1960s (Cooper 1996, Schmidt 2007). A focus on labour and urbanisation has furthermore illuminated the ways that gender norms and particular models of the household configured conflicts between union members and employers about workers' rights, responsibilities, and living standards (Cooper 1996, Lindsay 2003).

This research has done a great deal to illuminate the rich history of organised labour in Africa, as well as the intertwined relationship of labour to migration, industrialisation, and urbanisation. But the emphasis on wage labour in the formal sector leaves unexplored another vast sector of the labour market, that of the informal economy. Keith Hart (1973) is generally credited with identifying 'informal income opportunities' – or what has come to be known as the informal sector – in an article on ethnicity and urban employment in Ghana. In that piece, Hart points out that 'many of the essential services' (1973, 68) of urban life in Accra were provided by economic actors who were not formally employed and did not draw regular wages. Broadly speaking, the informal sector is characterised by small-scale entrepreneurship, self-employment, and often flexible and personalised networks of credit and exchange (Light 2004).[1] The people who make their living in this sector typically operate in a highly unstable economic environment that is vulnerable to devastating shocks of both global and local origins, from worldwide price fluctuations and environmental disasters to political crises and urban redevelopment schemes aimed at improving the urban landscape. (Such redevelopment schemes almost inevitably squeeze out those who operate on the fringes of the formal economy and who exercise tenuous land and property rights.) Members of the informal sector are also susceptible to the often arbitrary and unpredictable actions of proximate actors, such as government bureaucrats, landlords, and family members.

When the informal sector first became the subject of systematic study in the 1970s and 1980s, many academics and policy analysts argued that it was a transitory phase, a step through which developing economies would necessarily pass on their way to becoming developed economies. According to this line of thinking, regularised wage labour would increase with economic expansion and the informal margins of the economy would be reconfigured and incorporated into the formal sector. But the passage of time has not borne out this particular developmentalist narrative and the informal sector is instead recognised as a permanent feature of economies all over the globe (Pillay 2007). As Donald Light (2004, 717) notes, '[c]ontrary to the expectations of some analysts, informal economic activity did not fade away with advanced capitalism, but has thrived in major economies as well as in developing nations'. In Brazil, for example, 8 of 10 new jobs created in the 1990s were located in the informal sector (Munck 2004, 244).

That the informal economy continues to be a dynamic and growing site of work and production – albeit a sector where some of the poorest people in the world eke out a living – contrasts sharply with the place of salaried work and organised labour in Africa which, as in other parts of the world, has suffered a sharp decline in recent years.[2] A number of processes account for the shrinkage of formal-sector employment in Africa. Foreign direct investment, structural adjustment programmes, and neo-liberal reforms that stress individual property rights, free trade, and market deregulation have increased the influence of international corporations and foreign investors and contributed to 'jobless economic growth' (Pillay 2007, 2). These processes have also diminished the state's role in labour regulation and undercut the capacity of labour unions to agitate to maintain or improve the working conditions and salaries of their members.[3] At the same time, democratic reforms have diluted the political influence of organised labour, as greater participation in the electoral process has expanded the number of interest groups who exert political pressure on elected officials (Pitcher 2007).

The eroding influence of labour unions and the reduction in formal-sector employment indicate that it is critical for students of African labour history to expand the scope of their analyses to include the informal sector, where a substantial proportion of the population make a living. Studying the history of aluminium casting shows how fruitful this approach can be. Aluminium casting illuminates the ways that skilled labour is acquired and disseminated outside of formal institutions of learning and employment in Africa. It also shows how people respond to economic pressures and opportunities, for the sector has been created and sustained by processes that cut across colonial and national boundaries. The work of aluminium casters further exposes the unexpected ties that West African artisans share with some of the most sophisticated forms of industrial production in the global North.

The diffusion of aluminium casting in Africa

That artisans in Africa manage a dynamic sector devoted to metal is not surprising. Metalworking has long been practised in Africa and the topic has emerged as an important and productive subject of study. While scholars have documented various technologies of metal manipulation and recycling in Africa, little attention has thus been paid to artisanal sand-casting. Sand-casting is distinct from other widely-studied metallurgical technologies, such as that of blacksmithing used to work iron, or that of lost-wax casting which made possible the famous Benin bronzes, or the post-colonial craft of making toys and briefcases from flattened cans and tins (Kriger 2000, Herbert 1993, McNaughton 1988, Nevadomsky 2005, Cerny and Seriff 1996, Eisenhofer et al. 2004). Aluminium casting in Africa certainly shares ties to older metalworking traditions such as blacksmithing, but aluminium is a twentieth-century metal and its story in Africa, as it is most everywhere else in the world, is a twentieth-century one.[4] Although aluminium's history in Africa has garnered little attention from academics, its relatively recent introduction to the world of metalworking generate a considerable advantage to researchers, for its recent vintage meant that it is possible to pinpoint the origins of aluminium use in West Africa and, more precisely, the beginnings of the craft of aluminium casting.

The explanation for aluminium casting's origins, as told by casters themselves, is quite straightforward. During World War II, two industrialised foundries operated in Dakar. Those foundries made iron products using sand-casting technology.[5] Some of the Senegalese wage-labourers who worked in these foundries realised that the technique of sand-casting could be used to manipulate other types of metal besides iron. They started to experiment with sand-casting using different types of metal that they collected around the city and they discovered that the process worked particularly well with scrap aluminium, which could be found in abundance in Dakar at that time. Soon thereafter, some of these wage-labourers left their jobs at the industrialised foundries and opened their own sand-casting workshops in Dakar, where they started to make cooking pots and other items which they sold on the local market. These casters soon took on and trained apprentices, young men and boys who wanted to learn the trade. Some of those apprentices were Senegalese, while others came from neighbouring colonies, including the French Soudan (present-day Mali) and Guinée Française (present-day Guinea-Conakry). Other Senegalese chose not to stay home, but to go elsewhere with their skills, and they travelled to other regions and colonies to work. There they set up workshops and trained apprentices in aluminium casting.

El hajj Mohamed N'Diaye is an example of one of the Senegalese casters who helped to diffuse the technology of aluminium casting from Senegal to other parts of West Africa. Born in Senegal, N'Diaye learned casting in Dakar and then travelled to Conakry in the 1950s, where he established an aluminium casting workshop and started to sell cast aluminium products on the local market. At that time, N'Diaye was the fourth aluminium caster to work in the city. The three casters who had preceded him were older 'brothers', that is, they were also Senegalese.[6] Like the other master casters, N'Diaye took on Guinean apprentices, and he and his cohort trained the first Guinean contingent of aluminium casters. The predominance of Senegalese in the formation of the Guinean casting sector is made evident by a notable linguistic legacy: one of N'Diaye's first Guinean apprentices, Moussa Baldé, speaks fluent Wolof, a Senegalese language, although he has never lived in or visited Senegal.

A similar narrative is told about the origins of casting in other cities and regions. The earliest casters to set up shop in Bamako, Mali also did so in the 1950s, and they too were either Senegalese or they were Malians who had trained in Senegal. This 'first generation' of aluminium casters from Senegal did not, however, simply confine themselves to other colonies of the French West African empire. Senegalese casters ventured into Anglophone and Lusophone colonies as well. One Senegalese caster took up residence in the 1950s in the town of Hastings, located just outside of Freetown, the capital of the British colony of Sierra Leone. Residents of Hastings note that Pa Diouf, as he was known, spent decades in Hastings making cast aluminium wares and training a number of Sierra Leoneans in the craft before he eventually returned to Senegal to retire.[7] Some Senegalese casters also went much further afield, taking their expertise with aluminium as far as Congo-Kinshasa. The narratives told about castings origins thus converge around a common portrait of the craft's original practitioners: the first generation of aluminium casters was constituted by Senegalese men or by men from elsewhere in West Africa who learned the craft in Senegal. Together, these Senegalese and Senegalese-trained casters travelled with their technological know-how, creating a new market for locally-produced cast aluminium goods and creating a new sector of the informal economy.

Historical context of the diffusion

It is clear that the presence of aluminium casting in West Africa owes a great deal to the entrepreneurial spirit of a handful of men who had the insight to adapt an industrialised technology to the artisanal sector and the initiative to set up workshops and produce cast aluminium goods in different parts of West Africa. While the enterprise of these artisans certainly cannot be denied, a number of other forces played a critical role in the diffusion of the craft. These forces include the technologies and materials of production, local systems of training, and deep-rooted patterns of migration, as well as a series of relationships and hierarchies produced by the French colonial regime. The emergence of the aluminium casting sector did not simply arise, in other words, because of the ingenuity, hard work, and luck of a few intrepid men, but because a material – aluminium – and a technology – sand-casting – came into dynamic interaction in a colonial context with particular practices of work, travel, and knowledge transmission.

Of fundamental importance to the aluminium casting sector and the artisans who managed it was the metal itself. Goods made from aluminium possess many useful characteristics: they are resistant to corrosion, conduct heat well, possess a high ratio of strength relative to weight, and they are not affected adversely by extreme cold. In addition, and of particular importance to West African artisans who work the metal, is the ease with which aluminium can be re-used. Aluminium has no structural memory and rendering it into molten form does not reduce its mass, which means that aluminium can be infinitely recycled. Aluminium also has a low melting point: unlike other metals such as steel and iron that require heat of more than 2000° Fahrenheit (about 1370° Celsius), aluminium liquefies at 660° Fahrenheit (349° Celsius). Aluminium's durability and malleability is essential to the West African aluminium artisanal market because these attributes mean that casters can manipulate the metal with the use of fairly basic technologies and relatively little energy.

The timing of the emergence of this artisanal sector, at the tail-end of World War II, is also not a coincidence, for aluminium's circulation increased dramatically during the war. Although aluminium was isolated and identified as a metal nearly a century and a half before, in the early nineteenth century, it remained exorbitantly expensive to make until the 1880s, when processes were discovered which rendered more efficient and cost-effective the method for transforming bauxite (aluminium ore), into aluminium.[8] The applications for aluminium proliferated in subsequent decades, but it was the demand for aluminium-bodied airplanes during World War II that substantially augmented aluminium production in industrialised countries. Germany took the early lead in producing aluminium, but that country was subsequently overtaken by the United States. Since that time, aluminium manufacturing has remained an activity that takes place principally in industrialised countries, for the energy resources and infrastructural capacities needed to run bauxite processing plants are enormous. (Notably, the cost and energy needed to render aluminium from bauxite is vastly greater than the cost and energy needed to recycle it, once the state of aluminium has been achieved.)

But the difficulty and expense of processing bauxite did not restrict the circulation of finished aluminium goods. Aluminium seems to have made its appearance in Africa by the early 1900s, after the European colonial conquest of the continent. At that time, colonial officials and merchant interests imported aluminium products – plates, cups, motor parts – for their personal use, as well as for sale. Those aluminium products did not necessarily endure in their original imported forms, however, as West African jewellers and smiths quickly adopted the metal and incorporated it into their artisanal repertoires. A French colonial official noted in a 1921 article on Kankan, an important interior town and commercial centre in Guinée Française, that within the span of the previous decade, 'aluminium, introduced by commerce, has achieved an extraordinary success' and that it had replaced copper and silver in the trinkets and adornments made by local jewellers (Humblot 1921, 155). In Nigeria, Nupe metalsmiths made aluminium bracelets and rings since at least the 1930s and perhaps as early as the 1910s (Nagel 1942, Perani 1973 cited by Wolff 1986). It is not altogether clear how artisans acquired aluminium with which to work although it seems logical to assume, as Humblot suggests, that a commercial market had grown up around the metal. It also seems clear that the metal was treated as a luxury good, and that artisans worked it with the same techniques that they employed to fashion other valuable metals, like copper and silver. That is, they created plugs of aluminium which they shaped by hand into the desired form.[9] Put simply, the medium was new, but the technique used to manipulate it was not.

As the uses to which aluminium was put in the industrialised world expanded, the possible applications for aluminium in Africa also expanded. The incorporation of aluminium into the manufacture of everything from airplanes to food-storage containers ultimately increased the circulation of aluminium and ultimately resulted in more scrap, as those aluminium cans, parts, and fuselages met the end of their life-use. The larger volume of scrap moved aluminium from the realm of a luxury metal to that of quotidian one. But the full potential of all that scrap could not be realised by the technologies for working aluminium that had heretofore prevailed, in which small nuggets of aluminium were bent and shaped by hand into new forms. It was not until the technology of sand-casting entered the skill-set of West Africa's artisans that larger quantities of scrap aluminium could be manipulated and more substantial objects, such as cooking pots, be produced.

Sand-casting technology enabled artisans to take full advantage of the increased availability of scrap while exploiting the major strength of the informal sector, which is rich in labour but not in capital. Sand-casting demands skill, strength, and a few physical inputs and it can, therefore, be carried out by people who have sparse financial resources and limited infrastructural access. To sand-cast, casters need a physical workshop, which is typically a simple, covered structure with a dirt floor layered with a thick layer of sand, and a few tools: a small furnace; hoes and trowels; wooden frames, or casks; patterns, or models, of the items to be fabricated; and a good supply of sand and water.

To sand-cast an object, casters follow a few basic steps. Casters render aluminium molten in locally-constructed furnaces, which are typically a covered oil drum loaded with wood or a charcoal stove which is fed oxygen via a hand-crank. While the aluminium is melting, casters prepare the sand moulds inside the workshop. Casters make their moulds by selecting a pattern – a cooking pot, lid, or part – which they wish to duplicate. They then use the dampened sand and wooden flasks, or braces, to make internal and external impressions of the original pattern. The caster then extracts the original pattern from the packed sand impressions and carefully reassembles the mould. This creates a cavity of air in the shape of the original pattern. The molten aluminium is poured into the mould and, in a matter of seconds, the mould can be broken, exposing a replica of the original cooking pot or lid that had been used to make the mould. After the object has cooled, it is then finished, that is, the rough edges are rubbed off and any gaps or holes are plugged. If the final product is marred by too many imperfections, it is simply melted down again and used in the next batch.

Casters use this same basic process to make the most of their products: lids, mechanical parts, pipes, platters, teapots, and mortar and pestles. What makes sand-casting so labour-intensive is that casters must make an individual mould for each cooking pot, lid, pipe or part that they produce, and that mould must be broken to release the finished product. Moulds cannot be re-used (although it is possible to fabricate re-usable moulds for some smaller items, such as spoons). Depending upon the size and model, casters may have to take extra steps or draw upon on more labour to make their moulds. Manoeuvring the heavy, sand-packed flasks to make very large cooking pots (of 40, 50, and even 60 kilos) requires up to four strong men.

While a number of inputs are necessary to make products using this process, one of the most important components of sand-casting is the technical know-how. The way in which knowledge about sand-casting has been produced and reproduced thus opens up another vantage point on the history of this informal economic sector activity. To ensure the controlled dissemination of knowledge about sand-casting aluminium, casters rely upon the apprenticeship system. The apprenticeship system is a reciprocal relationship in which the apprentice provides labour for the master caster, while the master caster trains the apprentice in the trade. The apprenticeship system not only serves to educate boys and young men in the craft but it also ensures a cheap labour supply for the master caster while limiting, to some degree, competition among casters. In addition, apprenticeships help to mitigate broader economic pressures for, as Light notes, personalised networks within the informal sector 'provide norms, key linkages, social capital and various forms of cooperation' (Light 2004, 712). In an environment marked by economic insecurity and unpredictability, the apprenticeship system functions as a social and economic safety-net that offers protections to both the apprentice and the master caster.

The organisation of aluminium workshops reflects the labour and training required to successfully produce sand-cast aluminium products. Most workshops are headed by a senior caster, or master caster, who is typically a middle-aged or older man. (In West Africa, casting is an exclusively male profession.) The master caster supervises anywhere from two to fifteen apprentices. Apprentices typically spend a number of years working under a master caster, and once an apprentice has achieved a high level of competence he can, in principle, strike out on his own and set up an independent workshop. But that normative ideal is not necessarily achieved: some apprentices prefer to stay with their master and move up the hierarchy of a workshop with the hopes of one day becoming the chief apprentice. Other apprentices stay in their master's workshop because their master is their father and they are carrying on a familial tradition of metalworking that dates to the era when ironwork predominated, as many aluminium casters come from families that once specialised in blacksmithing.[10] In this situation, the son or sons involved in aluminium casting will inherit the workshop upon the father's retirement. Yet other casters may sometimes work for themselves and then work for someone else, perhaps on a piece-work basis, depending upon changing circumstances and pressures in their own lives. Indeed, it would be mistaken to assume that all casters remain forever in the profession – as with other sectors of the informal sector, men may work as casters for a time, then take up another occupation, to perhaps return again one day to casting.

The apprenticeship system reveals that while the material and technology with which casters worked may have been new, the aluminium casting sector owes a great deal to training practices that had deep roots in West Africa's social and economic landscape. In its training method, aluminium casting shares ties with older artisanal trades, such as blacksmithing and leatherworking – professions that are similarly organised around an exchange of labour for expertise. But unlike apprenticeship systems elsewhere in the world, West African apprentices do not enter into a regulated, formalised course of learning where they are evaluated according to a certain standard and awarded a certificate or licence upon their completion. Nor do these apprenticeships indicate the existence of a larger corporate structure of skilled labour that restricted membership and accorded to its constituents particular legal rights, as in the European artisanal worlds of yesteryear (Sewell 1980). The relations of apprentices and masters in West Africa are (and seem to have long been) highly personalised, paternalistic, and negotiable. But while West African apprenticeships in the aluminium casting sector may be flexible, they are also absolutely obligatory. Every master caster working today in West Africa once served as an apprentice.

The apprenticeship system is not only important because it provides for the future of the profession. It also generates a living archive of the profession's past. By asking casters questions about their training and background, it is possible to trace how casters moved and settled in different cities, regions, and countries of West Africa and to generate a temporal and geographic record of aluminium casting's history. To illustrate this point, consider the case of a caster named Namory Kondé, who works and lives in the city of Kankan, in Upper Guinée (Guinea-Conakry). Kondé learned to cast from another master caster in Kankan, who had himself trained with Bankaly Baro, the man who is identified as Kankan's first caster. As a young man in the 1950s, Bankaly Baro had left Guinea for Abidjan, Côte d'Ivoire, where he learned casting from a master caster named Yaro. Yaro was Senegalese and a member of the 'first generation' of aluminium casters who had played such a key role in diffusing casting from Senegal to other parts of West Africa.[11] Thus by tracing Kondé's professional genealogy, it is possible to uncover a transnational process of labour migration that spans four generations, fifty years of time, and three different colonies and countries.

That Kondé's casting lineage stretches over such a vast geographic expanse suggests another critical aspect of casting's history, which is that the diffusion of the craft also depended upon the mobility of men with expertise in it. Professional casting genealogies often extend over great distances and feature men of various nationalities and ethnicities. But that a young man like Bankaly Baro travelled and moved in search of new opportunities is certainly not a phenomena exclusive to the late colonial period or to the casting profession. Indeed, the motif of young men striking out on their own to find their way in the world is a common one in West African cultural traditions. In Mande, a large sociolinguistic group made of many different related languages and ethnicities from the interior savanna region of West Africa, the figure of the fearless male traveller crops up in epic traditions as well as in memoirs and narratives that men tell about themselves and their male relatives and ancestors. The men who partake in this sort of autonomous voyaging are typically unmarried younger brothers who are unconstrained by the familial obligations and responsibilities that burden older brothers (Jansen 1996).

The destinations to which young men travelled 'on adventure' changed, however, as the result of colonial rule and the creation of new urban and economic centres. In the nineteenth century, young men from interior urban areas like Kankan were as likely to go 'on adventure' to centres of commerce and Islamic scholarship, like Jenné and Timbuktu, as they were to head to coastal trading centres, such as Saint Louis. But by the 1950s, colonial capitals overtook those older metropolises as preferred destinations, and men from interior regions of West Africa were likely to undertake this rite of passage by heading to Abidjan, Côte d'Ivoire, which was then emerging as a shining modern metropolis, or to Dakar, Senegal, the capital of French West Africa and a vibrant and cosmopolitan centre of culture and commerce. It was in these cities that young men could make new connections and learn new trades with which they sometimes, as did Baro, return to their original home.

It was not only young men from West Africa's interior who struck out 'on adventure', however. Casters from coastal Senegal also pursued the opportunities generated by taking their skills to other cities and regions. In so doing, those casters participated in a well-established pattern of Senegalese labour migration, one that had been fortified and broadened by the period of colonial rule. Considering the dynamics and history of French West Africa more generally shows that the prominent role that Senegal and Senegalese men play in aluminium casting's history is not, in fact, simply the result of fortuitous luck and daring enterprise. Rather, a number of very precise forces helped make possible the Senegalese origin of the craft and the success of its Senegalese practitioners in diffusing the craft.

In migrating to and establishing casting workshops in other colonies, Senegalese casters followed a path of labour migration that had been well worn by their compatriots. That path had been laid in the late nineteenth century, when the French started to aggressively expand their colonial holdings in sub-Saharan West Africa. As one of France's oldest possessions in West Africa, the French relied heavily in their territorial ambitions upon the manpower of Senegalese slaves and ex-slaves who filled the ranks of the French army (Klein 1998, Kanya-Forstner 1969). When the colonisers sought to solidify colonial conquest into a colonial occupation, the French continued to rely upon Senegalese employees to man, literally, the apparatus of colonial rule. Senegalese men worked as bureaucrats, clerks, and soldiers throughout the different colonies of French West Africa (FWA), while they also facilitated road-building projects in these other colonies and worked as engineers and mechanics on FWA's colonial railroads. Senegalese merchants also followed the French flag, some of them doing so in the employ of metropolitan commercial houses, while others established their own independent ventures. The persistent presence of Senegalese men within the bureaucratic hierarchies and commercial networks of France's West African colonies is due largely to Dakar's physical proximity to France and to the status of that city as the capital of French West Africa. But informal and intangible processes – daily practices, personal relationships, and entrenched habits – were equally important in ensuring Dakar's primacy as the educational, political, and social hub of France's West African empire.

Indeed, considering aluminium casting against this historical backdrop reveals that the birth of this craft in the capital of French West Africa was not just a quirky coincidence, but was a direct result of Dakar's status as the jewel of France's West African empire. With a fairly sizable number of French settlers (in comparison to the other colonies of French West Africa), Dakar became home to a small manufacturing sector, including the two French-owned industrialised metal foundries where Senegalese wage-labourers first learned the technique of sand-casting. When Senegalese casters moved with their skills into other regions of West Africa, they were indeed professional pioneers of sorts, but those casters were certainly not the only representatives of their homeland when they set up shop in other cities such as Conakry, Guinea or Abidjan, Côte d'Ivoire. Those casters were part of a much larger stream of Senegalese professionals, merchants, and skilled labourers who moved into other parts of Africa to make use of their education, connections, and expertise. This process left a terminological legacy in Conakry, where so many Senegalese took up residence in the city during the colonial period that a whole *quartier* was named after them.

The diffusion of casting from Dakar to other parts of West Africa in the aftermath of World War II does not simply tell the story of a metal, a technology, and an entrepreneurial group of artisans, however. The diffusion of aluminium casting through West Africa also sheds light on the limits of colonial rule and the efforts by the state to manage and control its subjects. The voyages of casters indicate that 60 or so years on, the colonisers had still not managed to bring Africans on board with some of the major premises of colonial rule, including ideas about the impermeability of territorial boundaries and the alleged homogeneity and rural orientation of African ethnicities and linguistic groupings (or 'tribes' in colonial terminology). On the contrary, colonial borders and the spectre of ethnic or linguistic difference did not hinder casters in the least from migrating to new regions and territories. Indeed, the migrations of casters offer a microcosm of a larger challenge with which the colonial state grappled throughout the colonial period: despite concerted efforts by the colonial state to subordinate its subjects within colonial economic and political regimes, the colonisers often faced great practical difficulties in managing the mobility and labour of the inhabitants of their colonies.

The diffusion of casting in West Africa thus exposes the limitations of both colonial and post-colonial governments to control the mobility of populations. As such, casting generates a transnational perspective on change and transformation in West Africa, a perspective that is often obscured in the historiography by the tendency to use a particular colony or nation-state as a unit of analysis, as well as by the focus on migration from Africa to other parts of the world, such as Europe. Aluminium casting serves as a reminder, however, of the frequency with which men (and women too) 'voted with their feet' in the twentieth century not to travel across the ocean, but to go next door. Indeed, many aluminium casters responded to political and economic pressures at home by seeking opportunities in other parts of West Africa. The inability of African governments to staunch these movements and benefit from the skills and resources of their own people is strikingly demonstrated by the Guinean 'diaspora' of aluminium casters that emerged in the 1970s. At that time, Sekou Touré was the president of Guinea, and his repressive economic and political policies provoked a massive emigration of people to neighbouring colonies. Among those waves of people were men and boys who took up aluminium casting. Since then, Guineans, particularly ethnic Fulbe from the Futa Jallon, have managed to carve out a robust portion of the casting sector in coastal towns and cities from Dakar, Senegal to Abidjan, Côte d'Ivoire. That the Guinean casting diaspora is constantly rejuvenated by 'new arrivals' shows that out-migration has remained a significant feature of Guinean life since the 1970s. Those Guinean casters living 'on the outside' thus show the inability of the Guinean state to marshal and manage its human resources, while they also offer evidence of Guinea's persistently abysmal economic circumstances.

But it is not only political and economic circumstances or systems of knowledge production which have shaped the diffusion of aluminium casting in West Africa. Material factors have also played an important role in the process, for casters cannot practise their craft without scrap aluminium. The progression of aluminium casting from coastal regions to smaller interior cities and towns since the 1960s has taken place at a pace determined not by a lack of expertise, but by scant scrap aluminium. Historically, casters set up shop in areas where scrap could be most easily obtained, which meant those urban areas and port cities where aluminium was imported, circulated, and most likely to become scrap. By contrast, obtaining scrap in the interior of West Africa has historically been and continues to be a great challenge, even in large urban centres such as Bamako.

The demand for scrap aluminium from the casting sector has become so intense in recent decades that it has spawned an ancillary profession: scrap-metal dealers, or (in French) *fournisseurs*. *Fournisseurs* travel widely to acquire aluminium, such as Mohamed Samaké, from Mopti, Mali, who takes two to three trips annually to buy aluminium in Ghana, Nigeria and even across the Sahara in Algeria.[12] Travelling alone or with other *fournisseurs*, Samake purchases aluminium by the ton and then hires a semi-truck and driver to transport it back to Mopti. But casters and *fournisseurs* face increasingly serious competition in their efforts to acquire scrap aluminium. In the twenty-first century, that competition is coming from Indian, Chinese, and Lebanese scrap dealers who have set up export businesses in West Africa's port cities. Those expatriate metal-buyers focus principally on scrap iron, but when possible they also purchase scrap aluminium.[13] The heated competition for scrap metal the world over has served to integrate West African casters into the global scrap-metal market, and when West African casters buy scrap they pay a price per kilo that is comparable to that paid elsewhere in the world.

The circuits of recycling and reuse that have emerged around the casting profession indicate how aluminium casters and *fournisseurs* have professionalised recycling and transformed refuse into resources. But like other people who make their living in the informal sector, aluminium casters do so by operating on razor-thin margins. Most of them labour with the support of very little, if any, modern infrastructure, such as electricity or running water. That casters can work without such resources means that they can establish their workshops in a variety of different contexts and environments, but this capability also bespeaks the very precariousness of casters' socio-economic position. Casters often set up shop in areas where few people desire to live or work, but where many people are nevertheless compelled to do just that: next to railroad tracks and busy freeways, at the rugged edges of manufacturing districts, on hillsides prone to washouts in the rainy season, and in the newer slums that have grown up in the gorges and gullies that surround older neighbourhoods. Casters often try to locate their workshops near other economic sectors with whom they share (or once shared) mutually beneficial relations. In Conakry, for example, the oldest casting shops are within throwing distance of the (now inoperative) maintenance shop for the (now inoperative) railroad built during the colonial period. It is also very common in both large and mid-sized cities to find casters operating near transportation hubs, auto repair shops, and garbage dumps. Close proximity to those sites provides casters with a market for their finished products, or a source for scrap, or both: mechanics and drivers sometimes need aluminium parts for their vehicles, which casters can make for them, while mechanics and drivers may also sell to casters aluminium parts that are no longer operable. Likewise, casters working near garbage dumps can take first dibs on aluminium collected and sold by weight by *recuperators*, adults and children who specialize in salvaging scrap aluminium and other reusable resources from garbage dumps.

Because casters frequently squat on the land where they operate, the locations of their workshops help to illuminate the shifting economic fortunes of the urban areas in which they live. Many of the older casters in Abidjan, Côte d'Ivoire, could tick off the names of the several locations where they had built workshops over the previous two or three decades, and they would then describe the new buildings, businesses, or governmental projects that had pushed them out. Casters have been long gone from one of the original sites where casting was practised in Abidjan in the 1950s, for example, because that neighbourhood underwent 'improvement'. By contrast, there are still groups of casters in Conakry who work near the now dilapidated railroad, which is one of the original sites where casters started working in that port city. That *quartier* is located in a part of downtown Conakry that – like much of the rest of downtown – has remained untouched by new building projects or efforts of rejuvenation or renewal. The forced transfers of Abidjan's casters and the permanence of Conakry's thus suggests that the status of casting workshops on the urban landscape presents a sort of inverse index to prosperity and development within the formal economic sector.

Conclusion

The market niche that aluminium casters have carved out in the second half of the twentieth century reveals that the labour of the informal-sector economy must be incorporated into our understanding of work and its history in Africa. The history of aluminium casting shows that participants in informal economic activities, such as artisans and craftspeople, are as likely to respond to the economic opportunities of migration – as well as to move away from various pressures and constraints at home – as are wage-earning participants in the formal sector of the economy, such as mineworkers. The recent vintage of sand-casting means that its history and early diffusion, in the aftermath of World War II, can be quite precisely detailed. Key to the diffusion of sand-casting has been material conditions, that is, the availability and circulation of scrap aluminium, as well as technological know-how. Expertise in the craft has been disseminated through the apprenticeship system, a tradition of learning that has deep roots in West Africa and which helps to mitigate against the uncertainty of the informal sector. Tracing the history of aluminium casting thus sheds light on an understudied sector of the informal economy while it opens up a fresh perspective on the intertwined histories of labour and migration in West Africa.

Notes

1. Donald Light notes the difficulties that researchers have had in precisely defining informal economic behaviour but he emphasises its 'relational and reciprocal' character (Light 2004, 710). A spate of studies have been conducted on various specialities within the informal sector in Africa, such as Peace et al. (1988).
2. In Zambia, for example, formal market employment rates shrank from 17% in 1992 to 10.4% in 1999, while the number of people with union membership in the copper mines fell from 62,000 in 1990 to 25,000 in 1999 (Pitcher 2007, 135, 143).
3. Pitcher notes that, 'changes in production processes, the restructuring of distribution networks and technological improvements' has fostered more competition, mobility, and a 'casualization of labor' (Pitcher 2007, 135–136). For a case study of neo-liberal reforms and international investment, see Haglund (2008). These processes are certainly not unique to Africa, as demonstrated by Brazil, where neo-liberal reforms, monetary stabilisation policies, and increased foreign investment have produced a 'significant decline in union-led strikes' (Sandoval 2007, 64).
4. Art historians and anthropologists have made passing references to aluminium bangles and earrings worn in different parts of Africa, while Norma Wolff has written one of the only pieces devoted to artisanal aluminium production in a 1985 article in *African Arts* on the ornate aluminium spoons produced by smiths in Kura, Nigeria. But the artisans with whom Wolff worked used a wholly different technique for manipulating the aluminium than that which casters use to make cooking pots (Wolff 1986). Short references to aluminium casting can be found in Bocoum (2005) and Morice (1981).
5. Youssouf Thiombane and Souleyman Touré, interview with author, Dakar, Senegal, 13 May 2006.
6. *El hajj* N'Diaye, interview with author, Gbessia, Conakry, 16 March 2006.
7. Baba Camara, interview with author, Hastings, Sierra Leone, 26 April 2006; Chief Pa Almamy Kano, Mamadi Cisse, and Santigi Fofana, interview with author, Hastings, Sierra Leone, 26 April 2006.
8. The 1886 Hall-Herault method used a system of electrolysis to make more efficient the process of making aluminium from alumina, while the Bayer process developed in 1888 simplified the extraction of alumina from bauxite ore.
9. This technique is the one that Wolff witnessed in the making of decorative spoons in Kura, Nigeria (Wolff 1986).
10. This process has taken place extensively in the village of Kulatokosere in the Futa Jallon, which used to be a blacksmithing village but many of whose male residents now specialise in aluminium.

11. Namory Condé and other casters, interviews with author, Kankan, Guinea, November, December, January 2005–06.
12. Mohamed Samaké, interview with author, Mopti, Mali, 14 March 2006.
13. KMCI metals company, interview with author, Abidjan, République de Côte d'Ivoire, 9 June 2006.

References

Bocoum, H., 2005. Annexe: emergence et développement des fonderies artisanales. *In*: M. Niang, ed. *Participation paysanne et developpement rural au Senegal*. Dakar: Codesria.

Cerny, C. and Seriff, S., 1996. *Recycled, re-seen: folk art from the global scrap heap*. New York: Harry N. Abrams.

Cooper, F., 1987. *On the African waterfront: urban disorder and the transformation of work in colonial Mombasa*. New Haven, CT: Yale University Press.

Cooper, F., 1996. *Decolonization and African society: the labor question in French and British Africa*. Cambridge: Cambridge University Press.

Eisenhofer, S., Guggeis, K., and Froidevaux, J., 2004. *Africa on the move: toys from West Africa*. Stuttgart: Arnoldsche.

Haglund, D., 2008. Regulating FDI in weak African states: a case study of Chinese copper mining in Zambia. *The journal of modern African studies*, 46 (4), 547–575.

Harries, P., 1994. *Work, culture and identity: migrant laborers in Mozambique and South Africa*. 186–1910. Portsmouth, NH: Heinemann Press.

Hart, K., 1973. Informal income opportunities and urban employment in Ghana. *The journal of modern African studies*, 11 (1), 61–89.

Herbert, Eugenia, 1993. *Iron, gender, and power: rituals of transformation in African societies*. Bloomington, IN: Indiana University Press.

Humblot, P., 1921. Kankan, métropole de la haute Guinée. *Bulletin de l'Afrique française: le comité de l'Afrique française et le comité du Maroc*, 6, 128–140, 153–164.

Jansen, J., 1996. The younger brother and the stranger: in search of a status discourse for Mande. *Cahiers d'études africaines*, 144 (4), 659–688.

Jones, J., 2002. *Industrial labor in the colonial world: workers of the* Chemin de Fer *Dakar–Niger 1881–1963*. Portsmouth, NH: Heinemann.

Kanya-Forstner, A.S., 1969. *The conquest of the western Sudan: a study in French military imperialism*. Cambridge: Cambridge University Press.

Klein, M., 1998. *Slavery and colonial rule in French West Africa*. Cambridge: Cambridge University Press.

Kriger, C., 2000. *Pride of men: nineteenth century ironworking*. Portsmouth, NH: Heinemann.

Light, D., 2004. From migrant enclaves to mainstream: reconceptualizing informal economic behavior. *Theory and society*, 33 (6), 705–737.

Lindsay, L., 2003. *Working with gender*. Portsmouth, NH: Heinemann.

Moodie, D., 1994. *Going for gold: men, mines and migration*. Berkeley, CA: University of California Press.

Morice, A., 1981. *Les petites activités urbaines: reflexions à partir de deux etudes de cas: les vélos taxis et les travailleurs du metal de Kaolack (Senegal)*. Paris: IEDES.

Munck, R., 2004. Reconceptualizing labour in the era of globalization: from labour and 'developing area studies' to globalization and labour? *Labour, capital and society*, 37 (1/2), 236–257.

Nevadomsky, J., 2005. Casting in contemporary Benin art. *African arts*, 38 (2), 66–95.

McNaughton, P., 1988. *The Mande blacksmiths: knowledge, power and art in West Africa*. Bloomington, IN: Indiana University Press.

Peace, T.O., Kujore, O. and Agboh-Bankole, V.A., 1988. Generating an income in the urban environment: the experience of street food vendors in Ile-Ife, Nigeria. *Africa*, 58 (4), 385–400.

Pillay, D., 2007. Introduction. *Work, capital, and society* (special issue on 'Globalization and the challenges to labour and development'), 40 (1 and 2), 2–15.

Pitcher, A., 2007. What has happened to organized labor in Southern Africa. *International labor and working class history*, 72 (Fall), 134–160.

Sandoval, S., 2007. Alternative forms of working class organization and the mobilization of informal sector workers in Brazil in the era of neoliberalism. *International labor and working-class history*, 72 (Fall), 63–89.

Schmidt, E., 2007. *Cold war and decolonization in Guinea, 1946–1958*. Athens, OH: Ohio University Press.

Sewell, W., 1980. *Work and revolution in France: the language of labor from the old regime to 1848*. Cambridge: Cambridge University Press.

Van Onselen, C., 1976. *Chibaro: African mine labour in Southern Rhodesia, 1900–1933*. London: Pluto Press.

Wolff, N.H., 1986. A Hausa aluminium spoon industry. *African arts*, 19 (3), 40–44, 82.

Transnationalism and nationalism in the Nigerian Seamen's Union

Lynn Schler

Department of Politics and Government, Ben Gurion University of the Negev, Beer-Sheva, Israel

This article will examine the shifting tactics employed by Nigerian seamen in their struggles to improve their working conditions onboard Elder Dempster vessels in the late colonial period. Nigerian seamen successfully exploited opportunities arising within the context of colonialism to participate in globalised economies and cultures, exposing them to new solidarities and empowering them to seek an improvement in their lives. In crafting their onboard protests, African seamen historically forged ideological and organisational alliances with the wider world of the black diaspora. But the era of decolonisation shifted the balance of power between seamen and the union leadership as they negotiated with colonial shipping companies in the transition to independence. As ruling elites in both Europe and Nigeria took political, economic and ideological actions to secure lasting power and influence for themselves, seamen experienced a profound disempowerment. Although intent on engaging with the globalised world, African seamen were ultimately prevented from securing for themselves positions of power and autonomy as an effective labour movement in the post-colonial context.

The struggles conducted by African labour throughout the colonial and postcolonial eras have reflected ongoing efforts to maximise opportunities through dynamic processes of coalition-building. Either individually or through the official channels of unions, cultural organisations or political parties, African working-class struggles have tapped into fluid and evolving solidarities and alliances to overcome disempowerment and to advance their particular cultural, ideological and economic agendas. These alliances have varied in their scope, duration and significance, and in the extent to which they have coincided or conflicted with larger political, cultural, or ideological movements. While African working classes have mobilised creative strategies and exploited networks as part of larger efforts of organising, they have continually confronted limitations in their ability to assemble and exploit solidarities when these came into direct conflict with the political and ideological agendas of power elites. Thus, the history of labour organising in Africa must consider the limitations imposed upon rank-and-file labour in envisioning and implementing opportunities for collaborative efforts that threatened the political, ideological or racial borders upholding more powerful hegemonic interests.

Particularly in the shadow of nation-building in the era of decolonisation, African labour was corralled into allegiances reflecting the political programmes of the African power elite in collusion with colonial capitalist interests. Both local and transnational imaginaries lost ground to the nationalist perspectives, and it was ultimately the nation-state that became the pre-eminent framework within which class struggles were negotiated and fought in the postcolonial era. Thus, the triumph of colonial and African elite interests in preserving national political and ideological borders had far-reaching implications for how African organised labour could envision and exploit solidarities in the postcolonial era. This article will provide a close examination of organising among Nigerian seamen and demonstrate how political developments associated with the transition from colonialism to independence ultimately limited the autonomy of African labour in crafting strategies of protest.

Seamen provide a unique but highly informative opportunity for studying the impact of nationalisation on African labour precisely because their experiences leading up to decolonisation cut across geopolitical and cultural landscapes. In framing and responding to their local contexts, seamen exploited their mobility and drew upon ideological currents and material support circulating around what Paul Gilroy (1993) has termed the 'Black Atlantic'. Gilroy's notion of the Black Atlantic provides a powerful tool for emphasising fluidity and displacement as foundational features of black experiences, and foregrounds the transnational solidarities that arise from these historical positions. The creolisation of African seamen's identities had deep historical roots dating to the very origins of African seafaring on European vessels in the era of the slave trade. As Peter Linebaugh and Marcus Rediker (2001) have shown, black seamen exploited class and gender-based solidarities and participated in a multi-ethnic 'Atlantic proletariat' that ultimately challenged relations of power throughout the Atlantic world. Jeffrey Bolster (1997, 39) has argued that the work of seafaring was the catalyst for defining a new black ethnicity throughout the diaspora, as sailors embodied 'a mode of communication integrating local communities into the larger community of color'. But while seamen across time were inspired and invigorated by universalist currents, their autonomous organising strategies were deeply embedded in the local, finite context they occupied onboard ships. Thus, while Nigerian seamen of the colonial era embraced political and cultural ideologies emanating from the black diaspora, their organising efforts were constructed and played out within the tight quarters of colonial merchant vessels, and reflected a distinctly local agenda.

While rank-and-file seamen demonstrated their adaptability and creativity in formulating their ideological positions, union leadership in Lagos increasingly sought to subordinate seamen's protest efforts to further their own quest for influence in the shifting political landscape associated with decolonisation. This article will examine the shifting tactics employed by Nigerian seamen in their struggles to improve their working conditions onboard Elder Dempster vessels in the late colonial period. An examination of their organising efforts and demands reveals how some cultural, religious, and ideological discourses attracted them, inspired them and shaped their worldviews. In studying their defeats and failures, we can understand precisely how power was consolidated in the processes of decolonisation at the expense of these workers, and how deals struck between European and African elites on the eve of independence continue to limit the choices and opportunities available to African working classes today.

Recruitment and organising among Nigerian seamen

From the time commerce began between Britain and the coast of West Africa, British shipping interests looked to hire African seamen as a cheap supplement to crews recruited in Europe. In the initial stages of trade, the overwhelming majority of these recruits came from the ethnic Kru, who as early as the eighteenth century were recruited in Liberia and later Freetown, Sierra Leone. European shipping companies would routinely stop in Freetown to pick up Kru deckhands and firemen before continuing down the coast (Frost 1999, 27). Over time, the Kru developed a tightly organised recruitment system, and headmen overseeing groups of seamen protected their interests and negotiated relatively favourable terms of employment. Due to their experience in seafaring and efficient organising efforts, British shipping companies relied heavily on Kru recruits, and they constituted the majority of seafaring African labour signed on in West Africa prior to World War II (Frost 1999, 102).

From the outbreak of World War II, shipping giants such as Elder Dempster, which controlled the majority of cargo, mail and passenger shipping between the United Kingdom (UK) and the West African coast, began diverting their African recruitment efforts to Lagos. The war had greatly increased demands on the company, and the need for seamen was acute. Janet J. Ewald (2000) has argued that, particularly in times of economic hardship, European shipping companies historically sought out fresh sources of coloured seamen to recruit throughout the maritime world, and tapped them to offset rising costs of labour. Elder Dempster's move to hire in Lagos was thus designed to circumvent the demands of Kru seamen hired in Freetown, with poorly organised Lagos recruits willing to sign on for lower salaries (Sherwood 1995, Davies 2000). Elder Dempster thus established a four-tiered pay scale during World War II. At the bottom were Nigerians recruited in Nigeria, followed by Africans recruited in Freetown. The third level of pay was given to Africans employed from Liverpool, while the highest salaries were reserved for European seamen, who were paid the National Maritime Board rates.

Thus, seamen recruited in Nigeria were embraced by colonial shipping companies as the cheap alternative to the Kru, with the additional benefit of being unorganised and inexperienced in labour contract negotiating. What the colonial employers did not anticipate, however, was the quick turnaround among the Lagos-based recruits from easily exploited and inexperienced manpower to agents of industrial discord and protest. Already in 1942, the seamen recruited in Nigeria formed their own union, the West African Union of Seamen. In the early years this was hardly a broad-based organisation, with membership dropping to an all-time low of six in 1946. But reorganisation came in 1947 and, along with it, a name change to the 'Nigerian Union of Seamen'. Following this spirit of revival was a swift climb in due-paying membership, reaching 2250 by 1953. But the union's declared objectives remained the same from the earliest years: to protect the interests of its members, regulate work hours and wages, ensure adequate accommodation for all seamen on vessels and ashore, to promote the general welfare of seamen and to regulate relations between employers and employees (*Report of Board of Enquiry* 1959).

At first Elder Dempster attempted to avoid any recognition or contact with the organisation. This was not hard to do, as the union was often more concerned with infighting than actually representing seamen in their conflicts with the shipping companies. As one government review from the period stated:

> The record of the Union's activities over the years makes a most pathetic reading. Almost from its inception, there have always been instances of endless strife, distrust, intrigues, tribal discrimination, police arrests, litigation, rifts of members into factions, one faction trying at one time or the other, and often quite successfully, to overthrow the other from office, and to install itself into power. No set of officials of the union would appear to have held office happily together for any reasonable length of time. (*Report of Board of Enquiry* 1959, 4–5)

But, suddenly in 1948, in what appeared a stark turnaround, Elder Dempster conceded recognition of the Nigerian Union of Seamen as the sole representative of seamen engaged in Lagos. The two sides formed a local board with representation from the union, the shipping companies and local government to monitor the recruitment and supply of seamen working out of Lagos. The board was to establish and maintain a register of seamen, and West African ratings were to be recruited only from those whose names were on the register. Both parties agreed that all matters pertaining to Nigerian seamen should be decided in Lagos.

The change in the shipping companies' position towards the Nigerian Seamen's Union was in line with an overall shift in colonial policy towards African labour unions in the post-World War II period. A wave of strikes across the continent forced colonial governments and business interests to make some concessions in their stance toward organised labour. But while recognising the need for reform, Frederick Cooper (1996, 3) has argued that governments and employers

> wanted to confine the labour question to a set of institutions and practices familiar to them from the industrial relations experience of the metropole: to treat labour as [separate] from politics. The threat of a labour crisis becoming unbound – linked to people other than waged workers... made governments especially willing to pay the costs of resolving labour issues [through recognised unions].

Thus, the decision to engage with the Nigerian Union of Seamen was a calculated attempt at making limited yet controlled concessions to Nigerian seamen, but did not represent any fundamental shift in the shipping companies' views on seamen's rights, and the whole endeavour was undertaken with a frustrated yearning for the good old pre-war days when African seamen had not yet awoken to claim their rights. As one Elder Dempster official wrote in 1959:

> We have looked through the rules of the Nigerian Union of Seamen ... It is a shocking document and much of what the Union appears to be aiming to do could not possibly be accepted by the [shipping] lines. I am referring to ship committees and so forth. I suppose in the old days there would have been someone in Nigeria who would have told the Unions not to be silly in framing rules of this kind, but I do not know whether there is anyone bold enough or authoritative enough to do so at the present time. (Merseyside Maritime Museum 1959c)

Despite the sporadic rhetoric of demands, throughout the 1950s the Nigerian Union of Seamen did not pose a serious threat to the shipping companies' designs of maintaining the status quo, because union leaders in Lagos remained preoccupied with internal political struggles for control over the organisation. The focus of the leadership constituted a colossal divide between the concerns of union officials and the everyday experiences of seamen on ships. This divide was partly unavoidable, as the unique nature of seamen's work took them away from Lagos and union headquarters for most of the time they were under contract. On the other hand, those based in Lagos were either Westernised elites posing as professional trade unionists and never actually employed as seamen, or seamen who had been denied work due to disciplinary actions taken against them onboard or criminal activity such as smuggling or drug trafficking (Merseyside Maritime Museum 1954). Thus, the gap separating the rank-and-file seamen from the leadership and decision-making organs of the union was exceptionally wide. In May 1959, President Ekore of the union, in an effort to discredit a resolution calling for his removal, described the problematic situation:

> The Seamen's Union is not like any other and why trouble always finds a way easy, is because when a resolution has passed and [been] adopted by a handful of members ashore without the knowledge of members at sea, on arrival they will declare their stand

of ignorance and thereby seek to oppose the adopted resolution which actually is right. (Merseyside Maritime Museum 1959b)

Local struggles, transnational networks

While union officials in the 1950s might have been preoccupied with petty politics, the seamen working on colonial ships often faced miserable working conditions, replete with racial discrimination and dehumanising treatment. Many black seamen suffered physical abuse, name-calling, and random punishments by the officers who they served under, and group beatings or other violent attacks by their fellow white seamen, such as one seamen who was burnt in the fire-room by a white crew member who threw boiling water on him (Merseyside Maritime Museum 1958). Often, these incidents would land black seamen in the hospital, but the majority suffered these abuses and remained on board, lacking any record or verifiable proof against those who perpetrated these crimes. African seamen who did seek justice usually came up against an uninterested or unconvinced captain, and when it was a case of a black seaman's word against that of a white seaman, there was little hope that any justice would be served.

The insecurity faced by black seamen and the lack of retribution for white offenders clearly infuriated Africans, and primed them for embracing ideologies of liberation circulating in the contemporary black diaspora. As can be seen in the following letter written to the Elder Dempster shipping company in 1958, seamen's acts of protests revealed the development of a transnational perspective:

> For your information, the African crews have long hesitated from retaliating not because they are cowards but because the Union has been continually telling them that they should obey before complaining. If by any chance you think that they are afraid of being defeated by the English offenders on board ships, you can refer to boxing history and see what Joe Louis and Sugar Ray Robinson did to their white opponents. Today, Hogan Kid Bassey another black man is showing the world how he can handle the white man.
>
> And while the [Shipping Master] sits back with his English friends from shipping companies, who carry away our raw material and minerals and enjoys this paradise of sunshine, our men – Africans and West Indians, are being slashed with knives and beaten with pokers in England.
>
> Does this not prove conclusively that colour prejudice is rampant on all ships, particularly those of the Elder Dempster Lines? What is happening and what we have related here is no different from the incidents taking place in Little Rock, Arkansas, and London and Nottingham, England.
>
> ... If the Elder Dempster Lines and other shipping companies continue to send the English seamen to beat up African crews, we will show them that Africans are no cowards. (Merseyside Maritime Museum 1958)

Yet, while seamen aligned themselves ideologically to a wider world of black protest, most responses to onboard discrimination remained confined to single ships. Individual seamen or small groups would react to beatings or unfair treatment either by complaining through official channels onboard or through spontaneous physical violence, neither of which reaped any great results. While borrowing from broader political trends, seamen conceived of the ship as their ideological battleground, and sought solutions and dreamed of a better world on deck. For this reason, the Seamen's Union leadership, preoccupied with Lagos-based politics, remained largely useless and irrelevant in organising and initiating seamen's protests.

Yet, the end of the 1950s resulted in significant changes in the role the Seamen's Union played as representative of seamen's struggles. Two major incidents resulted in a significant change in the status of the union as an equal negotiating partner with shipping companies, and this had far-reaching consequences for ship-based protests, and in turn, the status of individual seamen. The rest of this paper will examine first, the hiring of Sidi Khayam, a new general secretary for the union in 1958, and second, the strike that began on board the *M.V. Apapa* in Liverpool in 1959. The events and outcomes surrounding these two incidents will be evaluated for what they teach us about seamen's organising efforts and opportunities, and their successes and failures in the shadow of decolonisation. This examination will shed light on the long-term implications of decolonisation on African seamen in particular, and on African labour movements in general.

New union leadership: General Secretary Sidi Khayam

Sidi Khayam, born in Nigeria, had lived, worked and studied in England for nearly 10 years before he was recruited by the Nigerian Union of Seamen to be their new general secretary in 1958. Khayam was actually recruited in Liverpool, where some local African residents and Nigerian seamen persuaded him to return to Nigeria and head the Seamen's Union. Khayam had studied economics and law, although he did not complete any degree, and had scattered experience with trade union membership as he worked in various factories and industries throughout England. Khayam's appointment to the position of General Secretary was a great annoyance to the shipping companies, particularly because of the confrontational manner he adopted towards the employers from the beginning of his term. Attempting to solidify his position, Khayam was initially uncompromising in his attitude toward the shipping company, making strong demands for salary increases, payment for overtime and improved lodging for seamen onboard ships and ashore. But what was truly disturbing to the management of Elder Dempster was Khayam's habit of flying into a rage in his meetings with management, and frequently accusing them of racial discrimination. While the shipping companies were willing to enter into a dialogue with a legitimate representative of African labour to negotiate compromises with regard to pay scales or benefits, the employers were not willing to engage with an incendiary racial discourse. Thus, Elder Dempster refused to officially recognise him, claiming that he was appointed illegitimately. Unofficially, they schemed to get him deported from Nigeria (Merseyside Maritime Museum 1959–1962).

But the changes in the balance and nature of power in the era of decolonisation meant that simply deporting Khayam was not an option. Nigerian government officials, a group of anti-radical Westernised elites owing their positions of influence to their proximity to colonial rulers, were equally in favour of getting rid of Khayam in theory. They realised, however, that he could be discredited and hence neutralised through legitimate means. As the Minister of Labour, Nwokedi, suggested to the Elder Dempster representative in Lagos in 1959:

> Khayam is unfavourable and it would be best to see him out of the country. But the ministry would like the seamen themselves to get rid of Khayam and they consider that the only way to achieve this would be for Khayam to be shown up beyond doubt, on a wider screen than at present, as an irresponsible person not working in the seamen's best interests. The proposed method for 'exposing' Khayam would be to have a 'trade dispute' and for the Labour Department to appoint a conciliator. It could be expected that Khayam's behaviour during conciliation meetings would finally make clear to all his unreasonableness and irresponsibility … resulting in the seamen denouncing and dismissing him. (Merseyside Maritime Museum 1959–1962)

Thus, in the era of decolonisation, the rules of the game had changed and both the shipping companies and the government had to endure Khayam.

As it turns out, Sidi Khayam's relationship to the rank-and-file membership of the union was no less antagonistic and his approach toward them was equally belligerent. A few months after taking office, he issued a statement to the general membership, instituting an uncompromising expression of his rule over the organisation and demanding unambiguous obedience from the Seamen's Union members. As the statement said:

Our plan is to run the Nigerian Union of Seamen on a pattern different from the gangster-tactics of yesteryears .... We have had enough complaints, some are true, some are not. But the damn truth is, that there is [an] absence of evidence that some of us are really serious seamen. From now [on] the union will take steps to rub in some discipline for those who are caught on petty-theft, underhanded business, smart rackets and fishy deals. It's none of our business to defend such mess.

... Any person whose acts will likely prevent all seamen from getting their rights and respect, who wants to clown around his job and shows us up as drones to shipping captains will get a fast punch out the union door. He will get a black eye from the union before the shipping company does it. Any guy who is feeling lazy can drop on shore to doze or booze about the place, but he is not going to pull down our prestige or weaken the effort the Nigerian Union of Seamen wants to put up for decent and hardworking African crews.

Members who feel a bit big or want to bluff their way by looking too sulky for instructions can just ask themselves how much they get for the same job white crews perform.

... And anyone who figures we don't mean business can start the stew and see how it tastes. We mean every damn decision we have put down here - that he will be thrown out of the NUS picture outright. (Merseyside Maritime Museum 1959)

Khayam's sharp approach aimed at gaining him respect both from seamen and the union did not do much to further his cause, and it seemed each rebuff from above and below sent him into a new rage. His luck changed, however, in the aftermath of the *Apapa* strike of 1959, an event he played no role in initiating, but one that he masterfully managed to exploit to his advantage.

The *M.V. Apapa* strike of 1959

On 27 May 1959, the *M.V. Apapa* vessel arrived in Lagos. The crew met with the General Secretary of the Nigerian Union of Seamen, Sidi Khayam, to complain of ill-treatment of the African crew during their most recent voyage. At the root of the seamen's grievances was what they identified as the systematic discrimination of black seamen onboard Elder Dempster ships. They had several specific examples of this discrimination, claiming, for instance, that African seamen were limited to purchasing only Woodbines, Senior Service and Capstan cigarettes, while the European crew was allowed to have any available brand. The seamen also complained that the bartender watered down the beer of Africans, but not the European crew's. They charged that the newly-appointed Chief Steward denied Africans steak, chicken and turkey, and instead served them only pork. The crew also suspected that the chief steward had ordered customs officers to perform in-depth searches of the belongings of crew members who had complained of the new arrangements regarding food, cigarettes and beer. The most serious allegations were made against the second steward, who had become violent with crew, 'pushing men about with his hands, cursing them and almost causing a physical fight'. This same second steward demanded that the crew wash his car during working hours and when the men refused he threatened to blacklist them from further employment (*Report of the Board of Enquiry* 1959a).

In the weeks leading up to the strike, Sidi Khayam was busy trying to oust the executive officers from the union and organised a no-confidence vote in a Delegates Conference, and, although he had met with the *Apapa* crew, he actually discouraged a walk-out and persuaded them to sail again with the *Apapa* on 2 June for Liverpool

(*Daily Telegraph* (Lagos), 27 May 1959). The *Apapa* arrived in Liverpool on 15 June 1959. On 17 June, the Nigerian crew, represented by a local African resident of Liverpool, submitted a letter to Malcolm Glasier, director of Elder Dempster, detailing their complaints and demanding the removal of the *Apapa*'s European chief steward, second steward and chief storekeeper from the ship. Not surprisingly, the company refused this request. Some attempts were made at negotiating with the crew, but when the demand for removing the European bosses from the ship was refused, 75 members of the African crew walked off the ship on Wednesday, 24 June. They went from the docks to Stanley House, a community centre for African seamen in the city of Liverpool.

It was also reported on this day that a 'shore-African' named Ogun went to the docks to collect men from five other ships to join the striking *Apapa* crew at the Stanley House. A meeting was called that night of all the African crews in port, hosted by a few local African residents of Liverpool, and with Ogun acting as chairman. Unable to force the crew back to work, Elder Dempster decided on Thursday, 25 June 25, that the *Apapa* would sail without her African crew. On Sunday, 28 June, the *Apapa* crew was repatriated to Nigeria via airplane, and the rest of the striking crews returned to their ships. The arrival of the *Apapa* crew in Lagos was followed by a mass protest of all crews in port, marching to the prime minister's house and demanding a meeting. The prime minister, Tafawa Balewa, went into the street to hear their grievances, and then invited a delegation of representatives, including Sidi Khayam, in for a meeting. In the aftermath, it was agreed that a committee of inquiry would be formed to investigate the seamen's grievances.

This strike that began in Liverpool was initiated by the seamen, but there were clearly influences from local Liverpool residents, including members of the Socialist Labour League, with both local British and African members in contact with ships' crews and representing their interests to Elder Dempster (Merseyside Maritime Museum 1959e). The role of diaspora Africans and British communists in the inspiration, organisation, leadership and carrying-out of the *M.V. Apapa* strike is highly significant, particularly when compared to the inaction of the Nigerian Seamen's Union's leadership. Liverpool-based Africans, such as a Mr Akinsanya, from an organisation known as the National Union of Nigeria, began meeting with representatives of Elder Dempster to complain about working conditions onboard the *Apapa* over one month before the strike. When the strike broke out, it was members of the National Union of Nigeria in Liverpool that organised crew protests and rallied seamen from other ships to join in the walkout. As soon as the strike broke out, they also sent a written protest to the company, calling themselves the 'African Defence Association'. The letter declared that their group was made up of the 'African Intelligentsia and Literary Detectives of this city' for the purpose of 'protecting the socio-economic interests of our Nigerian Seafaring brothers' and was symbolically signed 'Sojourner Truth'. In make-up and intent, the organisation represented a solidarity bridging Nigerians across the diaspora, and reflected an alliance moving beyond the borders of the mother country, as they wrote: 'In defense of Reason and In Honour's Cause, we speak of Africa and golden joys and as Nigerian Ambassadors of Goodwill we remain in friendships' garden always' (Merseyside Maritime Museum 1959d).

Nigerian seamen in the aftermath of the *Apapa* strike

As far as Elder Dempster was concerned, the strike onboard the *Apapa* did not create any immediate disaster. In fact, the news of the ship that sailed without its African crew provided some comic relief for the British press, which recounted harrowing tales of *Apapa* passengers cleaning their own rooms and serving their own food. The passengers themselves apparently approached the whole incident with equal amusement, and were duly pleased to receive an 'inconvenience compensation' from Elder Dempster at the end of the voyage.

But from the Nigerian government's perspective, the lingering threat of masses of discontented seamen fuelled the decision to appoint a committee of inquiry. This was a typical response of late-colonial regimes faced with strikes during this period. As Cooper (1996, 16) has argued, 'Commissions of inquiry into major strikes were used to delineate ... problem areas' and determine the 'techniques and resources' that would be used 'to set things right.' Investigations conducted in the framework of these inquiries and the final reports they produced 'became apparatuses of surveillance, shapers of discourse, and definers of spaces for legitimate contestation'. In bestowing all authority and judgement in the hands of a commission of inquiry, colonial regimes 'were also saying that Africa's forms of knowledge were irrelevant'.

The establishment of the Board of Enquiry in the case of the *M.V. Apapa* set very clear boundaries for the terrain of the conflict, confining what was being discussed, and who was being represented. 'The Board of the Enquiry into the Trade Dispute between the Elder Dempster Limited Lines and the Nigerian Union of Seamen,' as the investigation was called, was headed by two Nigerian conservatives: the Industrial Relations Commissioner, Thompson Edogbeji Salubi, and the Secretary General of the Trade Union Congress of Nigeria, L.L. Borha, a declared anti-communist. Also on the board was Alfred McClatchey, the secretary of the Employers Consultative Association.

Publicly, Elder Dempster supported the investigation, while privately the company was kept abreast of the committee's work directly from chairman Salubi. Officials at Elder Dempster attempted to have the report serve as a firm condemnation of Sidi Khayam, and hoped that he would be removed in the aftermath. But despite the efforts of the company, the Board of Enquiry was not willing to make any resounding condemnations of the union's general secretary in their report, which was finally released in 1960. In fact, the report had quite the opposite effect, with the recommendations actually forcing Elder Dempster to fully recognise Khayam and to co-operate with him in the establishment of formal mechanisms for representing the interests of both the union and management. Khayam was now a full partner in any future negotiations. The union was to be the official channel for representing all seamen, and responsible for recruitment, registration of seamen, and for negotiating with management.

Following the publication of the report, Khayam marked his decisive victory by celebrating the *Apapa* crisis, as he reminisced:

'It was this incident which led to the inauguration, to the setting up of specific machineries for negotiations and settlement of problems, to the real recognition of the Nigerian Union of Seamen, to more respect of Nigerian Seamen because they had proved they are not cowards but can stand up, protest and demonstrate and assert their views before management. We mustered our families, sons, daughters, wives in the most spectacular demonstration ever held in our country.' The Salubi report, then, had the unintended consequence of bestowing in Khayam a sense of proprietorship over the official narrative of the seamen's victory, and enabled him to boldly re-write the history of his role in it.

Thus, the published report empowered Khayam, and he in turn reminded seamen of his new power: 'From now on, we must devote all our energies in working harder, in improving our skill and mastery of the job, in maintaining respect for our superiors and preserving patience until we are on port to report our grievances to the union.' (Merseyside Maritime Museum 1960)

The granting of legitimacy also meant that Khayam had to adopt a more conciliatory tone with Elder Dempster. The change did not go unnoticed by management, but not everyone was convinced, as one official wrote:

> On the few occasions that I have personally met him, Khayam has always been well behaved. I still, however, subscribe to the view that leopards do not usually change their spots. It may well be that Khayam will reform and I am quite ready to give him this opportunity. I will not, however, disguise the fact that doubts still linger. (Merseyside Maritime Museum 1960a)

The shift in Khayam's position was an outcome of the new alliance with Elder Dempster's management, and this came at the expense of his willingness to represent seamen's concerns. As put by one Elder Dempster official:

> There is a very cordial atmosphere prevailing in our day to day relations with the Nigerian Union of Seamen. Several times in the past few weeks Mr Khayam and other senior Union officials have been in contact with us on various subjects and a great deal of good sense and goodwill has been shown and without going into great detail there have been occasions when misinformed seamen making unreasonable demands have been sharply cautioned in our presence by the Union. (Merseyside Maritime Museum 1960b)

The new proximity to management required that Khayam and the union give up the rhetoric of racial oppression, and one of the successful outcomes of the new order was a narrowing of the union's agenda away from race issues. As Khayam now explained to union members: 'We must effectively learn more and more that it is not only colour. People cheat and oppress others because they believe in oppression which gives them profits, and whether black or white' (Merseyside Maritime Museum 1960).

For the colonial regime, the abandonment of racial discourse provided security that conflicts with African labour would remain within a moderate range of disputes between employers and wage earners. As this was a prerequisite for securing his own position, Sidi Khayam was willing to make this compromise. The move away from racial discourse also helped Khayam justify his demand that seamen turn their gaze toward Lagos rather than Liverpool in their search for leadership. Seeking the unambiguous loyalty of the Nigerian seamen, Khayam began to see Liverpool activists as bad influences, and worked with Elder Dempster to cut ties between seamen and the Nigerian National Union based in Liverpool. Under the banner of 'Nigerianisation', the union leadership was able to consolidate its power over the rank-and file membership. 'Nigerianisation' enabled the union to refuse contact with international seamen's unions, and remove dissident Freetown ratings from the Lagos registers. Independence thus justified a turn inwards, and a hardening of ideological, discursive, and identity borders around new states and away from alternative communities. The shift in Khayam's attitude and tactics was in line with the political manoeuvres of many African elites in the era of decolonisation, ultimately impacting the nature of political regimes in the post-colonial era. As Cooper (1996, 5) claimed:

> the study of labour in the period of decolonisation can give us some kind of indication of how Africans ended up with the kind of independence [they] got – politically assertive and socially conservative regimes focused on their control of the coercive, patronage, and symbolic apparatus of the state, distrustful of and hostile to the continued influence of social movements that once helped challenge the colonial state, fearful of groups that might make claims.

Conclusion

For Nigerian seamen, the political and ideological currents favoring the strengthening of the union served to disempower them in their ship-based protests, and the union's insistence that crews rely solely on a 'Nigerian' leadership rather than a fluid set of tools based in a multitude of locations represented a profound silencing. The imposition of Nigerianisation severed the historic racial and class links that seamen had forged between themselves and others beyond the borders of Nigeria. The *Apapa* strike, and hundreds of incidents leading up to this action, grew out of a belief among African seamen that they could achieve the vision of justice they constructed for themselves. Their struggles were not limited to concerns over pay scales and clothing allowances, but expressed deeper and more fundamental wishes for colour-blind camaraderie of men, perhaps similar to that enjoyed by black seamen in the days of sailing. Crews fought discrimination through transnational alliances, and their sense of empowerment led to creative and forceful initiatives such as walk-outs and demands for firing of their European bosses. The Salubi inquiry was a typical and effective tactic of the colonial regime and local westernised elites to eliminate the radical and destabilising creative force of African labourers that was so clearly evident in the *Apapa* strike.

In the era following the publication of the Salubi Report, seamen continued to suffer racial oppression, but they also internalised the fact that they could no longer protest for themselves. This can be seen in the following letter from the crew of the *M.V. Apapa* at port in Liverpool in 1961:

> to our greatest surprise, when we arrive at Las Palmas this trip .... the stewards who feel to buy drinks collect their money and give it to one man. The cleaners do likewise. On those men returning the ship, the captain was on the gangway himself and started to dump these drinks in the water before the passengers who were looking [at] the view of the town. Despite all the pleas by the head cleaner, he dump everything, including only one that Ibeji hold for himself. ... Despite all the explanations to the captain, the drinks were dumped. The attitude so provoked our minds. Because none of that of the [white] sailors were dumped so we [took] it for another discrimination so an emergency general meeting was called and it last 20 minutes. We took a decision the two head men were delegated to the captain that we the entire crew want our drinks or he pay for them. ... the captain promised to pay for the drinks. The headmen told him ... that he cannot take it upon himself to accept the money for the whole crew ... before we sail way on the Thursday the 20th we do not take any step either, we are just putting it to your knowledge at the same time we would like to know from you whether to receive the money from him or not. Reply not needed until our arrival. (Merseyside Maritime Museum 1961)

The seamen's letter is testimony to the entrenchment of the union's authority in the post-colonial era, and the recognition among seamen that they could no longer act for themselves. We have seen that Nigerian seamen successfully exploited opportunities arising within the context of colonialism to participate in globalised economies and cultures, exposing them to new solidarities and empowering them to seek an improvement in their lives. At the same time, ruling elites in both Europe and Nigeria took political, economic and ideological actions to secure lasting power and influence for themselves, and this occurred continually at the expense of seamen's autonomy. Although intent on engaging with the globalised world, African seamen were ultimately prevented from securing for themselves positions of power and autonomy as an effective labour movement in the post-colonial context. Thus, for ordinary seamen, changes with nationalisation did result in a change in the definition of the possible, but what was possible was, in many regards, far less.

References

Bolster, J., 1997. *Black Jacks: African American seamen in the age of sail*. Cambridge: Harvard University Press.

Cooper, F., 1996. *Decolonization and African society: the labor question in French and British Africa*. Cambridge: Cambridge University Press.

Davies, P.N., 2000. *The trade makers: Elder Dempster in West Africa, 1852–1972, 1973–1989*. St. John's, Newfoundland: International Maritime Economic History Association.

Ewald, J.J., 2000. Crossers of the sea: slaves, freedmen, and other migrants in the northwestern Indian Ocean, c. 1750–1914. *The American historical review*, 105 (1), 69–91.

Frost, D., 1999. *Work and community in among West African migrant workers since the nineteenth century*. Liverpool: Liverpool University Press.

Gilroy, P., 1993. *The black Atlantic: modernity and double consciousness*. Cambridge, MA: Harvard University Press.

Linebaugh, P. and Rediker, M., 2001. *The many-headed hydra: the hidden history of the revolutionary Atlantic*. Boston, MA: Beacon Press.

Merseyside Maritime Museum, 1954. 4C 1908 Nigerian Union of Seamen Apapa strike 1959. Letter from Elder Dempster representative in Lagos to M.B. Glasier, 19 February 1954.

Merseyside Maritime Museum, 1958. 4C 1908 Nigerian Union 1959–1962. Letter from A. Monday to M.B. Glasier, 10 October 1958.

Merseyside Maritime Museum, 1959. 4C 1908 Nigerian Union of Seamen 1959–1962. Letter from the Secretariat and Education Bureau to the general membership, 10 January 1959.

Merseyside Maritime Museum, 1959a. 4C 1908 Nigerian Union of Seamen 1959–1962. Letter from R.H. Chalcroft to M. Glasier, 10 February 1959.

Merseyside Maritime Museum, 1959b. 4C 1908 Nigerian Union of Seamen 1959–1962. Presidential address by S.M. Ekore, 15 May 1959.

Merseyside Maritime Museum, 1959c. 4C 1908 Nigerian Union of Seamen 1959–1962. Letter from the Shipping Federation to M.B. Glasier, 25 June 1959.

Merseyside Maritime Museum, 1959d. 4C 1908 Nigerian Union of Seamen 1959–1962. African Defence Association (signed from Sojourner Truth) to Mr Glasier, 30 June 1959.

Merseyside Maritime Museum, 1959e. 4C 1908 Nigerian Union of Seamen 1959–1962. Letter from M.B. Glasier to R.N. Chalcroft, 6 July 1959.

Merseyside Maritime Museum, 1959–1962. 4C 1908 Nigerian Union of Seamen 1959–1962.

Merseyside Maritime Museum, 1960. 4C 1908 Nigerian Seamen's Union. Sidi Khayam address to the First Delegates Conference. (No date, but must be in 1960 at the earliest because of reference to Salubi enquiry.)

Merseyside Maritime Museum, 1960a. The Nigeria Shipping Federation to M.B. Glasier, 9 January 1960.

Merseyside Maritime Museum, 1960b. Elder Dempster, Lagos. Robertson to Steamship Nautical Dept, Liverpool, 26 April 1960.

Merseyside Maritime Museum, 1961. 4C 1908 Nigerian Seamen's Union. Crew letter from the m.v. Apapa in Liverpool to Gen. Sec. Sidi Khayam, 18 July 1961.

Report of the Board of Enquiry into the trade dispute between the Elder Dempster Lines Limited and the Nigerian Union of Seamen, 1959. Lagos, Nigeria.

Report of the Board of Enquiry into the trade dispute, 1959a. Lagos, Nigeria, Appendix C.

Sherwood, M., 1995. Strikes! African seamen, Elder Dempster and the government 1940–42. *In*: D. Frost, ed. *Ethnic labour and British imperial trade: a history of ethnic seafarers in the UK*. London: Frank Cass.

What goes around, comes around: rotating credit associations among Ethiopian women in Israel

Hagar Salamon[a], Steven Kaplan[b] and Harvey Goldberg[c]

[a]Jewish and Comparative Folklore, The Mandel Institute of Jewish Studies, The Harry S. Truman Research Institute for the Advancement of Peace, The Hebrew University of Jerusalem, Jerusalem, Israel; [b]Comparative Religion and Middle Eastern and Islamic Studies, The Harry S. Truman Research Institute for the Advancement of Peace, The Hebrew University of Jerusalem, Jerusalem, Israel; [c]Sarah Allen Shaine Chair in Sociology and Anthropology, Department of Sociology and Anthropology (Emeritus), Jerusalem, Israel

This article looks at how working-class Ethiopian women, who have migrated to Israel, have sought empowerment and economic control through the establishment of rotating credit associations known as *iqqub*. In the changing world of Ethiopian Israeli women, *iqqub* associations and their specific cultural manifestations constitute a highly meaningful experience, whose building-blocks incorporate the financial, the social, the ritualistic, and the symbolic. It is a complex mechanism of tradition and renewal: its existence challenges paternalistic assumptions regarding the status of Ethiopian immigrants vis-à-vis the state and its institutions and the experience of Ethiopian Israeli women specifically. As we shall demonstrate, the *iqqub* serves as a generative focus for gender relations and the dramatic changes that have affected them. Ethnographic examination of the *iqqub* and its internal discourse expands our understanding of the dynamics of change among the group's cultural, gender, and power relations.

Once a month, on or around the 20th, a group of ten Ethiopian Israeli women meet in their neighbourhood in Israel. They are members of an *iqqub*, spending an evening during which, in their words, 'they drink with money'. The group's members all immigrated to Israel about 25 years ago, and have young children for whom they receive National Insurance child benefit payments on the 20th of every month. Another *iqqub* meets once a month, always after the 28th. It also has about 10 members, mostly mothers of adult children. The women in this second group do not work, but rather subsist on their old-age pension, which they receive on the 28th of each month. In both these cases, the *iqqub* serves as a member-organised financial and social support group. While not limited to women by definition, these are clearly gender-based organisations. This article will focus on *iqqubewoch*[1] of Ethiopian Israeli women.

An *iqqub* (sometimes referred to as *quve*) is established when a small group of 10 to 20 women come together to create a rotating financial circle, typically on a local or even neighbourhood basis. The amount of money to be contributed by each member at the monthly meeting is determined in advance by the participants, and the entire fund collected is awarded at each meeting to one participant who has been chosen by lottery. The amount paid by members per session varies widely among groups, ranging at the time of our research from 300 to 1000 sheqels. The length of an *iqqub* cycle is determined by the number of members, each of whom contributes a fixed sum at each meeting, and receives the entire pool once per cycle. A lottery held at the end of each meeting decides who among those who has not yet received the 'jackpot' will receive it at the next meeting. In most *iqqubewoch*, this lucky recipient is also the hostess of her 'jackpot' meeting. After a cycle is completed, members may choose either to dismantle the group or start a new cycle. These local organisations serve as group credit and savings mechanisms that are unique in their social and symbolic aspects. Each group formulates its own by-laws and holds its monthly ritual meeting, which adheres to binding rules (referred to by members as 'laws') that are recorded in an internal document specifically regulating the meetings' hosting, agenda and content.

While the world of Ethiopian Israeli women has been addressed in the literature on the Ethiopian community's integration in Israel, the *iqqub* and the central role of women within it has not yet been the subject of intensive research. Numerous reports, articles and dissertations have focused on domestic violence, divorce, single-parent families, menstrual purity, and the redrawing of gender relations, [2] but the cultural aspects of finances and financial initiatives by Ethiopian Israelis, and women in particular, have been neglected.[3] The one exception is the conventional wisdom that the Israeli system of *Bituach Leumi* (lit. National Insurance, the Israeli social security system) has afforded these women a degree of economic independence that they lacked in Ethiopia.

As we shall demonstrate, the study of the *iqqub* is of interest not merely because it can shed light on yet another feature of the lives of Ethiopian Israelis, but rather due to its nature as a complex mechanism of tradition and renewal: its existence challenges paternalistic assumptions regarding the status of Ethiopian immigrants vis-à-vis the state and its institutions and the experience of Ethiopian Israeli women specifically.[4] Our study examines a phenomenon that has gathered momentum over the years and which encompasses a significant percentage of Ethiopian Israeli women.[5] In addition, this financial association serves as a generative focus for gender relations and the dramatic changes that have affected them. Ethnographic examination of the *iqqub* and its internal discourse allows us to focus on our ever-expanding understanding of the dynamics of change among the group's cultural, gender, and power relations.

As several of the articles in this issue demonstrate, the process of migration for African labour has led to a break with life and opportunities in their homelands, but it has also afforded working classes and, in our example, women, new opportunities for cultural, personal and material renewal and empowerment. This article looks at how working-class Ethiopian women, including many who have been transformed from peasants and artisans to members of an urban working class, have sought empowerment and economic security through the establishment of independent credit and loan institutions.[6] Even those who have not formally entered the labour markets have benefited from stable incomes due to the social policies of the Israeli welfare state. Indeed, this case raises the interesting, general question of whether one needs to actually work in a paying job in either the formal or informal sector to be part of the working class.

Moreover, the example of the *iqqub* shows how African working classes in an African diaspora have established safety-nets that employ cultural practices and symbols from homeland traditions (Ethiopia – real or imagined) and synthesise these with local cultural and material circumstances in the host society. The article thus contributes to our understanding of how working classes borrow cultural forms to enhance and ensure their economic security as well as a sense of social belonging. We also get a sense of how material practices are linked to cultural practices.

In terms of literature on working classes in the African diaspora, Ethiopian Israelis present a particularly interesting case because their identity can be seen to be divided between two competing conceptions of homeland and diaspora. Ethiopian Israelis are obviously part of the Ethiopian diaspora in the plain sense of the dispersion of Ethiopian nationals from their homeland. As such they are the second-largest Ethiopian diaspora community, exceeded in numbers only by the United States.

However, while there is little question that Ethiopian Israelis should be discussed in any discussion of Ethiopians abroad – as refugees, immigrants, migrant labourers, or even transnationals – their place in the Ethiopian diaspora is far more complex. Virtually all the recent literature on diaspora is in agreement that 'diaspora' is not merely a product of geography, but also of worldview and cultural orientation – a 'diaspora consciousness' (Butler 2002, Safran 1991, 1999, 2005, Gilroy 1994, Clifford 1994). In this respect, it must be noted that Ethiopian Israelis to a significant extent portray themselves and are depicted by other Israelis not as an Ethiopian diaspora, but as a Jewish community which has returned 'home' after centuries in the African diaspora (Salamon 2003, Kaplan, forthcoming). Moreover, they are to an extent perhaps unequalled by any African migrant group in the world highly visible in their new surroundings. Prior to the immigration of the Ethiopians to Israel, the total number of residents in Israel of sub-Saharan African descent – including the Black Hebrews of Dimona (Markowitz et al. 2003), Muslims of African origin (Miles 1997) and Ethiopian Christians (Cerulli 1943–47, Pedersen 1983) probably did not exceed a thousand people. Even the influx of African guest workers from Ghana and Nigeria in the 1990s (Sabar 2004) only slightly altered this situation.

One consequence of this situation is that in Israel virtually all people of African descent are assumed to be Ethiopians by most other citizens of the country. Consequently, Ethiopian Israelis need to invest far less energy in the 'performance' of their Ethiopian identity than do their countrymen in other diaspora communities, in which other populations of African descent are well established (Salamon 2003). Thus the flourishing of the *iqqub* in Israel is not an attempt to make a public display of their Ethiopian identity, but rather as we shall discuss in greater detail below, an internal sharing of an intimate inner group sensibility.

The *iqqub* and similar financial associations

Rotating financial associations have been documented in varied cultural contexts. Termed ROSCAs (rotating savings and credit associations), they have been the subject of longitudinal studies whose results have been published in detailed quantitative reports and social and economic research, particularly of the functionalist anthropological school.

In 1962, Clifford Geertz published an article on ROSCAs in Java in which he suggested that they represent an 'intermediate stage', or the product of the transition from a traditionalist agrarian to a commercial society. Geertz viewed these associations as educational mechanisms by which traditional peasants learned to become traders in the broad cultural sense. Two years later, in 1964, the British anthropologist Shirley Ardener, who conducted research in Cameroon and Nigeria, published a comprehensive article describing the phenomenon's prevalence and diversity. Ardener defined a ROSCA as 'an association formed upon a core of participants who make regular contributions to a fund which is given, in whole or in part, to each contributor in rotation' (Ardener and Burman 1995, p. 1).

Some 40 years later, Ardener re-examined the phenomenon in the opening chapter of a volume which she co-edited. This collection of papers edited by Ardener and Burman (1995) focused on contemporary, exclusively female groups. Its comparative perspective emphasised the need to understand the phenomenon of the different ROSCAs in each of their own particular cultural contexts.

Although *iqqub* associations are not documented in Ethiopia prior to the late nineteenth and early twentieth centuries, they are nonetheless customarily treated as a 'traditional' Ethiopian institution. Based on evidence for the existence of similar associations in India, Southeast Asia and Africa, it has been claimed that the institution was imported into Ethiopia via Indian traders. Others have asserted that the Ethiopian *iqqub* originated in the country itself and spread among the different ethnic groups, thus becoming a pan-Ethiopian cultural institution that includes Ethiopians regardless of religion, ethnicity, class or gender.[7] Whatever its origin, the research literature is in agreement regarding the *iqqub's* prevalence during the second half of the twentieth century in urban Ethiopia, and the inroads made by similar rural Ethiopian associations. The flourishing of such associations in Ethiopia is typically explained by the proliferation of the use of money, financial instability, and the absence of a formal banking system.[8]

Iqqub associations are ubiquitous in present-day urban Ethiopia, as well as in many rural areas where a money-based economy has been established. Moreover, similar associations have been documented among Ethiopian immigrants to the West, as well as in the Ethiopian diaspora in a number of cities including Boston, Los Angeles, Washington, and New York in the USA, Toronto, Canada, and Oxford, England. Previously, many of these Ethiopian émigrés were well-off city-dwellers, primarily from Addis Ababa (Ornguze 1997, Taa 2003, Almedom 1995, Worku 2002).

Complex references to the Israeli banking system, welfare, and National Insurance authorities figure prominently in the discourse of Ethiopian Israeli *iqqub* associations. These references dismantle the dichotomy that positions formal against informal economic reasoning. The present study examines the way *iqqub* members perceive the phenomenon in its entirety as a system whose financial and symbolic threads are interwoven, forming a unified, flexible, and virtuosic cultural entity which invokes references to both Ethiopian and Israeli contexts.

Economic considerations

In our interviews, particularly at the outset of each conversation on this topic, interviewees were often ill at ease. Apparently, this had to do with their concern that the *iqqub* – which is not familiar to non-Ethiopian Israelis – is viewed as improper, perhaps even forbidden and illegal. The fact that use is often made of 'government-coloured' money – National Insurance money, which is exchanged outside the formal banking system – seems to add to this feeling of unease.[9] The concealed, loaded, internal, perhaps even subversive nature of these associations is perhaps an explanation for their near-total neglect in the vast literature documenting Ethiopian attempts to cope with the dramatic changes experienced in Israel.[10] Their existence was revealed to us by chance during interviews with Ethiopian Israelis on entirely different topics. One interviewee told us explicitly that: 'in Israel the *iqqub* is considered illegal, is considered gambling... Most Ethiopians do *iqqub* quietly, because they have heard maybe that here in Israel gambling is not allowed.'

Nonetheless, once we began asking directly about these credit associations, referring to them using Ethiopian terms, we heard about them repeatedly. Discussions of the topic became relaxed and more specific as the interviews progressed. Interviewees' initial hesitancy to discuss the phenomenon melted away, and they became increasingly proud as they described its financial advantages and even proposed – in an almost missionary tone – that the female interviewer join them in 'drinking with money'. In most interviews, the *iqqub's* social importance was explicitly stated. The interval between collecting and receiving the money is understood as an important component in sustaining the ongoing commitment between group members. In view of the shared financial arrangements, members are committed to maintaining stable relations between group members, and to helping each other in times of celebration and mourning, thereby adding a moral dimension to the *iqqub*. Thus, alongside the financial explanation – generally immediately following it – the interviewees stressed the associations' importance in both supporting their lives outside the meetings and in the social enjoyment of the meetings themselves. Through the ritual and symbolic mechanisms that encourage and process the codes that lie at the foundation of each group, the mutual commitment is validated anew at each meeting. One participant told us:

> The *quve* is not only for money. If you are in a *quve*, if God forbid something happens in your family, there is more support, [members] come, help with money, too, and with expenses, and with hosting guests, and in celebrations – you feel a more personal connection, more responsibility toward each other. In general – it is customary to help each other, to come visit when someone is sick, visiting when [someone] dies, especially. You make sure you go. If you don't go, no matter the reason, you are not forgiven! And that is hard. In Ethiopia it was easier to go to one another's [home], here – it's harder.

In summing up the *quve's* advantages she added: 'It's good. When you want to buy something and there's no money – the *quve* helps – it gives hope.'

As stated above, the characterisation of the *iqqub* as a 'traditional' association warrants careful consideration, all the more so as regards the Beta Israel in Ethiopia. While similar associations are found in many parts of Ethiopia, and some Ethiopian Israelis knew of and sometimes even participated in such groups, most of our interviewees stated that there was no *iqqub* in their villages in Ethiopia, and that they had learned of its existence only after making *aliyah* to Israel. This was explained by the practical aspect of a traditional rural economy that lacked significant use of money.[11] The Jews of Ethiopia immigrated to Israel in several waves and by a number of routes, and many of the Beta Israel began to take part in financial groups while awaiting *aliyah*.[12]

Another point touches upon terminology and the insights it reveals. While meetings are often conducted in a mixture of Hebrew, Amharic and Tigrinia, Hebrew is the language in which the group's rules are written, as it is most of the immigrants' primary written language. Nevertheless, the association is perceived as uniquely Ethiopian and is always referred to by its Ethiopian name. Use of Ethiopian terms to conceptualise the association is shared throughout the Ethiopian diaspora around the world, connecting Ethiopians outside of Ethiopia with Ethiopian cultural heritage. Thus, the *iqqub's* appearance in Israel can be largely viewed as yet another expression of the complexity embodied in the term 'preserving tradition' as applied to Ethiopian and other ethnic manifestations in Israel (Kaplan and Rosen 1993). Whether participants became familiar with the *iqqub* while still in their villages in Ethiopia, during their transition period via Addis Ababa or the Sudan, or only following *aliyah* to Israel, an ever-increasing number of Ethiopian-Israeli women appear to be utilising the support offered by these kinds of 'Ethiopian' associations in their new life in Israel.

This support, which relies on a mutual assistance mechanism that originated in Ethiopia, does not mean that *iqqub* participants are unfamiliar with the 'new' Israeli banking system. Rather they maintain a symbiotic relationship with the banking establishment; it is split in members' consciousness, as will be evidenced in their discourse, between the poles of the empowering and the threatening. State money deposited in the bank becomes the primary source of the female *iqqub*'s funds, while the bank itself is described in the 'male' terms of exploitation and hidden knowledge. Both these poles were repeatedly described as central to the foundations of *iqqub* associations in Israel.

Thus, for example, a female participant of about 70, who depends upon income supplements and her old-age pension, explains:

> Look, today it is hard with the banks. They take service fees and they are not 'okay' anymore. For every page you print out, they take a service fee. Even on savings there is a service fee of about 300 sheqels a year ... Maybe I if I lack something, or my son needs something ... he cannot get [a loan from a bank] because he is too young. This month it's my turn to receive [the *iqqub* fund] on the 29th.

In another interview, a young woman of about 20 explains, '... the adults here can't save money in the bank – they don't work – so they can have something like "savings" from the National Insurance'.

Further, as a member of another *iqqub* indicated, the *iqqub* is intended to complement, not replace the banking system. In contrast to the bank, which is portrayed as alienating, forbidding and inaccessible, the *iqqub* is familiar, tailor-made to fit the participants' needs. The *iqqub* in Israel, whose timing is determined by the date on which National Insurance payments or employees' salaries are deposited in the bank, facilitates a connection between the two financial systems. Both practically and symbolically, it allows members to 'own' the alienating system, while assimilating it into the traditional institution. One participant explains:

> The advantage of the *quve* is that there's no 'minus' to close. When you take a loan from the bank, you pay back interest as well. There is no interest in the *quve*. If you need the money urgently, you can ask to be first. If you need quick cash to pay back loans or to cover your overdraft at the bank, you can quickly use the *quve* so you will have [money]. There is no overdraft with the *quve*. What there is, you get 'netto' [clear]. It helps you return money after you took a loan from the bank, you can cover it with the *quve*. And there is also the social aspect, which there isn't at the bank. They [the members] help with other things. They see that you have something urgent – talk to each other and decide how to help. The *quve* is not just money, but also help on a daily basis.

Another participant explains:

> We put in 600 sheqels each time. When there were two of us, it was 1200 sheqels. [Now] every month it's 600. I now receive 1000 sheqels a month from National Insurance. [I have] six children, so I receive 1000 sheqels. I put 600 in the *iqqub*. On the day of the party I have to bring the money. I receive money for the children on the 20th of the month. If this falls on a Thursday, we don't have [a meeting]. There are weddings, there are parties, so we meet as close as we can after the 20th, perhaps the 21st or 22nd ... as late as the 25th, but no later. We try not to be later, so there will still be money.

While the *iqqub* described above includes only mothers of children under 18, an older women's group holds its meetings according to the date of deposit of their income supplements[13]:

> We have an *iqqub*. Every month we hold it, girls only. They [the men] have one too – did you think they'd give it up? [Our *iqqub*] is of girls we trust. We've had it for three years already ... We always hold it on the 29th of the month. Do you want to join us? We'll collect you [take you on] ... Whoever drops money on time, collects money on time.

Another participant compares the *quve* in Gondar with one held in Israel, where employed men and women participate. She reiterates the arrangement whereby the *iqqub*'s dates coincide exactly with receipt of salaries in the participants' bank accounts:

In Israel, in my *quve*, everyone works … Once a month in Israel we get a salary on the 10th of the month, so the *quve* is on the Friday evening. We have the *quve* before Shabbat … In Ethiopia we would hold the *quve* at the home of a woman who sold *mashilla* [roasted corn kernels] and all kinds of things like that – a fixed place. We went to her place, and didn't know who would receive that evening. Here in Israel, wherever we hold it, the hosts receive the money that evening, unless someone asks to move up his turn – then we let him … Now there are 14 people in my *quve* – each person puts in 1000 sheqels a month, and receives 14,000 at his turn. We set the amount at the beginning. If someone wants [to give] 2000 sheqels, she'll put in her daughter and her name too. If someone wants to pay double, he'll get double on his name.

Social considerations

In the participants' discourse, the social support provided by the *iqqub* is fortified by the connection between the formal financial system and the informal social system. The close link between financial and social benefits, of which the *iqqub* constitutes a practical and ideological axis, has been identified in other cultural contexts as well. For example, Busha J. Taa quotes an interviewee, an immigrant from Ethiopia to Toronto, as follows: 'Indigenous organizations … are comfort zones that shelter immigrants from desperation. They support a positive start up in the new country … These organizations are good places of comfort' (Taa 2003, 255).

In contrast to the attitudes expressed by participants of the female *iqqub*, a male interviewee describes the enjoyment he derived from his family *iqqub* in connection with the topics raised by the group's men and women of all ages:

… People come to our *iqqub* from all over: from Netivot, from Jerusalem, from Haifa. It's a great pleasure. We tell stories, it connects us to Ethiopia. I was disconnected. For me it's been a history lesson. We talk about politics. Not personal, family matters.

This family *iqqub* always takes place on Saturday, and the money is transferred before Shabbat begins, corresponding with the group's historical and religious themes and its heterogeneous composition. But here as well an emphasis is placed on laughter as a central liberating component of the *iqqub*. He adds:

In my group, two older families live on National Insurance and all the rest work. The women and the men. We come on Friday, for the whole weekend [Friday and Saturday]. Each person brings some food. There is a *kiddush*, Shabbat songs, we sing a lot and exalt the Creator. The person in charge writes down whose turn it is at the beginning, then each person takes out money, it is counted and collected. The person in charge writes down that each person has given the host money. In Ethiopia, I don't know if it was done … I recommend having an *iqqub*. It connects you to your roots. It's not the same as at the bank. You need the human touch, the laughter. The material aspect is not the important thing. Everyone talks with everyone. The young people tell jokes. One of the pleasures there is telling jokes about the day-to-day blunders. It's spontaneous. Lots of laughter. Everyone laughs with everyone. They tell how it was in the villages, everyone tells how it used to be (in Ethiopia), we make comparisons.

Both the historical stories and the jokes about the blunders can be deciphered as a dismantling and reassembling of loaded themes in the lives of the Ethiopian community in Israel. The supportive group framework, along with the financial concretisation enabled by its ongoing commitment, is shared by the different *iqqubewoch* in Israel. Examination of the female *iqqubewoch*, their unique characteristic praxis and discourse, reveals explicit female empowerment. This issue, for which we found no parallel in the literature on ROSCAs around the world, was striking in its clarity for Ethiopian Israeli women. Expressions of empowerment are used to describe the very existence of the *iqqub* in Israel, as well as the specific content raised during its monthly meetings. A participant in a young mothers' *iqqub* recounts:

> So we drink, we chat, we talk ... all kinds [of talk]. Who was where, who did what, all kinds of things. Sometimes [laughs] about the husbands, too. Sometimes we tell about the [children's] kindergarten ... some work for the Jewish Agency and they tell about what goes on at the agency, or those who work in a kindergarten tell about the children at the Ethiopian children's kindergarten, or about the new immigrants, those from the Agency tell, about the Falashmura[14] they talk, they laugh, about how they behave, that they don't know [how to behave], and then we also drink *bun* [coffee]. Sometimes maybe a little about clothes. We dress nicely with a little bit of gold. I wear nail polish, but not too much, not like for a wedding. I take a shower, put on perfume, wear jewellery from here, not from Ethiopia. It gives a feeling of fun.

The immigration theme is processed at the young mothers' group meetings: fixed topics are discussed, accompanied by liberating laughter. Other subjects exclusive to the female *iqqub* include references to family life, intimate relations between men and women, as well as couples' financial arrangements and use of their money. The marking of the *iqqub* money as 'female' is central to the interpretation of the issues processed within its framework. A clearly empowering connection is created between the state and the women by means of the designated funds that are transferred on fixed dates from the state to the women and from the women to the *iqqub*, using the funds in a way that corresponds with the state's original intent. Another participant spoke explicitly of female empowerment:

> There's *quve* for women only. There's also *quve* for men only. In every aspect, when it is mixed, the women are not free. They won't feel free. So usually there are men separately and women separately ... The *quve* betters her status. First of all, she gets self-confidence. She can buy things for herself, and she can buy for the house and the children.

Indeed, in the present study, the *iqqub*'s image as an institution of women's empowerment clearly emerges from the words of many participants. For example, a female participant in a mixed *iqqub* recounts:

> Most important are the meetings. The money is worthwhile too. Now, here, we want to be with each other. The women love to be together and stay after the [financial part of] the *quve* and talk to each other. The men leave right after the *quve*. When the men are present – [we] are guarded, like your religious people, even with eyes open, we don't look [at members of the opposite sex]. Even me, and I was born in a city ... when the men leave, the women speak, talk about their husbands, 'He doesn't give me money, he doesn't act nicely.' There is no embarrassment, everything is on the table. Anger between husbands and wives – we tell each other about that, too.

The *iqqub* offers Ethiopian Israeli women both support and enjoyment. The women extol the liberating framework of the association in general, and of each meeting. If, however, the ROSCA is by its very nature a supportive, empowering counter-institutional framework, then the ethnographic study enables us to decipher particular manifestations of this empowerment. The remainder of the discussion will, then, provide an in-depth examination of *iqqub*'s meetings, symbolic and ritual aspects, and discourse.

Founding and rules

The founding of an *iqqub* group typically comes out of an initial conversation between two or more women. They propose additional participants, usually from among their neighbours or relatives who live nearby. One participant recounts:

> Those who have means build a group for others with means, money follows money. Those who have go to those who have ... Anyone can set up a *quve*. It doesn't have to be family,

it can be acquaintances or neighbours. But from the same region. But it's kind of a problem to stop – if I received a sum of money, I have to continue the round until everyone has received, and only when it's my turn to receive, I'm allowed to leave.

In the Israeli *iqqub*, the founders choose women similar to them financially, that is, with the same funding sources. At the founding meeting, they set a rigid framework of binding rules that are formulated in writing in a detailed contract, and which are not to be revoked. While typically, women (and men) in rural Ethiopia did not know how to read or write, most of the younger women in Israel have acquired a degree of literacy. However, this important resource is still not to be taken for granted among the community. The group's dynamic components are set carefully at the outset as well. A female member discusses evasion, social sanctions and discontinuation of membership:

Whoever wants to join, the most important thing is to bring money. She has to pay, there is no such thing [as not paying]. So far this has not happened. You know what they would do to her? They'd finish her until she paid. They'd send the 'big ones' [respected members of the community] to her, to tell her that she owes money and if she doesn't pay … or else, she can say she has no money so she can't continue – that's different. If she can't, we'll return her money as long as she hasn't taken [from the fund] yet.

Another member lends a tough, obligatory aspect to participation in the *iqqub*: 'Whoever wants to stop, can't! If he returns what he received – then he can leave, but there's no chance, because it's a lot of money.'

In another interview a female member added:

Everyone has [an *iqqub*]; there are a lot of them. I'm in one, for instance, but there are some who drink at several. There's one woman who has a 600 sheqel *iqqub* with us, and another of 700 sheqels, so every month she puts in 1300 sheqels for both her *iqqubewoch*. Over there [at the second *iqqub*] there are 16 people, so whenever it's hers [her turn to receive the fund] it's a lot of money! … But there are some who talk, there are a lot of them. There are girls who badmouth, or just come and talk, so you understand? We don't want them. Look, we've been drinking now for, how long? Five years. So five years we've been. There was just one who participated and left, and she's already come back. She came back again. Because [when she left], she didn't have enough money. She was drinking for two, so she didn't have enough money. So she said she didn't have enough. Now she's back. Because she was with us on the first list, we let her come back, but if she hadn't been with us, we wouldn't have let her back. Got it?

This description indicates the group commitment that is established at the group's founding meeting and exemplified in the participant's interpretation of the term '*iqqub*' as fixed, a binding obligation.[15] While this obligation is a moral one, it also finds expression in the group's by-laws. Members can be added to the circle only if all members agree. Often, the newest member will be marked separately, and will participate in the group's financial aspects only, not its social aspects. Conversely, a participant who was herself present at the founding of the group is allowed to return after leaving the *iqqub*.

Another expression of this attitude is found in the words of another male participant, who describes members' strong commitment to each other:

The original group has continued from 1998 until today, nine years without interruption. We have become a family already. It has happened that people met and even got married. Connections have been made. During mourning or celebration, the *iqqub*'s people come and help. I, for example, was abroad, and I intend to return to the same *iqqub*. A special place is reserved for me. They will be offended. If I go to another *iqqub*, they'll be offended. That's because a good connection was made between everyone … Whoever is late pays a fine. It is set ahead of time. At our *iqqub* it was 100 sheqels. If you didn't notify 24 hours before the meeting that you'll be late or that you cannot come, you're fined. If you don't come, depending on the reason, if it is justified. That evening we'd call him and maybe forgo his fine. If someone was ill, couldn't make it, we'd understand, in general we believe them.

The *iqqub* is indeed characterised by a binding set of rules and regulations, which may be classified by the formality of their formulation. Interviewees have described the recording of *iqqub* rules in by-laws or a contract of sorts, typically at the group's founding meeting. This document is usually kept by the *iqqub*'s founding members.[16] The documented rules exist alongside those set verbally at the same meeting and rules of conventional behavior that do not need to be put in writing. One participant talks about the rules:

> We also have a letter, we wrote everything down. We wrote down what needs to be brought, that whoever is late has to bring ten sheqels ... The money [for being late] goes into the fund. We already have 300 sheqels in late fees [laughs]. I actually pay a lot for being late. Yes, I've already paid about 60 sheqels, over the five years I have had to pay. You're late, so you pay. Because it's not good to be late. Let's say we start at 6:30, then if you arrive at 7:30 ... then it's good to come on time, not be late. Because let's say we want to eat, some let's say came straight from work and haven't eaten. So we want to start and wait until she comes. So if she pays, she'll come on time. Everyone comes on time. They come in panting [demonstrates]. Running, kind of. Everyone really looks at their watches. Five minutes late, they already pay ten sheqels. So we now that if we are five minutes late, we pay. Then you may even come earlier. You need to come at 6:30, so you'll come at 6:25, maybe 6:00. Doesn't matter. The important thing is not come after 6:30. That's how it's done, that's how we wrote it. We also wrote in the beginning about the food, what to make. We wrote that there needs to be chicken, *injera* [a pan-fried Ethiopian bread], and eggs to put inside, hard-boiled eggs. And fruit and drink. About food and lateness we wrote.

The commitment is intensified by setting the rules alongside the sanctions which follow in the event of their violation.[17] Using a somewhat functional approach, the 'late fees' may be interpreted as a form of 'practising' punctuality, among other modern skills needed for a bureaucratised, legalised world, within a supportive framework. This component of adapting to Israeli society may be linked with participants' description of adherence to the rules that they have created for themselves, and the empowerment created by the very ability to shape for themselves rules that are typically imposed upon them from above. Here the narrator describes the meeting's liberating elements. In another conversation we held on the topic, she explained that it was important not to be offended by the teasing that goes on in *iqqub* meetings, which is well known among participants: 'We already know that we don't have to be offended.'

Below we present two descriptions of what constitutes proper, customary participants' behaviour, from two male participants in mixed-gender family *iqqubewoch*:

> ... Each person comes with groceries for Friday and Shabbat: seeds, beverages, cookies. My offering was simple. I was a soldier, and I wasn't ashamed. Each according to his ability. There are no fixed things – not necessarily. When I was a soldier, I prepared chicken – all parts. If there are the funds, someone makes mutton – it's recommended. I was a soldier then, and I couldn't afford it. Some made meat instead of chicken. *Tella* [beer] – a very, very strong drink, like champagne. Only Ethiopians have it. Some women drink it, but mostly men. *Tella*, *injera*, *buna*, coffee. On Saturday night we drink *buna*, *kulu* [roasted seeds], popcorn. Humous if someone brings it. When we come to someone's house, we sit, whoever wants asks for water, drinks, and later refreshments are brought, and only afterwards chicken. We eat. We eat after collecting money, after, only after.

In another example, which demonstrates the range of rule-making, another male participant recounts:

> When we had the *iqqub* we had a lottery, but what did we do? We would give like this: 100 sheqels. Now 20 sheqels to help out the person who invited us, to make the food, to buy food and drink, to cover the expenses for food. He brings *injera*, *wat* [general term for Ethiopian spicy sauce], he buys beer, and things like that. [laughs] So now we said we would add another 20 sheqels. The same day we give [the money] to whoever prepares. Oh, I remember now! Then it was 100 sheqels that we distributed like that. What did we do? Out of the 100 sheqels,

20 went for food and I think 50 sheqels went to the person [who hosted us] and with another 30 sheqels we opened a bank account and kept it there … We also said that if someone's, say, father or mother dies, we'd give them 300 sheqels. If a brother or someone dies, we'd give them 200 sheqels. We made a kind of ranking of how much to give … I myself sat and wrote it! [Laughs] It was the first time I received a list in Amharic, I think I still have the list of rules. I still have that list … I need to look for it … Yes, we made rules and by the way, we also got certification that so and so's father died, so everything is documented [laughs].

The second description illustrates a creative merging of *iqqub* and *iddir* (an Ethiopian burial society providing financial support in the case of death). Money intended to assist in death ceremonies has been linked to the transfer of funds for savings and credit. The detail and meticulousness of examination and documentation 'emulate' the relationship between the individual and the authorities. For this interviewee, himself a researcher of Ethiopian culture, an expression of the uniqueness of this merging is revealed from and within itself in his embarrassed laughter that explodes following mention of the kinds of food to be served according to the binding list; the explicit documentation of the sum to be given when a relative dies, quantifying grief according to familial relationship; and the presentation of an official death certificate to the members of the family group.

Ritualistic and symbolic aspects

A participant in a young mothers' *iqqub* explains:

When there is an *iqqub*, you'll see how neat the house is. The girls come. They tidy up the house, prepare food. They prepare chicken, sauce, *injera*, spicy sauce, they prepare one vegetable salad, and beverages, they buy beverages. Except for beer. We need only black [malt] beer. We need a regular cola – Coca-cola, and we need all flavours of Prigat [fruit drink]: mango, orange and melon, we need them all. There are eight of us. Only eight of us drink. There are others who participate in the money so they send it with them [the 'drinking' participants]. Let's say, she takes her husband's [money] too, so she'll host [the *iqqub*] twice, what can we do. She'll hold it twice a year. So that's how it goes … Mom was in, but I took her out. There's not enough money. But she wouldn't come [to the meeting itself], she only put in the money, and later I took her out … We who drink the money [all of us] are my age, no older. It's kind of like, free, nice, without getting so offended. We try, we say what we want, but you can't get offended. But if someone insults you, you'll retaliate, but don't get hurt.[18] There are some who really talk nonsense. There are a lot who want to join but we don't let them in. We talk about the man, what he does, what he doesn't do. We drink *bun*, drinks and everything. We speak in Hebrew.

This thick description touches upon issues central to the female *iqqub* in Israel. The list of food to be served is conveyed with an almost magical meticulousness, accompanied by terms such as 'we need,' 'we need only black beer,' 'we need them all'. Thus a transformation occurs from the social and economic obligations of the *iqqub* to its food, whose substance as an offering for the guests, contains two stakes of obligation: social and financial.

The meeting is of women of similar age and family status. Not random, this uniformity is embodied in ritual rather than money. Others, such as female relatives who do not fit the group profile, or male relatives, may take part in the group only if another member serves as agent on their behalf. They may thereby enjoy the group's financial benefits, but not its social and ritualistic aspects. In the changing world of Ethiopian Israeli women, *iqqub* associations and their specific cultural manifestations constitute a highly meaningful experience, whose building-blocks incorporate the financial, the social, the ritualistic, and the symbolic. In the attempt to understand the depth of meaning of their experience, we wish to refer to the lottery held at the closing part of each meeting. This component encapsulates complex, at times contradictory, themes that sometimes stand in contrast to the phenomenon as a whole. In addition to its above-mentioned features, the lottery determines the order of the financial and ritualistic rotation, and while all members are included, only the *iqqub*'s social core takes part in the ritual. Thus, the lottery creates a split between the financial and the social.

In a few cases, the order of rotation is set ahead of time, sometimes even at the group's founding meeting. However, most *iqqubewoch* choose to determine the order by monthly lottery, in a procedure that is a central pivot of *iqqub* meetings. The lottery is conducted as follows: the names of all members, even those who do not attend meetings, are written on small pieces of paper, which are then carefully folded into tiny, uniform paper squares, and are placed in a bowl. A representative is sent out of the room (this could be a member who has already won the fund, or the hostess' child, for example) and then called back in to pull out a square. The winner's name is revealed: she will receive next month's fund and usually, if she is a full 'drinking' member, host the group at her home. At the next meeting, only members who have not yet won the jackpot will participate in the lottery. All interviewees noted the option of negotiating the order of rotation that has been drawn, in the case of a member who urgently needs the funds.

Close scrutiny of the lottery procedure reveals perceptions that are connected with the *iqqub* and cultural understandings enfolded therein, that warrant viewing the lottery as a substantial key to the entire *iqqub*. In this manner, we assert, the juncture of the lottery is particularly loaded with symbolic meaning as regards the world, its existing order and the illusive, arbitrary nature of fate. As social order is determined by chance, it contains a tense, loaded, constant pivot at the intersection of certainty and randomness. The lottery and its unique characteristics are connected by way of encoding with the remainder of the *iqqub*'s components. One member described the lottery as the most pleasurable part of an entirely pleasurable *iqqub* meeting. Despite the concrete financial expectations the lottery evokes, it is described in terms of sisterhood, corresponding with the relative satiety experienced by the women in Israel.[19] The discourse of the lottery reveals oral references to the *iqqub*, attaching relaxed, 'satiated' terms to it as well. One participant recounts:

> Let's say that today I did the *iqqub*. So after we eat, everyone puts in the money and we have a lottery. Now I, let's say that I have already eaten [received the fund], then I'm out. Whoever has already eaten, has taken the money, [is] not in the lottery. We call the lottery *ija...ija* means lottery. OK, so if I go out [to act as the drawer of the lottery], my name is not in the lottery. So we take little pieces of paper, and write on each one the names of those who haven't yet eaten in this round. We put them on a plate and someone chooses. This is how, each time, we choose the hostess for the next time.

She goes on to explain:

> We have a lottery for those who haven't eaten yet ... whoever did not see, pulls out. Opens up whatever she draws. The name is written of whoever's turn it is next month. We pull out just one for next month. Next time, [we do it] again, from those who have not been in this round. In the next round, everyone again, again from the beginning, there's everyone, until it ends. The last one doesn't need a lottery.

Concluding words

The paternalistic view, which dominates most of the literature, portrays the arrival of the Beta Israel from Ethiopia as a manifestation of sponsorship by the state of Israel and world Jewry, which has left them little control over their lives. All financial aspects of the immigrants' lives appear to be dictated 'from above'. Through varied support and welfare mechanisms, the state views itself as the primary factor exercising control over the funding sources of passive, needy groups. Thus, without detracting from the importance of this support, and in practical and symbolic reciprocity with it, the phenomenon of Ethiopian financial associations presents an important alternative that has emerged 'from below'. Alongside the symbolic processing of broad cultural themes, these associations also embody empowerment and change.

Although rooted in a particular Ethiopian experience, the flourishing of the *iqqub* and its framing as an Ethiopian institution – both in structure and terminology – should not lead us to invoke simplistic notions of continuity or preservation. As the material above shows, these cultural practices emerge from a far more complex matrix of creativity in which elements of 'tradition' mobilised in a new setting, not to preserve the past, but to confront the challenges of a new future. For many of the participants their only first-hand experience of the *iqqub* takes place after their arrival in Israel.

Conceptualisation of the financial circle by means of oral terms, can be deciphered as a moderate double-bind of feeding and eating, between satiating the other and satiating one's self. As the *iqqubewoch* we have chosen to examine are women's groups, the symbols of nourishing are coloured by themes that are connected with relationships between women and the financial establishment, relationships among women, relationships between women and men and relationships between women and children. Multi-directional encoding is also found in the conceptual system connecting the lottery with eating, while concepts of eating and drinking ('drinking with money') transform the winner/eater into a 'feeder', by virtue of the very act of her winning. In addition, the *iqqub* and the lottery at its heart are a game, a show of the potential for change. The very drawing of the lots exhibits ambiguity. It is not excessively dangerous, as the gamble does not pose a risk of real uncertainty. There is only uncertainty regarding the order in which the 'jackpot' is received; there is no risk of not receiving at all. Thus, the ritualised lottery with its precise rules, moderately processes themes that lie between certainty and uncertainty, between the individual and society, between suspicion and trust, between control and loss of control, and above all between the individual and his or her fate. In the world of the *iqqub*, these contrastive pairs co-exist, representing for participants the intertwining of past and present, the ensuing potential for change, the social accompaniment that enables this change, as well as its limitations.

Acknowledgements

We thank the *iqqub* participants who shared their financial and ritualistic world with us, and Michal Nefesh for helping with the interviews. We also thank the Shain Center for Research in the Social Sciences of the Hebrew University of Jerusalem for their support.

Notes

1. The plural of *iqqub*. Our interviewees usually use the singular form even when speaking of multiple groups.
2. See, for example, Weil (1991, 2004), Shabtay and Kacen (2005), Leitman (1993), Leitman and Weinbaum (1998) and Phillips-Davids (1998, 1999).
3. The cultural research is heavily loaded with exoticism. We would like to suggest that issues on which Ethiopian Israelis' rationality and agency is so central, may tend to be ignored.
4. For research on the state's paternalistic attitudes, see especially Hertzog (1998).
5. While similar frameworks exist, comparisons between the various *iqqub/quve* in Israel show that they differ from one another in their composition and rules. In some cases, a number of participants share a single membership; in others, one participant may wish to double her share in the circle, or to deposit and receive money for a 'covert member', typically a female relative who is unable to be an active participant at meetings. In such cases, the active representative

is also the host of the covert member's *iqqub* meeting. The amounts of money deposited also vary among groups, as do group size and make-up. Sometimes, a participant wishes to exchange her turn to receive the fund with that of another member. In one interviewee's words: 'There is a list, there is a lottery, but even more we take into account who has asked for the money today,' while another interviewee said: 'Usually, even if there is a lottery, if there is a person who gave a little, if there is a person who needs the money … I give him my turn. He says, he asks for his turn [to receive the money] so [we] put him now.'

6. We are grateful to Dr Chaim Rosen for pointing out the dramatic rise in the percentage of Ethiopian women participating in the workforce over the past decade. According to the Israeli Central Bureau of Statistics 52% of Ethiopian women between ages 22 and 64 in 2007, as opposed to only 22.8% in 1995/96.

7. For a broader discussion of these institutions, see Schaefer and Amsalu (2005), Tubiana *et al.* (1958), and Dejene (1993).

8. See also Dejene (1993), Asfaw (1958), and Levine (1965, 278–279). For essays published primarily for their linguistic content, but concerned with the topic, see Leslau (1968, 209–215) (Gurage), and Leslau and Kane (2001). Varying types of ROSCAs are prevalent in Ethiopia, and are based on religion, locality, occupation and gender. Apparently, their fundamental similarities enable flexibility and facilitate transition between types of associations. In most of Beta Israel's villages, where money was used only minimally, there were no such savings and credit associations without immediate, defined objectives. Mutual assistance organisations, however, did exist, and were even commonplace in these rural areas. These organisations assisted with agricultural manpower, food preparation, or payment for events such as weddings or burials (*iddir*), when one-time fundraising of a relatively large sum was required. These customs were an integral part of the lives of Beta Israel in Ethiopia. The practice of helping to pay for weddings or burials still exists among Ethiopian Israelis, retaining clear elements of reciprocity and group commitment. Carefully documented amounts of money are involved, serving in fact, as some community members who are invited once and again to celebrations have helplessly remarked, to reimburse the host's contributions to previous celebrators.

9. Interviewees often revealed that many Ethiopian Israelis avoid depositing money in the bank or taking out bank loans, due to their difficulties in managing a relationship with a bank, their mistrust of the banking system, as well as their objection to paying interest. This phenomenon is particularly prevalent among the older generation and is connected with Ethiopian Jews' 'everyday resistance' as presented by Kaplan 1997.

10. In the entire and rather broad body of published research on Ethiopian Israelis, we found a marginal reference to the phenomenon in Schwarz (2001, 56–58). It is also discussed in Haim Rosen's unpublished essay on economic life in the town of Kiryat Malachi (Rosen 2001, 9–10).

11. An *iqqub* participant who came to Israel in 1983 from Walqayt through Sudan, recounts: 'There, in Ethiopia, we didn't have such a thing [*iqqub*]. No one had it. Maybe in the city they had it, but in the village they didn't have it. We didn't have it. Also, there was no money, we didn't use money. Everyone did for himself. Everyone had cows. They would milk them, maybe only *bun* [coffee] they would go and buy, but otherwise they didn't buy anything.'

12. For example, as Anbesa explains: '*Iqqub* is a custom that comes from there, so you don't change the name. Now even people who come from Ethiopia today, they come after seven, eight years in the big cities, so they're not like those who came during Operation Moshe or straight from the villages. So new things have come into the community this way, too.'

13. At the time of our research, National Insurance benefits were paid as follows: children's benefits on the 20th of the month, old age and dependents' pensions on the 28th.

14. The Falashmura are a group of people related to Beta Israel, who were converted to Christianity in the past, while living in Ethiopia. Many of them have returned to Judaism and have subsequently been brought to Israel. The relations between the Falashmura and Beta Israel are highly complex. On the complexity of these relations, see Salamon (1999, 56–73).

15. Linguistic references were made only when participants were explicitly questioned on the topic. Most did not respond to the challenge, explaining only that this was the name of the association in Ethiopia. We received varied responses, containing popular linguistic interpretations that in some cases relied even on Hebrew. For example, while one participant used Leslau's dictionary for his linguistic interpretation: 'Where does the word *iqqub* come from? It comes from *aqabba*, which is to guard, that has to do with guarding …', a Tigrinian-speaking participant proposed her own explanation, connected with the Hebrew

root k.b.a. 'to set' or 'set' ['fixed'] and corresponding in her consciousness with her group's binding nature, regularity and carefully-followed rules. Differentiating between *mehaber* and *iqqub*, she says: '*Iqqub* is like *mehaber*. It means to drink without money, that's the meaning of the word *mehaber*. It's just [taking] turns. But *iqqub* is always with money. *Iqqub* is fixed, [a determination].'

16. This is an essentially symbolic, rather than legal, document. Cognisant of the rules, members do not typically go back and refer to the document.

17. In Ethiopia, certain functionaries were appointed at the time of the group's founding. This has not been the case at any *iqqub* we have encountered in Israel. In Ethiopia, the functions were: judge or chairman [*musa*], elected by all members, to be responsible for supervising the group's smooth management and adherence to the rules; secretary, in the event that the judge is illiterate, whose role is to record all monies and prepare the lottery; treasurer, mentioned in two interviews; and alternating guarantors were filled by members who have not yet received the fund and are therefore not yet debtors. The rationale for the absence of functionaries in the *iqqub* in Israel is that the risk of non-payment is mitigated by several factors: selection of participants according to the means of payment available to them; the infeasibility of evasion following the drawing of the lottery and winning the jackpot; and participants' shared literacy skills.

18. This is a particularly apt description of the 'joking' relationships illustrated in Radcliffe-Brown's classic comparative research. On joking relationships as a characteristic of states of structured tension, see Radcliffe-Brown's classic functionalist analysis.

19. While the *iqqub* in Ethiopia usually occurred on market days, whose revenue was by no means guaranteed, the connection in Israel, with reliable, fixed state funds contributes to the sense of satiety.

References

Almedom, A.M., 1995. A note on ROSCAS among Ethiopian women in Addis Ababa and Eritrean women in Oxford. *In*: S. Ardener and S. Burman, eds. *Money-go-rounds*. Oxford and Herndon, VA: Berg, 71–76.

Ardener, S.G., 1964. The comparative study of rotating credit associations. *Journal of the Anthropological Institute*, 94 (2), 201–228.

Ardener, S. and Burman, S., 1995. Women making money go round; ROSCAS revisted. *In*: S. Ardener and S. Burman, eds. *Money-go-rounds: the importance of rotating savings and credit associations for women*. Oxford and Herndon, VA: Berg, 1–20.

Asfaw, D., 1958. Ǝkub. *University College of Addis Ababa ethnological society bulletin*, 8 (July), 63–76.

Butler, K.D., 2002. Defining diaspora, refining a discourse. *Diaspora*, 10 (2), 189–219.

Cerulli, E., 1943–47. *Etiopi in Palestine storia della communita di Gerusalemme*, 2 vols. Rome: Libreria dello Stato.

Clifford, J., 1994. Diasporas. *Cultural anthropology*, 9, 302–338.

Dejene, A., 1993. The informal and semi-formal sectors in Ethiopia: a study of the Iqqub, Iddir and credit co-operatives. *Africa research consortium research paper*, 21.

Geertz, C., 1962. The rotating credit association: a 'middle rung' in development. *Economic development and cultural change*, 10, 241–263.

Gilroy, P., 1994. Diaspora. *Paragraph*, 17 (3), 207–212.

Hertzog, E., 1998. *Bureaucrats and immigrants in an absorption center*. Tel Aviv: Tcherikover. [Hebrew]

Kaplan, S., 1997. Everyday resistance and the study of Ethiopian Jews. *Theory and criticism: an Israeli forum*, 10, 163–173 [in Hebrew].

Kaplan, S., (forthcoming). Tama galut Etiopia: the Ethiopian exile is over. *Diaspora*.

Kaplan, S. and Rosen, C., 1993. Ethiopian immigrants in Israel: between preservation of culture and invention of tradition. *Jewish journal of sociology*, 35 (1), 35–48.

Leitman, E.M., 1993. *Ethiopian immigrant women: transition to a new Israeli identity*, PhD thesis. Ohio State University.

Leitman, E.M. and Weinbaum, E., 1998. Israeli women of Ethiopian descent. *In*: T. Parfitt and E. Trevisan Semi, eds. *Ethiopian Jews in Ethiopia and Israel*. London: Curzon, 128–136.

Leslau, W., 1968. *Ethiopians speak: studies in cultural background. Part 3: Soddo*. Near Eastern Studies, vol. 11. Berkeley, CA: University of California Press.

Leslau, W. and Kane, T., 2001. *Amharic cultural reader*. Wiesbaden: Harrassowitz.

Levine, D., 1965. *Wax and gold: tradition and innovation in Ethiopian culture*. Chicago, IL: University of Chicago Press.

Markowitz, F., Helman, S. and Shir-Vertish, D., 2003. Soul citizenship: black Hebrews and the state of Israel. *American anthropologist*, 105, 302–312.

Miles, W.F., 1997. Black Muslim Africans in the Jewish state: lessons of colonial Nigeria for contemporary Jerusalem. *Issues*, 35, 39–42.

Ornguze, E.D., 1997. *The adaptation of Ethiopian political refugees in New York City (1985–1995)*. PhD thesis. New York, New School for Social Research.

Pedersen, K., 1983. *The history of Ethiopian community in the Holy Land from the time of Tewodros II till 1974*. Jerusalem: Tantur.

Phillips-Davids, J., 1998. Fertility decline and changes in the life course among Ethiopian Jewish women. *In*: T. Parfitt and E. Trevisan Semi, eds. *Ethiopian Jews in Ethiopia and Israel*. London: Curzon, 137–159.

Phillips-Davids, J., 1999. *Migration and fertility transition and changes in the life cycle among Ethiopian Jewish women in Israel*. PhD thesis. Emory University.

Radcliffe-Brown, A., 1940. On joking relationships. *Africa: journal of the International African Institute*, 13 (3), 195–210.

Rosen, H., 2001. *Hedgehogs and foxes among the Ethiopian Olim in Keriyat Malachi*. Report submitted to the Planning and Research Division, Israeli Ministry of Immigrant Absorption, May.

Sabar, G., 2004. African Christianity in the Jewish state: adaptation, accommodation and legitimization of migrant workers, 1990–2003. *Journal of religion in Africa*, 34, 407–437.

Safran, W., 1991. Diasporas in modern societies: myths of homeland and return. *Diaspora*, 1 (1), 83–99.

Safran, W., 1999. Comparing diasporas: a review essay. *Diasporas*, 8 (3), 255–291.

Safran, W., 2005. The Jewish diaspora in a comparative and theoretical perspective. *Israel studies*, 10 (1), 36–60.

Salamon, H., 1999. *The hyena people: Ethiopian Jews in Christian Ethiopia*. Los Angeles, CA: University of California Press.

Salamon, H., 2003. Blackness in transition: decoding racial constructs through stories of Ethiopian Jews. *Journal of folklore research*, 40, 3–32.

Schaefer, C.G.H. and Amsalu, A., 2005. Eqqub. *Encylopaedia Aethiopica*, vol. 2, 346–347.

Schwarz, T., 2001. *Ethiopian Jewish immigrants: the homeland postponed*. Richmond: Curzon.

Shabtay, M. and Kacen, L., 2005. *Mulualem: Ethiopian women and girls in spaces, worlds and journeys between cultures*. Tel Aviv: Leshon Tseha.

Taa, B.J., 2003. *The role of knowledge in the integration experience of Ethiopian immigrants in Toronto*. PhD thesis. University of Toronto.

Tubiana, J., Pankhurst, R. and Eshete, E., 1958. Self-help in Ethiopia. *Ethiopian observer*, 2 (1), 354–364.

Weil, S., 1991. *One-parent families among Ethiopian immigrants in Israel*. Jerusalem: NCJW Research Institute for Innovation in Education, The Hebrew University. [Hebrew]

Weil, S., 2004. Ethiopian Jewish women: trends and transformations in the context of transnational change. *Nashim: a journal of Jewish women's studies and gender issues*, 8, 73–86.

Worku, N., 2002. An ethnographic study of Equb: Ethiopian rotating savings and credit associations in Los Angeles (LA). *45th annual meeting of the African studies association*. Washington, DC, 5–8 December 2002.

Park pictures: on the work of photography in Johannesburg

Louise Bethlehem[a] and Terry Kurgan[b]

[a]Department of English and the Programme in Cultural Studies, The Harry S. Truman Research Institute for the Advancement of Peace, The Hebrew University of Jerusalem, Jerusalem, Israel; [b]Independent artist, Johannesburg, South Africa

This article investigates the cultural economy of an inner-city Johannesburg park through tracking the work of itinerant photographers who operate there. The authors revisit Johannesburg artist Terry Kurgan's interactions with the photographers of Joubert Park in order to raise questions relating to their material and symbolic – or 'immaterial' – labour. They point to the mnemonic or archival dimensions of this labour and investigate the visual idioms in which inner-city migrants conduct their self-fashioning, forging modes of vernacular urbanity in the photographic encounter.

Terry Kurgan is a visual artist who has lived and worked in Johannesburg for many years. Her practice over the course of her involvement with the city has been strongly oriented to a range of public-realm art projects. Many of these have engaged with people, community and place within the rapidly transforming culture and built environment of Johannesburg's inner city. In 2001, a series of cultural projects was launched in Johannesburg at the initiative of the City of Johannesburg and the Johannesburg Development Agency, linked to broader urban regeneration and economic growth interventions. Within this framework, the curators of one such project, the Joubert Park Public Art Project, commissioned over 50 local and international artists to respond to an inner-city park, an adjacent art museum and the surrounding precinct.[1] Terry Kurgan's participation in the Joubert Park Public Art Project set in motion a repeated series of engagements with the cultural economy of Joubert Park. Her initial involvement would catalyse further interventions showcased some years later in an exhibition and associated volume entitled *Johannesburg circa now: photography and the city* (Kurgan and Ractliffe 2005).

In this photo-essay, Terry Kurgan and Louise Bethlehem revisit Kurgan's interactions with the photographers of Joubert Park in order to tease out certain themes immanent in her encounters with them: strands of engagement whose reframing here enables the labour – material and symbolic – of the Park's photographers to be articulated as a form of commentary on the concerns of this special issue.

I

Joubert Park is one of very few green spaces in the dense inner city of Johannesburg. It is surrounded by what was once a thriving retail and business centre for the city's white middle class abandoned in the early 1980s for the suburbs, with their decentralised malls and business parks. In today's inner city, non-national African immigrants, refugees, poor and working-class South Africans now occupy derelict apartments and office buildings once designed for other uses. Their occupation is contested, and living quarters are typically dense and conditions fraught, with sometimes as many as 12 people living in a room designed for one. A 2003 survey of the inner city established that one-quarter of its inhabitants were born outside the boundaries of South Africa, while 68% of inner-city Johannesburg residents had moved to their present residence within the five previous years. In a similar vein, a 2001 population census reported that Johannesburg grew by 300,000 people between 1996 and 2001, with newly urbanised South Africans accounting for the majority of this growth (cited in Landau 2006, 130). These trends continue, exacerbating what hegemonic discourse in South Africa terms xenophobia as the competition for social and material resources between native-born South Africans and 'foreigners' is prolonged in the long stasis of transition that defines the post-apartheid moment.

Everyday life in such circumstances is restless, fractious even – leading one commentator to label Johannesburg an 'edgy city' defined by its 'its uneasy collocation of unevenly linked and possibly incompatible urban, sub-urban, and ex-urban forms'; a 'turbulent conurbation in which civic well-being appear[s] always to be out of reach' (Kruger 2006, 142, 143).[2] For all that this unease has become a form of widespread social malaise in a city preoccupied with threats of crime and with the violent reality of their enactment, the emergence of a new quotidian in the inner city, of new forms of mobility and access encoded in the everyday, must nevertheless be seen as one of the gains of the post-apartheid era. For Lindsay Bremner the passing of the apartheid city has allowed a different Johannesburg to emerge, characterised in its present incarnation by:

> messy intersections and overlapping realities. Ordinary, everyday lives, which were excluded from the city by Western urban management practices, town planning codes or by the legal and administrative apparatus of apartheid, have brought distant geographical, social and cultural worlds into contact. (Bremner 2004, 115)

Contact thus heightened is often scantly mediated. In the dense environment of the inner city characterised by the proximity of body-to-body, a constant, if tacit, calculus of engagement prevails between people on the street.[3] Street space is accordingly intense, seemingly chaotic and often perilous. The park, in this context, affords the opportunity of a rare breathing space, tenuous respite.

II

Although an open space, Joubert Park is not, itself, an empty space. It is pointedly replete with a history that reaches back to the segregated colonial city to which it owes its inception. The major institutional feature of the park is the Johannesburg Art Gallery (JAG), for many decades one of South Africa's premier Eurocentric art museums, whose holdings range from nineteenth-century European painting to modernist and contemporary South African artworks and material culture. Today, the Johannesburg Art Gallery maintains an extremely disjunctive relationship with the throbbing, contemporary African urban culture that surrounds it. Indeed, from the day it opened its doors in 1915, its interaction with the local has been an uncomfortable one. The Johannesburg Art Gallery was established in 1910 by Florence Phillips, wife of the British mining magnate Lionel Phillips, as part of an attempt

Figure 1.   Aerial map of Joubert Park and the Johannesburg Art Gallery (on right) showing the fixed
positions of 40 park photographers working out of the park in 2004.

to create a cultural infrastructure in Johannesburg that would encourage suitable English
families to settle there. An Anglo-Irish art dealer, Hugh Lane, assembled the collection and
recommended that the imperialist British architect, Edwin Lutyens, be commissioned to
design the building. The foundation collection of the gallery was funded by local mining
magnates, and promoted British cultural values to the exclusion of South African content at a
time when the need to consolidate the hegemony of these values was heightened by
economic crisis in the immediate aftermath of the South African War (see Carman 2003).
It would be 30 years until a South African work was purchased for the collection.

The sense that the Johannesburg Art Gallery, as a cultural institution, has consistently
spurned the local is reinforced by its emplacement. The gallery has always had its back to
Joubert Park instead of being in the centre of a grand and gorgeous garden. Urban legend
notwithstanding, the gallery was intentionally designed to face away from the park
towards what was planned – but never realised – as an extension of the park across an
underground railway (Carman 2003, 231). Efforts were made to change this arrangement
when the gallery was renovated in 1986, but unsuccessfully so. Spatial dissonance persists.
The entrance to the gallery is anomalously perched alongside a railway cutting and a busy
taxi rank, much to its disadvantage. A fence currently separates the park and gallery from
each other. When the wind blows in the right direction, plastic shopping bags discarded in
the park drift between it and the parking lot of the gallery, some to remain impaled on the
spikes of the fence that divides them. This incomplete negotiation, materialised in the
passage of debris between one cultural space and another, seems emblematic of so many

of Johannesburg's fragmented and conflicting networks of exchange, whether it is flows of capital, information or culture that are in question. In this respect, Johannesburg is as revealing of the uneven histories of the post-Fordist city as is Mumbai, in Arjun Appadurai's analysis, characterised like the latter by what Appadurai (2000, 627). calls 'disjunct, yet adjacent, histories and temporalities'.

III

This caesura enacted at, and as, the fence should not however be taken as commentary on something like the 'unmanageable' irrationality of the Joubert Park precinct (cf. Kruger 2006, 141) – such as it might appear in, say, the anxious over-the-shoulder retrospect of white former patrons who have largely deserted it. On the contrary, the park provides rich displays of that 'transactional rationality' which urban theorist Gary Bridge (2005, 2, 73–76) associates with the cosmopolitan 'city of difference'. This relational approach to the analysis of interactions in urban space sees the 'space-times' of the city as 'constituted by a range of communicative spheres comprising community "habits", transactions between bodies, and a range of discursive and non-discursive interactions (from the instrumental to the aesthetic) of varying intensities and durations' (Bridge 2005, 10).

The choreography of the park in fact discloses a surprising set of transactions focused precisely on the production of images of the self which blend aspiration, communicative intent and aesthetic address in varying degrees. Self-fashioning, in Stephen Greenblatt's (1980) well-known sense and individual acts of consumption converge here in the open-air exchanges between the street photographers of Joubert Park and their clientele. For it is photography, as Terry Kurgan soon discovered while exploring her 2001 curatorial brief, which lies at the very centre of the cultural economy of the park precinct. She recollects:

> Joubert Park was full of street photographers each displaying their own unique style and specialization on a sandwich board alongside their post. They occupy park benches or perch near photogenic plants or sculptural installations alongside a busy central thoroughfare as hundreds of people migrate past them each day, East-West across the park, and into and out of the inner city. The photographers earn their living by photographing the people who move through the park, and who mostly live illegally under fraught circumstances in mothballed former office buildings (personal communication).

Photography has had a long and contested history in Africa. Employed by the colonial state for control and surveillance (see, for example, Schler 2008, 85), the medium of portrait photography also intersected existing sculptural and performative art traditions in Africa (see Behrend 2002, 46–47). In postcolonial settings, as Heike Behrend has documented with respect to youth culture in Kenya, for instance, photography has become a 'technology of the self' in Michel Foucault's (1988) understanding, 'a means to objectify and at the same time to subjectify the photographed person' (Behrend 2002, 44). Photographic self-creation in Behrend's analysis both substitutes for other means of accumulating and maintaining status and, through invoking the cultural horizon of African-American rap and hip-hop culture, serves as oblique commentary on the repressive reification of ethnicity in Kenya under the government of President Arap Moi. The repertoires of individuation employed in the photographic portrait thus move in concert with 'a transcultural, global subjectivity' whose articulation constitutes a highly displaced form of social commentary (Behrend 2002, 53). The role of photography is also a mnemonic one, Behrend (2002, 57–59) stresses, whether for the individual whose capture of the display of reputation staged for the camera might be exceedingly tenuous, or for larger collectivities particularly at times of duress, associated with migration for instance (see Rosengarten 2005, 34). Kurgan foregrounds this mnemonic dimension of her fascination with the photographic archives of Joubert Park in the following terms:

> I have always been interested in the complex and elusive nature of photographic transactions and the street photographers' images compelled me. The photographers respond to the aspirations of the new residents of the area to create images of themselves as having 'made good' in the city that has so recently, so tenuously become home. In so doing, these photographers have inadvertently created an extraordinary 'social history' archive that documents the shifting demographics and transformation of this fragmented city. Their collective body of work, effectively thousands of snapshots produced over many years, has become a powerful means for many of their clients of shaping personal and cultural history, memory and identity (personal communication).

In conversation with a group of photographers about the conditions surrounding their work, it emerged that they had unsuccessfully been trying to persuade the city to allow them to use a small existing building in the park as a studio. Kurgan's response to this impasse unfolded in the context of a brief inviting her engagement with the culture and economy of the park. She approached an inner-city bank interested in supporting small business ideas and secured funding from them. Working with the business interests and ambitions of a core group of photographers, she designed a portable, mobile photographic studio for installation in the park. At 12 square metres, it was a durable, waterproof structure with lights, multiple backdrops and props for everyday use. The photographers chose the selection of images for the backdrops which were printed onto canvas from a library of stock images (see Figures 2 and 3). The inauguration of the studio redressed, to some extent, the invisibility of the photographers as a type of *ad hoc* professional guild whose legitimacy was not acknowledged by the formal institutions of spatial or economic governance in the city. It also spoke to the constraints operating on the material labour of image production in the particular setting of an inner-city park. The studio was shared by many photographers and was operational for almost three years until it grew too shabby,

Figure 2.   Installation view: Joubert Park Public Art Project, Photo Studio in Joubert Park. Photo credit: Terry Kurgan © 2001.

Figure 3.   Installation view: Joubert Park Public Art Project, Photo Studio in Joubert Park. Photo credit: Terry Kurgan © 2001.

shredded and weathered to use any longer. But the photographers' display boards still cite it in spectral visual form, as if it maintains a form of afterlife in the iconic imagination of the park.

To commission a photograph of the self is always to attest to a selfhood suspended in the dense solvent of sociality. This is the 'advent of myself as other' as Roland Barthes (1981, 12) famously puts it in *Camera lucida* or a depiction of 'myself not (only) as I would like to see myself, but as I am in turn seen, as I am perceived by the cultural gaze' in Ruth Rosengarten's (2005, 39) gloss. The terms of this exchange are latent in the photographers' negotiations around the choice of backdrops for use in the studio: from a radiant ocean sunset (this is a city devoid of sea and river, both) through theme-park Africa fetishised as the Lost City Hotel at the Sun City Complex in a former apartheid Bantustan. The photographers anticipated the iconic repertoires of their clients with great precision, isolating backdrops capable of bearing the aspirations of their clientele for particular forms of representation. 'People have a very specific notion of how (and what) they want to be photographed in or against', Kurgan observes (personal communication). The advent of the studio augmented the often playful enactments of identity construction already associated with the park. The conventions of the tourist exotic or of ethno-kitsch could now alternate readily with the fictionalisation of identity in various forms of role-playing sometimes enacted by clients in impromptu performances of the self – a man crouches for action and aims a pistol; another presents himself for depiction in tribal animal skins (see Figure 4). These, in turn, jostled with representations more pointedly designed to consolidate social and familial roles – young lovers embracing; proud mothers with children (see Figures 5 and 6). In each case, we see 'desire ... phrased in an idiom chosen with precision and specificity from a reservoir of cultural ideals,' as Ruth Rosengarten (2005, 39) reminds us. The park photographers' labour is manifestly that of making these vectors of desire material. That is also to say: it is the labour of rendering them visible.

Figure 4.   Unclaimed photograph by John Makua, subject unknown. Photo credit: © Terry Kurgan.

IV

Visibility and invisibility interact in complex ways in Johannesburg, a city which occults the hidden depths on which its wealth is literally built. Achille Mbembe and Sarah Nuttall cogently remind us that

> In Johannesburg, the underneath of the metropolis is akin to the world of extraction – the underground city of gold mining, with its own syntax, its arteries, its depth, its darkness, and the crucial figure of the *migrant worker*. Living in places and circumstances not of his or her choosing, the migrant worker is constrained to experience the metropolis as a site of radical uncertainty, unpredictability, and insecurity. ... In fact, seen from beneath, the migrant worker more than the flaneur is the paradoxical cultural figure of African modernity – the one who is both beneath the city and outside of its orders of visibility. (Mbembe and Nuttall 2004, 364)

Redressing this exclusion is as much a matter of theoretical or cultural as social intervention. Kurgan's repeated engagements with the life of photography in Joubert Park, indeed with the lives of its photographers, offers a possible corrective. From the vantage of the park, figured at street level through the lens of the photographer, the migrant worker is not completely excluded from lines of sight. In full cognizance of this fact, Kurgan returned to the park in 2004 to develop a new project.

   This project, Park Pictures responds once again, to the context of Joubert Park, but engages more specifically with the large community of resident photographers there, many

Figure 5. Unclaimed photograph by John Makua, subjects unknown. Photo credit: © Terry Kurgan.

of whom have spent their entire working lives operating from an inviolably fixed working position. In 2004, there were upwards of 40 photographers working in the park. Several of the photographers have worked from their spot in the park for over 20 years. They charge their clients 50% of their fee at the time of shooting the photograph, issue a receipt, and are paid the other half upon collection. At least half the photographs are never claimed. Kurgan bought many hundreds of these unclaimed photographs to use in her work, as if she were the missing client.

Park Pictures was initially conceived as a part of a group exhibition, *Johannesburg circa now*[4] and was designed specifically to be installed into the adjacent Johannesburg Art Gallery. Kurgan crafted photographic portraits of 40 photographers which were integrated into the exhibition alongside the unclaimed photographs of their clients, together with an aerial map showing the position of each photographer, and a selection of 15 modern British and European paintings from JAG's foundation collection – purchased and donated in 1910/12 by the mining magnates who built and funded JAG at its inception (see Figure 1). The reframing of the park photographers' *oeuvre* alongside the foundation collection foregrounded the dialectics of recognition and misrecognition, visibility and invisibility that obtain between elite and popular cultural practices in the Joubert Park precinct as emblematic of Johannesburg's disjunctive reordering in the post-apartheid moment. Visitors to the exhibition, who could themselves pose for and annotate their own portraits in a specially designated space in the studio became active participants

Figure 6. Unclaimed photograph by John Makua, subjects unknown. Photo credit: © Terry Kurgan.

Figure 7. *Park Pictures*, installation view, Johannesburg Art Gallery 2004. Photo credit: © Oscar Gutierrez.

Figure 8. *Park Pictures*, installation view, Johannesburg Art Gallery 2004. Photo credit: © Oscar Gutierrez.

2
Name: Jabulani Mpofu
Date of birth: 6 January 1978
Place of birth: Kwabulawayo, Zimbabwe
Relocation to Johannesburg: 2002
Currently resides: Joubert Park
Occupation: Photographer
Working in Joubert Park: 4 years

Figure 9.   Jabulani Mpofu's position in the park is marked on Figure 1 as number 2. Photo credit: © Terry Kurgan.

in refiguring themselves through and against the city's contradictions. These interlocking facets of the group exhibition rendered it both a performance of, and a form of commentary upon, the production and valorisation of the visual object in clearly differentiated economies of cultural and economic exchange (see Figures 7 and 8). 'The installation', Ruth Rosengarten observes, 'immediately confronts the spectator with the potentially disjunctive relationship between the activities within and without the gallery frame, but also with the representational conventions they may share' (Rosengarten 2005, 31).

V

In the context of this special issue, however, it is particularly the photographers who deserve emphasis in these vectors of circulation. Kurgan's own portraiture has thickened our grasp of an occluded sense of the photographer as worker by making the outlines of a professional archive part of the very substance of the visual field. Under each of her portraits of the photographers – but incorporated into the photographic print itself – is an abbreviated life history. It records name, date of birth, place of birth, date of relocation to Johannesburg, current Johannesburg residence and then lastly, the number of years each person has spent working from their spot in Joubert Park. The camera, placed *en abîme* in Kurgan's portraits, itself serves as a crucial trope of professional identity for all of her subjects who insisted through the device of its insertion on engaging with Kurgan in a dialogue of peers (see Figures 9, 10, 11 and 12). The necessary presence of the camera

6
Name: Robert Madamalala
Date of birth: 6 July 1968
Place of birth: Venda, South Africa
Relocation to Johannesburg: 1989
Currently resides: Diepkloof
Occupation: Photographer
Working in Joubert Park: 13 years

Figure 10.   Robert Madamalala's position in the park is marked on figure as number 6. Photo credit: © Terry Kurgan.

25
Name: Sbu Mchunu
Date of birth: 16 June 1975
Place of birth: Kwazulu Natal, South Africa
Relocation to Johannesburg: 1993
Currently resides: Joubert Park
Occupation: Photographer
Working in Joubert Park: 11 years

Figure 11. Sbu Mchunu's position in the park is marked on figure as number 25. Photo credit: © Terry Kurgan.

admits no vanishing point in the photographers' group portrait of their profession. The camera is the fixed locus of this particular staging of the self. Its fixity moreover, intersects still further domains of fixity and the corresponding extraction of professional agency, not without effort. Recall AbdouMaliq Simone's observation:

> It is important that we take seriously what is accomplished, even in the most deprived neighborhoods or cities, by those who spend their entire working lives in one place – the tea seller, the newspaper vendor ... especially in the poorest neighborhoods, cities or families, being stationary is an intense position – waiting for things to come to you, finding ways of exerting control over a specific place, exacting income from that control. (Simone 1999, 174)

Control entails regulation. The photographers constitute a complex and highly organised informal business sector – the principal economy of the park – and operate according to their own set of rules, exchanges and regulations. They all have their roots elsewhere and each has migrated to Johannesburg to find work. They mostly live in the inner city or close to it. The position each person occupies is sacred, and the process whereby they came to work as a photographer in the park is immensely complicated and is dependent upon far-reaching networks and flows of complicity, cooperation, family and other affiliations. 'Jabulani Mpofu from Kwabulawayo in Zimbabwe, explained to me that he came to work in his spot through his relationship with his uncle whom he assisted for several years before acquiring a position of his own' Kurgan recalls (personal communication). His accession to the status of an independent photographer with

1
Name: John Makua
Date of birth: 15 February 1950
Place of birth: Limpopo, South Africa
Relocation to Johannesburg: 1969
Currently resides: Hillbrow
Occupation: Photographer
Working in Joubert Park: 23 years

Figure 12.   John Makua's position in the park is marked on figure as number 1. Photo credit: © Terry Kurgan.

a standing, literally, all of his own, had to be carefully negotiated with the pre-existent group of photographers who had been there for many long years before him.

In contrast with the uncivil conduct of violence in a city where 'stories of crime ... became Johannesburg's defining genre of social commentary as well as artistic imagining' (Kruger 2006, 146), Joubert Park's photographers enclave a domain of civility in the city. Their collaborative negotiation of the contracts that allow an individual photographer to engage with a specific client speaks to just one aspect of the networks of sociality in which the photographers are embedded. Beyond this, we might point to the interplay of the fixed and the mobile in the circuits of exchange they facilitate. For all the fixity of their workaday emplacement, the photographers' own status as migrants often corresponds with the lived experience of their clients, at whose disposal they place a visual technology capable of rendering potentially shared aspirations concrete. These aspirations are drawn into the construction of a 'vernacular' urbanity (Kruger 2006) that literally comes into being on the city street as the aperture closes, the shutter clicks. But although the production of the visual forms of this vernacular urbanity are tied to the micro-locations whose intensely delimited circumference in the park Kurgan's aerial map lays bare, the diffusion of a selfhood modulated through the codes of this urbanity is far from local. Selves travel and so do photographic portraits linking the personae enacted in the city, this city, to other people, other places. The emergence of vernacular urbanity for the migrant might not be simultaneous with the tissue of lived experience at the point where the migrant's displacement began, but it should not be seen as discontinuous with this elsewhere. Instead it might be argued that the photograph, like other symbolic goods ferried between here and there, can come to be implicated in a metonymic relay of selfhood by means of which the 'working-class cosmopolitan', to use Pnina Werbner's (1999) phrase, apprehends the coordinates of subjectivity as transnational.[5]

It is against this background, that photography can be reframed as labour of a specific type: namely, as that form of work involving 'human contact and interaction' which Michael Hardt and Antonio Negri (2000) designate 'immaterial labour'. Immaterial labour serves to produce 'an immaterial good, such as a service, a cultural product, knowledge or communication' (Hardt and Negri 2000, p. 290) and must, they claim, be seen as a new form of productive force in the contemporary – globalised – economy (Hardt and Negri 2000, 29).[6] They draw on feminist analyses of women's care-giving, in the raising of children or caring for the aged, for example, to remind us that: 'What affective labour produces are social networks, forms of community, biopower (Hardt and Negri 2000, 293). Joubert Park's photographers must themselves be seen as nodal points in the creation of such social networks. They afford their clients a means of renegotiating the material scarcity in which they subsist through making available a visual syntax that allows the individual to experience and disseminate a range of emotions elicited precisely by the framing of the self in the camera lens. Thus, for instance, the migrant's tenuous purchase over housing and, by implication, over a private domestic sphere in the densely crowded inner city of Johannesburg may be renegotiated through the photographic capture, at once real and imagined, affective and tangibly corporeal, of plenitude and stability communicated through the well-formed portrait of a family group (see Figure 6).

But if the photograph becomes currency in the *fort-da* of the migrant's self-fashioning, it is also the case that the circuits of itinerant exchange sometimes fail to be properly constituted. The client does not return to retrieve the portrait commissioned. The projection of a self for future contemplation, by the self or by others, is arrested in the past perfect of the unclaimed photographic print. For Kurgan: 'These unclaimed photographs resonate with the paradoxical issues surrounding photographic representation and performance, which are particularly interesting as they are embedded in the ordinary, everyday domestic snap' (personal communication). The photographs have become superfluous in some of the dimensions of superfluity that Achille Mbembe reads off the surface of the particular metropolitan forms of Johannesburg: expendable, devoid of exchange or use value, hollowed out, haunted (see Mbembe 2004). The unclaimed portraits are orphaned, detached from the subjects who might imbue them with meaning and complete the circuit of address. They are, in other words, melancholic. In '[materialising] the photographic condition of capture and loss,' Ruth Rosengarten comments, they '[expose] the implicit melancholy inherent to all photographic transactions' (Rosengarten 2005, 43). This uncanny and incipiently traumatic excess persists despite Kurgan's reclamation of it through the surrogacy of her intervention. In a sense, however, the constraints of the park photographers' working lives have already anticipated this surrogacy as the routinisation of the warding-off of oblivion, since each photographer carries around, as a matter of course, a huge number of still-to-be-claimed photographs. The agency of the photographer–archivist can be glimpsed in these moments as apotropaic: a holding of the photographs in trust as the quotidian labour of witness. At street-level, the photographers precipitate what Ariella Azoulay has termed, in a different context of political saturation, 'the civil contract of photography' (Azoulay 2008).[7] The elaboration of new imaginaries of civility and singularity is no small part of (the) photographic work in contemporary Johannesburg.

Notes

1. The curators of the Joubert Park Public Art Project were Dorothee Kreutzfeldt, Bie Venter and Jo Ractliffe.
2. Kruger's witty reworking of Joel Garreau's (1991) notion of the 'edge' city stresses the city's anxious interpolation within global networks: 'Johannesburg may not appear on strictly defined lists of global cities, but it shares the global characteristics of transnational flows of capital and people, and the concentration of high-tech and high-touch nodes of social and economic exchange, made visible in the built environment of the high-rise office tower, as well as the concentration of cultural diversity on the street' (Kruger 2006, 142).
3. See AbdouMaliq Simone (2006, 72–74) for an evocative account of communication in the 'volatile' African city where, in specific circumstances, '[A] certain movement of … conversation and exchange is being rehearsed – not marked by the usual discursive or cognitive characteristics dependent upon the semiotic but by the referencing of the exchange to its own variations, its own changes in intensity, rhythm, and affect' (2006, 74). See also Gary Bridge (2005, 2, 73–76) for an elaboration of the cognitive and affective dimension of the 'transactional rationality' that grounds urban subjects, and references to Bridge, below.
4. *Johannesburg circa now: photography and the city* – an exhibition, education and book project curated by artists Terry Kurgan and Jo Ractliffe, Johannesburg Art Gallery, September–December 2004.
5. We draw here on Werbner's analysis of 'working-class Pakistani "cosmopolitans"': Pakistani migration involves the metonymic movement of ceremonial objects such as food, clothing, cosmetics and jewellery, which personify moral "places", and it is through these that new global ethnic social worlds are constituted' (Werbner 1999, 19). For the photographic portrait as metonymy and fetish, see Ruth Rosengarten (2005, 34).
6. In the political philosophy of Hardt and Negri, the term 'immaterial labour' registers a historical shift which has seen the 'central role previously occupied by the labour power of mass factory workers in the production of surplus value … today increasingly filled by intellectual, immaterial, and communicative labour power' (Hardt and Negri 2000, 28). In *Empire* (2000), they describe the three primary aspects of immaterial labour, namely: 'the communicative labour of industrial production that has newly become linked in informational networks, the interactive labour of symbolic analysis and problem solving, and the labour of the production and the manipulation of affects' (Hardt and Negri 2000, 30). For Negri, revisiting the term, immaterial labour can be considered 'the ensemble of intellectual, communicative, relational and affective activities which are expressed by subjects and social movements' implicated in the changed nature of contemporary relations of production (Negri 2008, 62). While conceding the value of the term for our purposes, we are nevertheless aware that some critics are uneasy concerning its applicability to African contexts. See particularly Kenneth Dunn (2004). For a related discussion of globalisation, see Lynn Schler, Louise Bethlehem and Galia Sabar in this volume.
7. Azoulay's work addresses the kinds of power relations in which photographic meanings subsist. She takes, as paradigmatic, the role of photography with respect to two major sites of the occlusion of visibility. The first relates to the presence/absence of the Palestinian non-citizen under the Israeli occupation and the second to the status of women, particularly the rape victim, in Western societies.

References

Appadurai, A., 2000. Spectral housing and urban cleansing: notes on millennial Mumbai. *Public culture*, 12 (3), 627–651.

Azoulay, A., 2008. *The civil contract of photography*. New York: Zone Books.

Barthes, R., 1981. *Camera lucida: reflections on photography*. Trans R. Howard. London: Vintage.

Behrend, H., 2002. 'I am like a movie star in my street': photographic self-creation in postcolonial Kenya. *In*: R. Werbner, ed. *Postcolonial subjectivities in Africa*. London and New York: Zed Books, 44–62.

Bremner, Linday, 2004. *Johannesburg: one city, colliding worlds*. Johannesburg: STE.

Bridge, G., 2005. *Reason in the city of difference: pragmatism, communicative action and contemporary urbanism*. London and New York: Routledge.

Carman, J., 2003. Johannesburg art gallery and the urban future. *In*: R. Tomlinson, R.A. Beauregard, L. Bremner and X. Mangcu, eds. *Emerging Johannesburg: perspectives on the postapartheid city*. Routledge: London and New York, 231–257.

Dunn, Kenneth, 2004. Africa's ambiguous relation to Empire and *Empire*. *In*: P.A. Passavant and J. Dean, eds. *Empire's new clothes: reading Hardt and Negri*. London and New York: Routledge, 143–162.

Foucault, M., 1988. *Technologies of the self: a seminar with Michel Foucault. In:* L.H. Martin, H. Gutmen and P.H. Hutton, eds. Amherst, MA: University of Massachusetts Press.

Garreau, J., 1991. *Edge city: life on the new frontier*. New York: Doubleday.

Greenblatt, Stephen, 1980. *Renaissance self-fashioning: from More to Shakespeare*. Chicago, IL: University of Chicago Press.

Hardt, M. and Negri, A., 2000. *Empire*. Cambridge, MA and London: Harvard University Press.

Kruger, L., 2006. Filming the edgy city: cinematic narrative and urban form in postapartheid Johannesburg. *Research in African literatures*, 37 (2), 141–163.

Kurgan, T. and Ractliffe, J., 2005. *Johannesburg circa now: photography and the city*. Johannesburg: Terry Kurgan and Jo Ractliffe.

Landau, L.B., 2006. Transplants and transients: idioms of belonging and dislocation in inner-city Johannesburg. *African studies review*, 49 (2), 125–145.

Mbembe, A., 2004. Aesthetics of superfluity. *Public culture*, 16 (3), 373–405.

Mbembe, A. and Nuttall, S., 2004. Writing the world from an African metropolis: introduction. *Public culture* (special issue on 'Johannesburg – the elusive metropolis', eds. A. Mbembe and S. Nuttall), 16 (3), 347–372.

Negri, A., 2008. *Reflections on Empire*. With contributions from M. Hardt and D. Zolo. Trans. E. Emery. London: Polity.

Rosengarten, R., 2005. Material ghosts: Terry Kurgan's park pictures. *In*: T. Kurgan and J. Ractliffe, eds. *Johannesburg circa now: photography and the city*. Johannesburg: Terry Kurgan and Jo Ractliffe, 30–43.

Schler, L., 2008. *The strangers of new bell: immigration, public space and community in colonial Douala, Cameroon, 1914–1960*. Pretoria: University of South Africa Press.

Simone, A., 1999. Globalisation and the identity of African urban practices. *In*: H. Judin and I. Vladislavic, eds. *Blank_architecture, apartheid and after*, section D8. Rotterdam: Nederlands Architectuurinstituut, 173–187.

Simone, A., 2006. Sacral spaces in two West African cities. *In*: P. Ahluwalia, L. Bethlehem and R. Ginio, eds. *Violence and non-violence in Africa*. London: Routledge, 63–83.

Werbner, P., 1999. Global pathways. Working class cosmopolitans and the creation of transnational ethnic worlds. *Social anthropology*, 7 (1), 17–35.

Index

Page numbers in **Bold** represent figures.
Page numbers followed by n represent endnotes.

For Product Safety Concerns and Information please contact our EU
representative GPSR@taylorandfrancis.com Taylor & Francis Verlag GmbH,
Kaufingerstraße 24, 80331 München, Germany

Batch number: 08151620

Printed by Printforce, the Netherlands